PASTOR AND PEOPLE

Fernley-Hartley Lecture, Liverpool, 1975

JOHN C. BOWMER

PASTOR AND PEOPLE

*A Study of Church and ministry
in Wesleyan Methodism
from the death of John Wesley (1791)
to the death of Jabez Bunting (1858)*

WIPF & STOCK · Eugene, Oregon

Wipf and Stock Publishers
199 W 8th Ave, Suite 3
Eugene, OR 97401

Pastor and People
A Study of Church and Ministry in Wesleyan Methodism
from the death of Jon Wesley (1791) to the death of Jabez Bunting (1858)
By Bowmer, John C.
Copyright©1975 Methodist Publishing - Epworth Press
ISBN 13: 978-1-5326-3824-4
Publication date 7/27/2017
Previously published by Epworth Press, 1975

Every effort has been made to trace the current copyright
owner of this publication but without success. If you have
any information or interest in the copyright, please contact the publishers.

TO

Michael and Eileen

FOREWORD

by the Rev. E. Gordon Rupp
FBA, MA, DD, DTheol
Dixie Professor of Ecclesiastical History, University of Cambridge

IT gives me pleasure to commend Dr Bowmer's learned study of 'Pastor and People' to as wide an audience as possible. To the Methodists he is well known as the man to whom, more than any other, we owe the putting in order of our archives, a signal service to the cause not only of the church, but to scholars all over the world. And as a brother beloved in the Methodist ministry, he has typified that pastoral office which has never been simply a badge of clericalism, but of true ministry. Dr Bowmer's studies will be read alongside other modern dissertations, notably those of Drs F. Baker and A. B. Lawson, and they take account of rather more destructive criticism from other directions. 'Pastoral Office' is certainly not a dirty word by reason of its invention by so-called 'Buntingites' of the nineteenth century, but it is an honourable seventeenth-century word which in its Methodist undertones and overtones can only be understood in the light of the first works of the Evangelical Revival and of John Wesley. Dr Bowmer is not given to exaggeration, and the acid cynicisms of some recent highflyers find their proper counterpoint in Dr Bowmer's careful learning and unwillingness to disparage honest edification. At a time when we are properly exploring the meaning of the ministry of the whole church, and the ministries of the laity, we need to remember the truth of F. D. Maurice's warning that if we take away from the significance of the calling of 'the' ministry, we inevitably depreciate the meaning of all other ministries in the church.

Cambridge GORDON RUPP

CONTENTS

Foreword	7
Preface	13

PART ONE
SEVEN STORMY YEARS
1791–7

1 Society or Church?	19
The Old Plan	20
The Providential Way	26
Are the Methodists Dissenters?	30
Reconciliation	34
2 The Nature of Episcopé	37
The Tentative Halifax Scheme	37
Attempts at District Superintendency	42
The Popular Front	45
3 The Form of Discipline (1797)	51
The Supremacy of the Conference	51
The District Chairman	52
The Circuit Superintendent	55
The Pastoral Office	57
The Role of the Laity	59
4 Summary	62
Wesley's Intentions	62
Why did Methodism adopt a Presbyterian Polity?	64

PART TWO
INTERLUDE
1797–1827

1 Minor Secessions	71
The Band-room Methodists	71
The Church Methodists	75
The Tent Methodists	80
The Primitive Methodists	82
The Bible Christians	84

CONTENTS

2 Polity and Temper — 88
   Admission of Members — 88
   Candidates for the Ministry — 89
   Ministerial Discipline — 91
   The Liverpool Minutes — 93
   The Conduct of Worship — 95
   Finance — 97
   The Laity — 98

PART THREE

THE CLASH
1827–49

1 The Leeds Organ Case — 103
   The Organ — 104
   The Constitution — 107
   The Ministry — 115
   Conclusion — 117

2 The Warrenite Secession — 119
   The Training of the Ministry — 121
   The Rules of 1797 — 125
   The Secessions — 134
   The Conference Rules of 1835 — 137
   Conclusion — 143

3 The Fly-sheet Controversy — 145
   The Methodist Reformers — 147
   Conference Methodism — 152
   The Significance of 1849 — 155

PART FOUR

CHURCH AND MINISTRY

1 The Resultant Polity — 163
   Structure — 163
   Its Nature — 177

2 The Pastoral Office — 198
   Wesley's Conception of the Ministry — 198

CONTENTS

After Wesley	202
The Office of a Pastor	207
Pastoral and Civil Rule	219
The Place of the Laity	221
The Free Methodist View	223
Conclusion	226
3 The Impact of the Oxford Movement	229
Methodists and Tractarians	230
Attack and Defence	235
Conclusion	247
4 Conclusions	249
Bibliography	263
Index	267

PREFACE

THIS is a new look at Wesleyan Methodism; 'new' in the sense that it is a look at the inside; 'new' also because, as a unique ecclesiastical structure, Wesleyan polity has never been analysed. The standard histories of Methodism are, as a rule, content to narrate events (plentiful and colourful enough!) but few go beneath the surface to consider the motives, tensions and strongly held convictions which shaped the institution they describe. Behind the fightings without and fears within, lay a world of ideas for which some fought, against which others rebelled, but which none should ignore. There were, of course, political and social factors which went to the moulding of Methodism and these are now attracting the attention of experts in these fields. Our concern will be to show how a certain doctrine—the doctrine of the Pastoral Office—influenced the shape of Wesleyan polity during the first half of the nineteenth century. Bernard Semmel, in his recent and provocative book, *The Methodist Revolution*, has rightly said, 'The Methodist polity was a remarkable structure, about which we need to know a great deal more than we do' (p. 115); so it is hoped that the present work will do something to supply that need.

Much use has been made of the vast storehouse of original material in the central archives of the Methodist Church. Pamphlets on the Reform Movement alone run to over 600 in number, while the letters of Bunting and his contemporaries number many thousands. The insights which this material gives to the inner working of the Wesleyans is what will probably give this study any special value it may come to possess.

Wesleyan Methodism of the period covered by this study has virtually disappeared. It has been so modified down the years that the 're-structured' Methodism of today can hardly be identified with what we have called 'Classical Wesleyanism'. The removal of the term 'Society' from the new *Constitutional Practice and Discipline of the Methodist Church* has virtually completed the process. If, therefore, this study serves any useful purpose at all, it may well be to set on record a body of ecclesiastical polity, doctrine and discipline which was unique in its way and deserving of a better fate than oblivion.

The substance of what follows in this book was delivered as the Fernley–Hartley Lecture at the Methodist Conference of 1975. A mere scanning of the names of those who have, from year to year, delivered these lectures is enough to daunt any newcomer to their ranks; sufficient is it also to quell any selfish pride—except, of course, the rightful pride and honour that one must feel, as I do, in being invited to deliver this lecture, especially as I do it in the city where I was ordained in 1939, and at the completion of my fortieth year in the ministry.

This work is a revised and abbreviated form of a thesis for which I was awarded the degree of Ph.D. at Leeds University. The full version of that thesis can be consulted in the original typescript in the University Library.

It would be impossible to mention all those who have helped me in this study. They are like the 'many blessings' of the old hymn, I could not count them, much less 'name them one by one'; but I must express gratitude to my friend and colleague, Dr Frank Cumbers, who read the script and thereby, time and time again, saved me from myself. I owe much also to Professor Gordon Rupp who has given me every encouragement to pursue this study of The Pastoral Office and has been kind enough to write a Foreword to the book. Dr W. R. Ward, who at present is Professor of Modern History at the university of my native city of Durham, has also helped me (often by not agreeing with me) in many conversations we have had together; and, as a sign that historians can differ and still remain friends, he presided over the lecture in its 'delivered' form. To Mr John A. Vickers, who in his usual painstaking way, has compiled the index, I owe a special debt of gratitude.

The usual chore of proof reading, together with the sufferance of endless hours of typing, has fallen again upon

PREFACE

my wife to whom I express an unrepayable debt of gratitude and affection.

The term 'Free Methodists', as used in this study, calls for an explanation. It is a generic term for a considerable number of Methodist bodies which had much in common in their protest against the constitution of Wesleyanism. It includes the Methodist New Connexion, the Protestant Methodists and the Wesleyan Association. The Bible Christians and the Primitive Methodists could also be classed as 'Free Methodists' in their conception of the Church and Ministry, but they originated as spontaneous evangelical revivals and not as protests against Wesleyan polity. The United Methodist Free Churches, formed by a union of the Protestant Methodists, the Wesleyan Association and some 1849 Reformers, did not come into existence until 1856, so they do not fall within our period.

The following abbreviations have been used, sometimes in the text, but mainly in the footnotes:

C.P.D.	*The Constitutional Practice and Discipline of the Methodist Church*
E.C.W.M.	Beecham, John: *An Essay on the Constitution of Wesleyan Methodism* (3rd edition)
F. of D.	*The Form of Discipline* authorized by the Methodist Conference of 1797.
L.Q.R.	*The London Quarterly Review*
M.C.A.	The Methodist Church Archives, 25–35, City Road, London, EC1Y 1AA.
Minutes	Minutes of the Wesleyan Conference (1862 edition)
M.M.	A Magazine which, in our period, assumed three successive titles: 1778–1797—*The Arminian Magazine* 1798–1821—*The Methodist Magazine* 1822–1913—*The Wesleyan Methodist Magazine*
M. & P.	Barrett, Alfred: *The Ministry and Polity of the Christian Church.*

PREFACE

P.O.   Barrett, Alfred: *The Pastoral Office.*
Proc. W.H.S. *The Proceedings of the Wesley Historical Society*
W.T.T.   *Wesleyan Tracts for the Times*

London 1975   JOHN C. BOWMER

PART ONE

Seven Stormy Years

1791-7

CHAPTER ONE

SOCIETY OR CHURCH?

ON the death of John Wesley, Methodism was still fundamentally societary in character and there was a strong party which held that this should be perpetuated; that services should not be held in church hours, that the sacraments should not be administered and that the Itinerants should not assume the role of ministers. At the same time there were signs that the movement was developing into a church with unmistakable characteristics of its own. The Deed of Declaration (1784) had, indeed, preserved the societary framework and terminology, but it gave the central governing body, the Conference, an independent identity which was recognized by the law. Again, while Wesley's ordinations were first performed on the plea that the men were to exercise their ministry in lands outside the jurisdiction of the Church of England, he later ordained others without sending them out of England. This opened the door to the argument that Methodism was now functioning as a church in its own right and therefore the sacraments should be administered in Methodist chapels by the men who, though technically known as preachers, were now becoming pastors. Furthermore, as Wesley's personal oversight had been transferred after his death to the legal Conference and not invested in a personal successor, it was left to the Itinerants to work out the implications of this situation. The root of the problem was, 'How was this new form of episcopé to be exercised and where was authority to lie?'

This was worked out in terms of three inter-related issues. First, the society-church problem turned on the administration of the sacraments and the conception of the ministry; second, the nature of episcopé had to be embodied in organization which, in turn (the third issue) needed to be defined in a code of law. These three problems will be discussed in part one of this work; but let us first consider the issue, Society or Church.

There were two main roads along which Methodism might have travelled when it found itself bereft of its leader in 1791. There was, first of all, what was called 'The Old Plan', by which Methodism would have remained, in essence, an appendage to the Church of England. On the other hand, there was what we might call 'The Providential Way' which involves the acknowledgement that after the death of Wesley, allegiance to the Anglican Church was sentimental rather than functional, doctrinal rather than practical. Supporters of this attitude, whom I have called 'The Makers of Methodism', argued that Wesley's plan was always 'to follow the openings of Providence'[1] and that in allowing services to be held in church hours, as well as in ordaining some of his preachers, Wesley himself had laid the foundations of a Methodist Church independent of the Church of England. We now examine these alternatives as Methodism stood at the cross-roads in 1791.

The Old Plan

The opening gambit was a move in Hull, just two months after Wesley's death. On 4th May, 1791, a letter over the signatures of 18 laymen,[2] 'Stewards, Leaders, Trustees and others' was circulated to the 'Stewards of every principal society in England'. The essence of the message was that the Itinerants must not administer the sacraments and that Methodist services must not be held during church hours. The signatories were, however, keen to preserve that system 'which had been so great a blessing both to preachers and people and one great means of preserving and increasing vital religion among the Methodists'.

[1] See, e.g., M.C.A. Letter from John Pawson to Joseph Benson, 4th May, 1791.
[2] No Itinerant seems to have any part in this circular, for there is a footnote which reads, 'It was also unanimously agreed that a copy be given to Mr Thomas Taylor and another to Mr John Shaw, the Preachers in the Hull circuit, from which they might express to the next Conference the sentiments of the society at Hull.'

SOCIETY OR CHURCH?

This was 'The Old Plan' clear and unmistakable. Methodism was regarded as a federation of religious societies related in some undefined way to the Church of England, the Itinerants as travelling preachers only and the people as members of the Established Church whether they were welcome there or not.[3]

Now we must take these 'Old Planners' quite seriously. The Hull signatories had many sympathizers, mainly among trustees in other parts of the country.[4] We cannot dismiss them as 'materially-minded', 'tyrannical'—epithets flung at them by their opponents. They had a cause to defend and a conscience to reckon with. Many of them were men of means (that is why they were trustees); hence, what is often overlooked, they were socially nearer the Church of England than most of the Itinerants and the rank and file of the Methodists. They were really Churchmen first and Methodists afterwards,[5] and they feared that now that Wesley was gone ties with the Established Church would be severed. Of course, encouraged perhaps by the more benevolent attitude which the clergy took towards Wesley in his later years, they may have still hoped that Methodism would be retained within the Anglican fold. Their hopes were ephemeral but their fears were real. Already some of the Itinerants were assuming the character of ministers. Ordinations had taken place without the permission of Conference.[6] The title 'Reverend' was frequently used,[7] and it was not unknown for some of them to appear in the pulpit

---

[3] Mr Robert Grey, of Newcastle upon Tyne, went so far as to argue that the administration of the sacraments was not part of original Methodism and not necessary for its continued existence—see *Letters from Robert Grey to Joseph Cownley* (1792), p. 8.

[4] Circulars were issued from Bristol (11th May), Birmingham (21st June) and Sheffield (27th June).

[5] See article (by J. S. Simon) in *The London Quarterly Review* for October 1884. Simon thinks that Methodist historians tend 'to overlook the friendly attitude of some of the parish clergy at the close of the century.'

[6] See *Letter from the Leeds Stewards*, 12th July, 1792; M.C.A. letter from Samuel Bradburn to Richard Rodda, 19th April, 1792 where Bradburn says he ordained in Manchester.

[7] M.C.A. letters from John Pawson addressed to 'The Rev.' Mr Atmore.

robed in cassock and surplice.[8] As the popular demand for the sacraments increased, the threat of a 'rival altar' became more real and the Old Planners felt compelled to take a stand. We shall now consider their reasons.

1. They felt that they were true to Wesley's intentions and freely quoted his *Farther Thoughts on Separation from the Church*, his sermon *On Laying the Foundation of the New Chapel* and *The Large Minutes* (1789). Wesley's words in the *Minutes* particularly suited their case—'Exhort all our people to keep close to the Church and Sacrament. Warn them ... against calling our Society the Church; against calling our Preachers ministers, our houses meeting houses. ...'[9]

It is true that when the Old Planners were confronted with the fact of Wesley's ordinations, they had to resort to arguments which their opponents did not find too difficult to rebut. Alexander Knox, for instance, maintained that in 1786 Wesley was 'enervated by age'; that in later years he 'was seduced from his better purposes'; that 'when he was left to himself his views returned to their old channels'; that Wesley's ordinations were, in fact, 'the effects of his own imbecility'.[10] Such arguments were easily answered by reference to Wesley's other activities until just a few days before his death!

The London Trustees believed that Wesley's ordinations were performed to meet a temporary and local situation only, not to be applied generally in the future economy of Methodism.[11] They stood by the maxim, so forcibly expressed by Lord Mansfield to Charles Wesley, that 'ordination is separation'.[12] John had justified his action on the ground that the Americans, for whom he had ordained his men, were 'totally disentangled from both

[8] The customary dress of an Anglican clergyman at this time was a surplice for the offices and a gown for the sermon. Bradburn in his *Answer to Embury Edwards' Letter* (1792), pp. 11 and 28, says he wore a gown and a surplice provided by the Trustees of Portland Place Chapel, Bristol.
[9] *Minutes*, i. 541.
[10] *Candid Animadversions* (1794), pp. 18–22; answered by Crowther, *The Crisis of Methodism*, p. 26.
[11] Address of the London Trustees, 17th July, 1793.
[12] Jackson, T., *Life of Charles Wesley*, ii. 391.

SOCIETY OR CHURCH?

State and from the English hierarchy . . .' and he intended that preachers thus ordained should shed whatever powers and privileges this conferred if they returned to England. It was an impossible position. The preachers maintained, quite logically, 'once ordained, always ordained', so the apprehensions of Knox were not unreasonable. As he put it rather colourfully, 'The seed of Presbyteral ordination being sown, the creeping plant of separation would spread wider and wider'.[13] Knox knew very well that during the year after Wesley's death, ordinations were getting out of hand; in fact some of the preachers also were concerned about this.[14]

2. The Old Planners contended that Methodism should be 'a kind of middle link between all religious parties, uniting them in the interests of experimental religion and scriptural holiness'.[15] They believed that if Methodists organized themselves as a separate church they would become just another denomination among many and 'lose their glory'. They were intended to be 'evangelists to all denominations'.[16]

3. They also had a fear of fragmentation if Methodism lost its anchorage in the Church of England, recalling Wesley's prediction that, after his death some of his followers would 'dwindle away into a dry, dull separate party'.[17] This fear was not groundless. The Old Planners had only to remember the pathetic fate of preachers who had hived off with a few followers to form little independent societies of their own; they had only to think of what happened in the cases of John Bennet, John Atlay and (as the Manchester Trustees did[18]) of Benjamin Ingham. They felt that Methodism needed the anchorage of the Church to preserve it from the fate of these splinter groups.

[13] *Candid Animadversions*, p. 18.
[14] M.C.A. Letter from William Thompson to Richard Rodda, 8th February, 1792.
[15] *Address of the London Trustees*.
[16] Ibid. See also, Knox, A., *Considerations on a Separation* (1794), pp. 6, 7.
[17] *Letter of London Trustees*, quoting Wesley's *Farther Thoughts on Separating*.
[18] *Address of the Trustees of Manchester, etc., to the Methodist Societies of Bristol* (1794), p. 9.

4. A material factor, but not without weight, was that the Trustees had invested money in the buildings entrusted to their care and they were legally bound to see that Methodist doctrine and discipline were not violated. Just exactly where authority lay for the enforcement of this discipline—that is, who were spiritual and who were temporal overlords, Trustees or Leaders—was a debatable point, as we shall discover in connection with the Leeds Organ Case, but even if the Trustees' conception of essential Methodism differed from that of the Preachers and most of the Leaders, there can be no doubt that they conscientiously endeavoured to discharge their trust.

5. They saw the danger of a struggle for power if the Preachers were to assume ministerial status. Again, the fear was not imaginary. One cannot read the letters of John Pawson, for example, without noting his suspicions of Alexander Mather who was the only one, apart from Dr Coke, who had been ordained Superintendent by Wesley; or of William Thompson, who had been the first President after Wesley. Yet Pawson himself was not above joining the band of self-appointed *episcopoi* under the Lichfield Plan. The Old Planners were convinced that the Itinerants should remain Preachers of the Gospel, as the temptation to self-aggrandizement (an oft-used word) would be too strong to be resisted.[19]

6. The Old Planners, finally, were afraid that if Methodism assumed ecclesiastical status, the Itinerant system would change into a 'settled ministry' and the lively Methodist Preacher approximate more and more to the

[19] *Primitive Methodism Defended* (1795), p. 32. See also a rather vituperative publication entitled, *A Letter to the Methodist Preachers* (1795) by 'A Member of the Methodist Conference', hence one of the Itinerants. Of Benson and Mather he says, 'the one struggled for universal dominion and the other for supreme power as Lord Bishop of our Connexion'. Undoubtedly, during the last few years of Wesley's life, Mather had occupied a commanding position. Joseph Sutcliffe, writing of Wesley's last Conference (1790), said, 'Mr Mather, as a sort of archdeacon, a man of clear head and commanding voice, conducted the whole business of the Conference' (*Proceedings of the W.H.S.*, xv. p. 58). Kilham said that while Wesley was alive, Mather was 'considered as Prime Minister in our Israel' (*Martin Luther Tract*, p. 4).

becalmed Parish Priest or the dry-as-dust Arian Dissenter.[20] There was never any real danger of this, but at least the Old Planners saw it as a possibility.

Such, then was the position of these Old Planners. It is difficult to assess just what measure of support they commanded. The long list of signatories to some of their Broadsheets looks very impressive, but one feels that they represent a small, select minority of the Methodist people, for it is certain that the Preachers, almost to a man, were in the opposite camp, backed by the majority of the rank and file. The truth is, the Old Planners were fighting a losing battle. We are not without hints as to what would have happened if they had prevailed. The infamous way in which the trustees of the Newcastle Orphan House kept the property in their own hands,[21] does not inspire confidence. In London even the most saintly and trustworthy of the Preachers were not allowed to administer the sacraments, and at Great Queen Street a 'pious clergyman' was extradited from the Fleet prison to perform this duty,[22] which must surely be considered the most ridiculous, if logical, conclusion of 'the Old Plan'.

No! Methodism could not enter a second time into its mother's womb. The Old Planners forgot that Wesley himself had moved on from the early days and that the Methodist people did not owe anything like the allegiance to the Church of England that the Old Plan assumed. Although they maintained a vigorous rearguard action until 1795—even later in some centres, like City Road and Great Queen Street, in London—the future lay not with

[20] See Taylor, T., *Defence of the Methodists*, p. 37 (1792).
[21] See Aquila & Priscilla, *An Humble Address* (1794), pp. 3ff; also M.C.A. Letters of William Smith to Joseph Benson, 9th November and 21st December, 1792.
[22] *The Methodist Recorder*, Winter Number, 1895, p. 33: 'The shifts to which the good but benighted people of Great Queen Street were sometimes reduced are startling. It is astounding that our Methodist fathers would not allow such men as Pawson, Clarke, Mather and Sutcliffe to perform the sacramental functions, but would rather send to the Fleet prison for a "pious" clergyman who was incarcerated for debt, to come and adminster to them the Holy Communion.' Alexander Kilham was not far from the truth when he wrote, 'this religious farce hinders the itinerancy' (Aquila & Priscilla, p. 5).

them and their backward-looking mentality, but with those who were convinced that the way forward was to do as Wesley did and 'follow the openings of Providence' and to this, 'The Providential Way', we must now turn.

The Providential Way

The opening move from Hull soon produced a reply which clearly set out the position of the other party. A circular from Newcastle upon Tyne dated 5th July, 1791 contains all the ingredients of what we are calling 'The Providential Way'.[23] In opposition to the Old Planners, the advocates of this way forward pleaded for the administration of the sacraments by ordained Itinerants where and when it was desired by the Society at large. They argued that 'The Old Plan' was not old at all, that the oldest plan of all was 'to follow the openings of Providence'[24] and that was just what Wesley had done from the beginning. They believed that the genius of Methodism was to meet the needs of the day with inspired improvisations and that the secret of its success lay in its flexibility. Samuel Bradburn pointed out that Wesley 'made alterations of one kind or another every year;[25] accordingly, now that Wesley was gone, the needs of the day must be met realistically, which meant the administration of the sacraments by Methodist Preachers in Methodist chapels. Kilham forcibly argued that unless this was done, the majority of the Methodist people would not receive the sacraments at all; besides, he said, it would be a positive gain to the Societies and build them up in fellowship.[26] Behind this sacramental controversy, how-

[23] The copy of this circular in the Methodist Archives is signed by Charles Atmore and Joseph Cownley. See also *An Address to the Members and Friends of the Methodist Society in Newcastle* (1792), anonymous, but certainly by Alexander Kilham; it forms part of the correspondence between Joseph Cownley, senior preacher in the Newcastle Circuit who had administered the sacrament at Byker, and Robert Grey, an Old Planner and a Trustee of the Orphan House.
[24] M.C.A. Letter of John Pawson to Chas. Atmore, 19th October, 1791, also by the same writer to Jos. Benson dated 4th May, 1791.
[25] Bradburn, S., *To the People Called Methodists* (1792).
[26] *Address to the Newcastle Society.*

ever, there were deeper principles involved. To these we now turn.

1. The Preachers, as well as the Old Planners, appealed to Wesley; the latter appealed to the Founder's original plans, the former looked to later developments and even thought they could discern his intentions for the future. On the question of separation from the Church of England, the Preachers attached considerable significance to Wesley's idea of 'a partial separation' when 'the minister of the parish wherein we dwell neither lives nor preaches the Gospel'. On the other hand they forgot (or did they?) that Wesley told his followers that they should not absent themselves from the Lord's Table just because the incumbent was an 'ungodly' man, for the character of the celebrant does not invalidate the sacrament.[27] Whatever the Methodists thought of the theology of this, they would not follow it in practice; in spite of Wesley's exhortations they could not bring themselves to receive the sacrament from an incumbent who did not live a godly life.

We are here touching upon a fundamental, but forgotten, cause of the separation of Methodism from the Anglican Church. Methodism had adopted certain codes of behaviour which were regarded as the essential marks of a Christian. In this respect it was a highly disciplined holiness movement, and the more it insisted on the observance of its rules, the more it became a closed shop. As far as the Lord's Supper was concerned, it meant not only that Methodists refused to attend the ministrations of a 'worldly' incumbent, but also that they would not communicate with 'worldly' men and women. They alleged that discipline in the Church of England had become so lax that there was no discrimination between the 'worldly' and the 'godly';[28] and there were still those who attended the Sacrament to qualify for civil office!

So at the end of the eighteenth century the Methodists

[27] See my former work, *The Sacrament of the Lord's Supper in Early Methodism*, p. 71. For Wesley's own words: *On Attending the Church Service*—Works, vii. 184. Sermons, ii. 19. Letter to Mary Bishop, 10th October, 1778; *Letters*, vi. 327.
[28] See, e.g., *Address to the Newcastle Society*, p. 10.

had the closed table and complained that the Anglicans were too hospitable. They wanted the sacraments in their own chapels so that they could receive it in the exclusive company of those of their own brand of holiness. To receive it 'along with openly profane and wicked people'[29] was quite repugnant to them. They were quite unanimous about this. Alexander Kilham in his *Martin Luther* tract said, 'admit none to communicate with you but those that belong to the Society'. Benson wrote, 'It is unlawful to communicate with the ungodly, as we generally must do if we receive it at the Church ... we ought to have it among ourselves.'[30] Henry Moore saw this as one of the chief reasons for the separation of Methodism from the Church of England.[31] Before Trowbridge Methodists received permission to have the sacrament in their chapel, they held the service 'in a friend's house' so as to avoid having to receive it in company with 'those who profane the Temple of God and pollute His ordinances by their unholy hands, impure lips and wicked lives'.[32]

2. Secondly, there is the question of the ministry. Wesley's ordinations could have prepared the way for a threefold order of ministers in Methodism; in fact, some of the preachers were convinced that Wesley intended this to happen.[33] The significant point is that Wesley himself had initiated much for which the Preachers contended. For instance, John Murlin maintained that he frequently administered the Sacraments at Norwich, 'till Mr Charles made a great outcry and put a stop to it for a time'.[34] John Pawson said that Wesley gave leave to some of his Preachers to wear gowns 'long since' and advised his friend to go ahead and administer the sacrament.[35] Even after the Conference of 1793 had banned clerical attire, Bradburn

[29] See Bradburn, S., *Answer to Embury Edwards*, p. 18, and *Letter to Preachers late in Connexion with Mr Wesley*.
[30] *A Farther Defence of the Methodists*, p. 47.
[31] *Reply to Considerations*, p. 6.
[32] *To Methodists in the Bradford Circuit*, p. 1.
[33] *Remarks on Several Passages in the Works of John Wesley*, p. 12. See also Crowther, J., *Crisis of Methodism*, p. 16.
[34] M.C.A., Letter to Joseph Benson, 23rd December, 1794.
[35] M.C.A., Letter to Charles Atmore, 19th October, 1791.

SOCIETY OR CHURCH?

had hopes of adopting some ecclesiastical form.[36] So the Preachers believed that they were not untrue to Wesley's intentions in providing Methodism with a regular ministry. Their people had been brought to Christ through the preaching and pastoral oversight of the men whom they now regarded as their ministers. Naturally, it was from these men (be they episcopally ordained or not) that they wished to receive the Lord's Supper. They never for a moment doubted their qualifications to do so. 'Who is he that dare say', wrote the Liverpudlians, 'those men whom God has thrust out into His vineyard and made their ministry the power of God unto the salvation of their souls ... are not equally qualified by Him to administer the other ordinances?'[37] Joseph Benson would have nothing to do with the priestly office for ministers; for the only priesthood known to the New Testament was that of Christ, the Great High Priest, and the Royal Priesthood of the People of God; but he held that those who were called to the Pastoral Office were thereby qualified to administer the Lord's Supper.[38] John Pawson, a fair-minded, middle-of-the-road man, to whom Methodism owed much in these turbulent years, was sure that the only way forward was to face facts and accede to the not unreasonable requests of the people. 'This will unite us', he said, adding, 'The people mourn the loss of that which was so blest to them.'[39]

But—and this is an important implication—did not this step of ordaining preachers and administering the sacraments independent of the Church of England imply that the Methodists were now DISSENTERS? The Old Planners said 'Yes'; the Preachers said 'No'—but to see how they argued the case, we must turn to the writings of the protagonists.

---

[36] *Life of Bradburn*, p. 152; also M.C.A. Letter to Richard Elliott, December, 1793.
[37] Isaac Marsh and the Leaders and Trustees of Liverpool, *A Letter to the Methodist People*, 27th March, 1792.
[38] *A Farther Defence of the Methodists*, p. 62.
[39] M.C.A., Letter to Richard Rodda, 29th January, 1793.

Are the Methodists Dissenters?

In spite of the fact that the law compelled Wesley to license his chapels as Dissenting Meeting Houses and his Itinerants as Dissenting Preachers, Dissent was a word he avoided as a plague; but his employment of lay preachers, his disregard of parish boundaries and, above all, his ordinations, rendered him easy prey to the clergy who needed no encouragement to call Methodists 'Dissenters'. Accordingly, when Wesley's death broke the most obvious link with the Anglican Church, the new leaders of Methodism found that it taxed all their ingenuity to sustain the arguments of their Founder.

Some of the Preachers were prepared to admit, without qualification, that the Methodists were Dissenters. Alexander Kilham confessed that he regarded himself as a Dissenter from the start of his itinerant career. Thomas Taylor maintained that Wesley was compelled to *act* as a Dissenter, whatever his professions might be, by which was meant generally acting without a Bishop's permission in preaching in the open air, raising societies, building chapels, admitting laymen to preach and, finally, ordaining some of them. Taylor concluded, 'Almost every step Mr Wesley has taken has been in opposition to the Canons' and 'If all this does not make a man a Dissenter, it is hard to tell what does'.[40]

Others admitted that Methodists were Dissenters, but with qualifications. The Newcastle circular, for example, agrees with Taylor, but concludes, 'We are Dissenters in fact, though not in profession', and mentions 'three grand causes of our differing from other Dissenters' which would continue even if we acknowledged separation from the Church. Doctrine, discipline and the Itinerant Plan were what distinguished Methodists from the Dissenters.[41]

Taylor was answered by Samuel Bradburn in a book entitled, *The Question, 'Are the Methodists Dissenters?' Fairly Examined* (1792), in which he maintained that no altera-

[40] *Defence of the Methodists*, pp. 37–8 and p. 49.
[41] *Reply to a Circular from Hull*, 5th July, 1791.

SOCIETY OR CHURCH?

tions had been made in the original Methodist Plan, so far as doctrine, practice and discipline were concerned. He alleged that it was Wesley's intention to install a clergyman in each of the main chapels, as in London. He said an attempt was made at Manchester, but it came to nothing through lack of clergymen and opposition from the Manchester Preachers. Furthermore, he points out, Methodists are not Dissenters in that they do not object to the Prayer Book, some even regret that so much has been omitted! Be that as it may, Bradburn was compelled to admit that Methodism had encroached upon Church hours, mixed clergy and laymen in conducting public worship, and ordained deacons, elders and 'bishops',[42] but he would not admit that these 'principal alterations' made Methodists Dissenters. They are Church people still because they have no objection to the hierarchical constitution of the Church, they believe all her doctrines and have no scruples about her forms of worship and, in fact, they go to Church. At the same time, though the Methodists are Church people, their constitution is Presbyterian. He then quotes Wesley's saying, 'As soon as I am dead, the Methodists will be a regular, Presbyterian Church', and comments:

> And he did not mean that we should become such by making any alterations in our government... but that *his death would make* us such. While he lived he was the head, the Bishop; but as soon as he died, all his power died with him. He left no successor, he could leave none.

After comparing the Methodist constitution with that of the Church of Scotland, he says:

> We are not Episcopalians, we cannot be. We are not Independents, we will not be. Therefore we must be Presbyterians. ... The Methodists are, in their judgement and affections, on the side of the Established Church; in their constitution... they are mild Presbyterians; in their practice some go regularly to Church, others occasionally conform, many are simply hearers of their own preachers.[43]

[42] *Op. cit.*, pp. 10–13.
[43] *Op. cit.*, p. 19. See also Bradburn's *An Answer to Embury Edwards*, p. 25.

Another apologist, Jonathan Crowther, says that the Methodists are no more Dissenters than they were before the divisions took place, and supports his contention by pointing out that Methodists do not have services in Church hours and celebrate the sacraments only as Conference permits; but within a few years of Crowther's writing, services were held in church hours and the sacraments administered in Methodist chapels, so this particular plea largely falls to the ground.[44]

As we have read this apologetic literature, we have gained the impression that much of it is special pleading and at times the arguments become severely strained. Perhaps 'it all depends upon what you mean by Dissent'. Certainly the Methodists were not Dissenters in the old Nonconformist traditions; i.e. as those who refused to conform to, or use, the Prayer Book.

Again, we are faced with the difficulty of placing Methodism in any previously known category, whereas the truth is that it was a 'new thing' in the religious world and there was no ready-made category into which it could conveniently fit. As Methodists performed their religious exercises together apart from the Church of England, they could be called 'Dissenters'; but if their links with the Church meant anything at all, they were good churchmen. So John Pawson could write:

> The design of Mr Wesley is clear. He wished to show to all the world that the Methodists, considered as a body, are not only a sound part of the Church of England, but that they are the very Church of England itself; and that were we to preach in Church hours (so called) and have the sacraments administered among ourselves, yet still, according to the article, we belong to that Church as much as ever.[45]

[44] Another strained argument is Henry Moore's *A Reply to Considerations*, p. 10. He argues that the Canons were not ratified by Parliament. Similar point-stretching exercises are found in Thomas Taylor's *Nature and Design of the Lord's Supper* (*c*. 1792) in which he says that in the early church any pious person could preside at the Lord's Supper; see p. 23. Benson too goes so far as to assert that the presence of a minister is not necessary for the celebration—see his *Farther Defence*, p. 96.

[45] *An Affectionate Address to the Methodist Societies*, p. 21; also *The Methodist*

SOCIETY OR CHURCH?

There we could leave the subject, were it not for the fact that the whole topic of Sacrament and Dissent was only part of a wider struggle. Professor W. R. Ward of Durham University, approaching the questions from the sociopolitical angle, points out that the clamour for the sacraments, although made in pietistic terms, was only the local aspect of a great divide—that is, between the Establishment and sectarianism, and that in the demand for separate Communion there was as much politics as religion.[46] Neither politically nor doctrinally did the Methodists wish to be classed among the Dissenters, who at this time were drifting theologically into Arianism and politically into Republicanism. Just after Wesley died, and before the Conference met in July, Coke wrote significantly to Joseph Benson:

> I see a separation from the Established Church, whether gradual or immediate, pregnant with all the evils you mention. It would probably drive away from us and from God thousands of our people. We should lose our grand field of action. When once the members of the Established Church had embraced a confirmed idea that we were a proper *Dissenting Body*, they would pass by the doors of our Meeting houses with the same unconcern with which they pass by the doors of the Presbyterian meeting House. But more than this, we should soon imbibe the political spirit of the Dissenters; nor should I be much surprised if, in a few years, some of our people, warmest in politics and coolest in religion, would toast (as I am informed a famous Society did lately in the short hours of the night) a bloody summer and a headless king.[47]

There was a certain security for Methodism as long as it remained within the fold of the Church of England. Nine years after Wesley's death, Joseph Benson was still regretting that they had abandoned 'the old way' by administering the sacraments, adding 'It is our making the

---

Magazine, 1833, pp. 186–91, article by 'A Layman' entitled, 'The Intolerance of Evangelical Clergymen'.
[46] Ward, W. R., *Religion and Society in England 1790–1850*, pp. 32–5.
[47] M.C.A. letter from Coke to Benson, 15th July, 1791.

people Dissenters that the Government is jealous of'.[48] Hence his sustained efforts, along with those of Coke and others, to maintain some show of loyalty to the Establishment, especially during the years of mob violence in the 1790s. Professor W. R. Ward interprets the expulsion of Alexander Kilham as a demonstration of that loyalty.[49]

Hence it would appear that, however much Preachers and people might clamour for the administration of the Sacraments (one of the certain marks of Dissent), it was not wise to pose as Dissenters for all the world, and especially the Government, to see.[50]

Reconciliation

At the beginning of 1795 there was a real danger of Methodism splitting into two; two parties, two Conferences.[51] Already there were two chapels in Bristol each representing its own interpretation of Methodism. The New Room followed the 'Old Plan' and would allow none but ordained clergymen to administer the sacraments. Portland Chapel represented what we have called 'The

---

[48] M.C.A., Joseph Benson to Zachariah Yewdall, 26th April, 1800. The passage reads, 'I believe we will all now find how much better it would have been if we had abode entirely in the old way and neither have introduced service in Church hours nor the Sacrament anywhere. It is our making the people Dissenters that the Government is jealous of.'

[49] *Op. cit.*, p. 35.

[50] For the attitude of the parish clergy to the Methodists, see Edwards, E., *A Letter to the Occasional Preachers at Portland Chapel* (1791) and Bradburn's *Answer to Embury Edwards*. Edwards said bluntly, 'You are Dissenters according to the strictest sense and meaning of the expression.' He was of the Evangelical wing of the Church and therefore a Calvinist. When John Pawson was asked, 'Are there no awakened clergy?' he replied, 'They are almost all Calvinists and therefore no friends to us.' Edward Tatham, in *A Sermon suitable for the Times* (1792) attacked the Methodists on the grounds that their preachers were 'self-ordained', to which Joseph Benson replied in his *Defence of the Methodists*.

[51] See Mather and Pawson, *A Letter to the Preachers Late in Connexion with Mr Wesley* (26th September, 1794); *Address of the Trustees of Manchester* (21st October, 1794); Knox, A., *Considerations on a Separation*. Entwisle feared 'two Conferences and two Connexions'; see his *Memoirs*, p. 73. It is not generally known that the Old Planners formed a secession at Birmingham with 13 classes with Andrew Inglis as their minister—see Entwisle's *Memoirs*, p. 102.

SOCIETY OR CHURCH?

Providential Way' and regularly had the sacrament administered by the Preachers.

Fortunately there were ties which were stronger than contrary opinions and between October 1794 and the Conference of 1795 the storm abated and serious consideration was given to means of reconciliation. The actual father of the *Plan of Pacification* would appear to have been William Thompson. Jonathan Edmondson, replying to the charge that the Plan was 'wrung from an unwilling Conference', says that Thompson set out some suggestions for reconciliation and sent them to Mather, Pawson, Benson and Coke for comment.[52] These suggestions, says Edmondson, became (after a few alterations) *The Plan of Pacification* as accepted by the Conference of 1795.[53]

So the two parties were reconciled, and Methodism emerged in one piece. The Trustees were satisfied that the sacrament should be administered only where a majority of Trustees and Leaders allow, and then only with the consent of the Conference.[54] The Preachers were satisfied, in so far as it did not deny the Sacrament to a society where there was no chapel (and therefore no trustees) and where a majority of the people desired it.[55] The main thing was that at every stage the Conference kept control; the lesson of placing too much power in the hands of either trustees or leaders had been learned.

Other provisions of the Plan can be briefly mentioned. In deference to the Trustees, it was decided that Methodist services should not normally be held during church hours; if they were, then the Church Service, or Wesley's *Abridgement* must be read. The Lord's Supper must never be administered in the Methodist Chapel 'on those Sundays on which it is administered in the parochial church'. These

[52] Letter in *The Methodist Magazine*, 1835, p. 131. Thompson was Edmondson's superintendent in London in 1794–5. For the committee appointed by the Conference to consider the Plan, see *Minutes*, i. 339 (1795).
[53] In the Methodist Archives there are many letters which passed between Pawson and Benson, but they do not (as far as we can tell) give Thompson the credit of originating the Plan.
[54] *Minutes*, i. 693.
[55] Ibid.

regulations concerning 'services during church hours' caused no hardship, for many Methodists customarily attended the parish church in the morning and their own chapel in the evening.

The long-term effect of the Plan was more serious. For one thing, it threw the main service into the evening where, generally speaking, it has remained to this day. Unlike both Presbyterians and Anglicans, Methodists have tended to neglect morning worship, and for this *The Plan of Pacification* can be blamed. More serious, perhaps, was the emergence of Sunday evening Communion services (unknown in Wesley's time). Wesley's glorious Sunday morning celebrations survived only as a memory.[56]

The Plan of Pacification was a compromise in the society/church situation. It attempted to satisfy those who wished to preserve the character of Methodism as a society in close association with the Church of England. At the same time it launched Methodism as a Church in its own right. Yet like every compromise it accomplished neither of these aims completely or satisfactorily. In a much less complicated situation, the American Methodists organized themselves as a Church with a threefold order of ministers in direct descent from Wesley. On this side of the Atlantic, in deference to the Church of England, the Methodists hesitated. The price of their hesitation and eventual compromise has been well expressed by T. H. Barratt. 'The Methodists', he wrote:

> have paid a sad price for the pathetic loyalty of their fathers to their old, unkindly mother ... and ... those four years of prohibition followed by the restrictions of 1795 created a tradition which went far to annul the teaching and example of John Wesley and sowed seeds of which we reap the harvest even to this day.[57]

---

[56] In my book, *The Lord's Supper in Methodism 1791–1962*, p. 14f, I have dealt with the almost total eclipse of Wesley's eucharistic theology.

[57] *The London Quarterly Review*, July 1923.

CHAPTER TWO

THE NATURE OF EPISCOPÉ

THERE were three distinct views in Methodism as to where episcopé should reside when Wesley's personal supervision was removed. The first two had much in common and differed only on whether it should lie with a number of District 'Episcopoi' who would have oversight of a group of circuits, or whether it should lie with the Superintendent[1] of each circuit. The third party believed that ultimate authority should rest in the will of the people—we shall call this 'The Popular Front'.

The Tentative 'Halifax' Scheme

John Wesley died on 2nd March, 1791 and on the same day the five Preachers of the London Circuit posted a short circular to the Assistants throughout the connexion, advising them of the event and reminding them of their late Leader's dying request that each remain in his station until the Conference meet. There were, however, nearly five months to go until Conference, so it was not to be expected that the Preachers would refrain from expressing an opinion about the future government of the connexion. Some of them were apprehensive lest the period be used for personal advantage, and this prompted quick action.[2] On 30th March, nine senior Preachers met at Halifax to consider 'our form or mode of government'. The result of the meeting was the publication of the well-known 'Halifax Circular'. The preamble began:

> There appears to us but two ways: either to appoint another king in Israel, or to be governed by the Conference Plan, by forming ourselves into committees. If you adopt the first, who is the man? What power is he to be invested with and what revenue is he to be allowed? But this is incompatible with the

[1] See ch. 3, n. 18.
[2] M.C.A. Letter, John Pawson to Charles Atmore, 9th March, 1791.

Divisions and reunion of Methodism in the nineteenth century

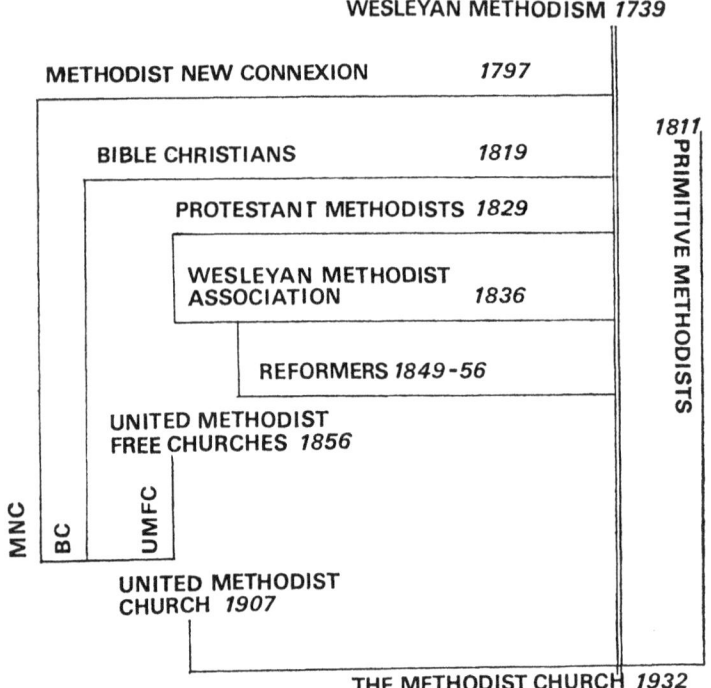

Other minor bodies of the nineteenth century include the Tent Methodists, the Church Methodists and the Arminian Methodists. The Independent Methodists and the Wesleyan Reform Union still exist as separate denominations.

Terminology differed very little from one Methodist body to another; but the following variations occur:

1. The U.M.F.C., used the term 'Annual Assembly' for the 'Conference'.
2. The P.M.C., referred to their circuits as 'Stations' and to their ministers as 'Travelling Preachers'.
3. The Bible Christians also spoke of 'Travelling Preachers' and often used the term 'Pastors' of their ministers. Unique among Methodist bodies, they had 'Elders' with regular 'Elders' Meetings'. Chairmen of Districts were known as 'Superintendents of Districts'.

Conference Deed. If the latter, we take the liberty to offer our thoughts upon the subject.

This well sensed the situation. In the nature of things, a new 'King in Israel' was out of the question. The Legal Conference was Wesley's true successor and all that remained to do was to carry out the provisions of the Deed of Declaration, which would provide the necessary oversight. The Halifax Circular suggested, *inter alia*, that the three kingdoms be divided into Districts, in each of which there would be a committee to manage local affairs until the following Conference. Each committee would annually elect its President, who would be accountable to the Conference for his own District. The District President had authority to convene the committee 'in case of the bad behaviour or death of a Preacher, or in any other emergency'.

The significance of the Halifax Circular was threefold—it formed a basis for discussion, it brought into the open the fears of autocratic rule and it suggested a means whereby discipline could be maintained between one Conference and the next. Naturally, replies and counter-suggestions were plentiful. Bristol, Leeds and Manchester approved the Halifax proposals, with Leeds suggesting that there should be a meeting just prior to Conference, similar to what we would now call the 'Stationing Committee'. This did not commend itself, so it was dropped—wisely so, for such a committee, meeting before the first Conference after Wesley's death, could easily have laid itself open to the charge of 'arranging things'. In a reply from Carmarthen, the Halifax Circular was thoroughly, though sensibly scrutinized. It was suggested that in addition to the Legal Hundred, all Assistants and every Preacher 'to be admitted' should attend Conference. This is significant, for it recognized that it was the Assistant who was responsible for executing the will of Conference in the circuits (as it had been in Wesley's day). The most farseeing comment from Carmarthen was that which dealt with the status of the District Chairman:

... is it not expedient that the power and authority of such

President should be particularly specified; or will not his office supersede that of the President (of the Conference) . . . and will it not be right to have his authority also explicitly stated according to the Deed enrolled in Chancery?

This was well said, for the Deed of Declaration made no mention of District Presidents (or Chairmen, as they were afterwards called).

So this was how matters stood when the Conference assembled on 26th July, 1791. The Halifax Circular had been generally approved, District Committees seemed to provide reasonable oversight, but the status and authority of the Chairman remained to be defined. When the matter was discussed by the Conference, it approved the setting up of District Committees, but an important alteration was made in Clause 6 of the Circular, thus:

Halifax	*Conference*
6. Let these committees, during the time of Conference, appoint their own Presidents for the ensuing year. And let their names be inserted in the Minutes that they may convene the Committee, in case of the bad behaviour, or death of a Preacher; or any other emergency.	The Assistant of a Circuit shall have authority to summon the Preachers of his District who are in Full Connexion, on any critical case, which, according to the best of his judgement, merits such an interference. And the said Preachers, or as many of them as can attend, shall assemble at the place and the time appointed by the Assistant aforesaid, and shall form a committee for the purpose of determining concerning the business on which they are called. They shall choose a chairman for the occasion, and their decision shall be final till the meeting of the next Conference, when the Chairman of the Committee shall lay the Minutes of their Proceedings before the Conference.

As Conference saw the situation, the authority to summon a District Meeting lay with the Assistant (i.e. the Circuit Superintendent) for it was more of an *ad hoc* meeting summoned to deal with a particular emergency.

In 1792 the District Chairman was given a little more power, in that the clause quoted above was amended to read:

> The Chairman ... shall have authority to call a meeting of the Committee of his District, on any application of the Preachers or people which appears to him to require it. But he must never individually interfere with any other circuit but his own.

That last sentence is worth noting. Whatever power the Chairman possessed, it must not diminish the authority of the circuit superintendent who was, and still is, the key man in the Methodist constitution.

In spite of the organization of District Committees, the need for tighter control was still felt and this seemed possible only by strengthening the authority of the Chairman of the District.[3] There were several attempts to do this. The basic idea was to install at the head of each District a person who should be free from circuit responsibility. Of course, the idea that a few senior Preachers should govern the connexion was embodied in an early plan of Wesley.[4] This laid it down that within six weeks of his death all the Preachers in England should meet in London and draw up articles of agreement. Those who felt that they must dissent were to be dismissed 'in the most friendly manner possible'. Those who remained were to elect a committee of 3 to 7, each to act as Moderator in turn. The duties of this select band was, 'to Propose preachers to be tried, admitted or excluded; fix the place of each Preacher for the ensuing year, and the time of the next Conference'. Before Wesley died, this oligarchical plan was set aside for the much more

---

[3] M.C.A. Letter of William Thompson to Richard Rodda, 8th February, 1792. William Thompson and John Pawson were both of the opinion that if proper Chairmen of Districts had been appointed in 1791, there would not have been so many unauthorized ordinations.

[4] *Large Minutes*, 1780 (*Minutes*, i. 587).

liberal Deed of Declaration. The earlier plan had only a semblance of suffrage, for while each Preacher had a vote at the initial stage, the actual government of the Connexion was in the hands of a small but powerful Committee. But there were later attempts to set up District Episcopoi, and to these we now turn.

Attempts at District Superintendency

The Lichfield Plan

The historical details of the clandestine meeting of eight[5] Preachers at Lichfield can be read in the standard histories of Methodism; our concern is with the ideas that inspired it. There are several versions of the minutes of the meeting,[6] but they all agree in the main suggestion that the Connexion be divided into seven or eight territorial divisions, over each of which a District Superintendent be appointed. His task would be:

> to execute, or see executed, all the branches of Methodist discipline, and to determine, after having consulted the Preachers who are with him, in all cases of difficulty, till the next Conference.

The rest of the Preachers are to be ordained Deacon on being admitted into Full Connexion and Elder later (though exactly when this takes place is not stated). At the same time, no Preacher is under any obligation to be ordained if he has scruples about it.

On many counts this would seem to be a reasonable scheme. To begin with, it had the support of the leading men in the Connexion and with such platform backing it should have experienced no difficulty in commending itself to the floor of the house. Furthermore, it would have given

---

[5] They were Coke, Mather, Thomas Taylor, Pawson, Bradburn, Rogers, Moore and Clarke.

[6] See M.C.A. letter from Samuel Bradburn to Dr Coke, 17th April, 1794; letter from John Pawson to Charles Atmore, 8th April, 1794; Smith's *History of Wesleyan Methodism*, ii. 703; a Ms. by Dr Adam Clarke formerly in Wesley College, Leeds, now at Wesley College, Bristol. A tabular arrangement of these versions will be found in Appendix I of my Ph.D. thesis, available at Leeds University.

Methodism a semblance of government which it very badly needed.[7] More cogent still, was the opinion, spelt out so confidently by John Pawson, that it was in line with Wesley's intentions:

> The design of Mr Wesley will weigh very much with many, both Preachers and people, which now evidently appears to have been this. He foresaw that the Methodists would soon after his death become a distinct body of people. He was deeply prejudiced against a Presbyterian, and was as much in favour of Episcopal government. In order therefore to preserve all that is valuable in the Church of England among the Methodists, he ordained Mr Mather and Dr Coke Bishops. These he undoubtedly designed should ordain others. Mr Mather told us so at the Manchester Conference, but we did not at all understand him. We could not see how a Scotch Presbyterian Bishop could support the Church of England.
>
> The mystery was here. By the Church of England was meant the body of Methodists who were to have the Doctrine and Discipline of the Church of England among them. . . .
>
> I do therefore sincerely wish that Dr Coke and Dr Mather may be allowed to be what they are, Bishops. . . .[8]

However, it is now a matter of history that, with so much in its favour, the Lichfield Scheme was decisively rejected by the Conference. As the Minutes do not give it even a passing mention, we must look elsewhere for the reasons for its rejection; fortunately, with the resources of the Archives at our disposal, these are not hard to come by.

In a letter dated 8th May, 1794, William Thompson reports to Joseph Benson that the secret of Lichfield had leaked out; in fact, it had been discussed at the London District Meeting. The feelings expressed there were first, 'that the meeting at Lichfield was entirely contrary to the existing constitution of Methodism and prejudicial to the

---

[7] M.C.A. letter of John Pawson to Charles Atmore, 2nd December, 1793, 'We really have no government. Our District Meetings do not answer the end'; also to Atmore, 18th February, 1794, 'Everyone may do what is right in his own eyes'. Pawson was satisfied that no one would have anything to fear from episcopal government, 'Any Bishop abusing his power would be unbishoped at once. . . .'—letter to Atmore, 21st January, 1794.

[8] M.C.A. Letter to Atmore, 13th December, 1793.

work of God in which we are engaged' and that it was 'contrary to the declaration of the last Conference'.[9] It was also said that it ought not to be discussed in Conference 'till the person or persons convening it be known'. Although Thompson was personally prejudiced against the Scheme[10] —perhaps annoyed at not being invited to Lichfield!—he did speak for the rank and file of the Preachers. Why, then, was the scheme rejected? We can think of at least six reasons.

1. The secrecy of the meeting angered the Preachers. It seemed too much of a *coup d'état*.[11] But Coke had a penchant for tempting Providence. Pawson admitted that, 'The Dr's design was to break the rules in order that the Conference might be obliged to call him . . . to account for so doing'.[12] 'Act and be damned' was his motto.

2. There was still tension between ordained and unordained Preachers, and in spite of the Conference ruling of 1793, ordinations were still taking place—Dr Coke being the chief miscreant!

3. When one compares the list of proposed Bishops with that of the men present at Lichfield, one can hardly exonerate them from place-seeking. The Scheme would certainly have stood a much better chance of success had it been left to the Conference to nominate the new Bishops (or Superintendents).

4. The rank and file of the Preachers were not for a change in the mode of government. They were content to let the District Chairmen retain what authority they had and to allow the circuit Superintendent to be the real executive.

5. There was a widespread fear of despotism. Opposition to Bishops came not only from the Kilhamites; moderates,

[9] i.e. that the title 'Reverend' be dropped and the distinction between ordained and unordained Preachers be ignored—see *Minutes* i. 290.
[10] M.C.A. Pawson writes to Atmore, 2nd December, 1793, '. . . the most profound secrecy must be observed or if Mr Thompson gets to know it, he will labour night and day to overturn it'.
[11] M.C.A. letter from Thompson to Rodda, 'I shall let you know whatever discoveries I can make of their dark designs'.
[12] M.C.A. letter to Atmore, 18th February, 1794; see also letter to Atmore, 21st January, 1794.

too, joined in and one of them, Jonathan Crowther, wrote:

> Should Bishops ever rise upon your humble hemisphere, as blazing and wandering stars, your sun of prosperity will quickly set. By a combination among themselves, they might, at any time, put you and the whole cause of Methodism at their disposal.[13]

6. Finally, there was a marked reluctance to create another order of ministers, another class of men who would be other than Itinerant Preachers without normal circuit responsibility. From the first Conference after Wesley's death, the Preachers took great care to stress the parity which must obtain among them—ordained or unordained, of the Legal Hundred or not. To appoint men with a roving commission seemed a dangerous step to take; and was it not laid down that any Preacher not appointed to a circuit[14] should not be eligible for the Legal Hundred?

So the Lichfield Scheme was rejected; but it was not the only or the last attempt to establish District episcopoi. At least two other attempts were made[15] but they met with no more success than Lichfield. The office of 'Separated Chairman' did not appear in an official form until the Conference of 1955.[16]

The Popular Front

While some of the Preachers were making their plans for the government of the Connexion, some of the people made known their feeling that they ought to have a share in that government. Among the circulars which were produced between Wesley's death and the Conference of 1791, one

[13] *Christian Order* (1796), p. 19.
[14] E.g. any clergyman who might remain in his parish, like Grimshaw or Venn, and still be in connexion with the Conference. See the 'Halifax' and 'Leeds' circulars of 1791.
[15] One was a scheme proposed by Samuel Bradburn to the Conference of 1795, and the other similar scheme put by Coke in 1797. For the former see the *Life of Alexander Kilham*, pp. 227–9; for the latter, M.C.A. Atmore's Ms. Notes on the Conference of 1797. Both schemes are discussed in my Ph.D. thesis, q.v.
[16] Before 1955, a few Districts had a Separated Chairman, but there was no office as such; he was designated 'District Missionary'.

from Redruth presaged events to come. Fifty-one delegates, meeting on 14th June, agreed that 'an amendment of our discipline is necessary' and suggested that Class Leaders should be chosen by the members themselves, and Society Stewards by the people; that members should not be admitted to, or expelled from, the Society without the consent of a majority of the members; that a majority vote of the Quarterly Meeting should determine such items as division of circuits, admission of Travelling Preachers; that delinquent Preachers should be tried before a mixed court consisting of an equal number of Preachers and Stewards.

This was not so much an amendment of the Wesleyan constitution, as a different one altogether; different in concept as well as in facts. But it expressed a point of view, the advocates of which were vociferous, if not numerous; and within a few years a champion was to arise and provide a rallying point for all who thought accordingly. The long and painful story of the disaffection, trial and expulsion of Alexander Kilham need not be repeated here, for what we are concerned with is the challenge his party presented to Wesleyan polity and ideas.

The Kilhamite protest began with the charge that 'the Preachers rule without consulting the people'. In evidence of this, he outlined the powers of an Assistant:

1. With[17] the help of a single leader, to receive members into, or exclude members from the Society; without consent of the people.
2. Alone to place or displace leaders, stewards or local preachers.
3. Alone to recommend new Travelling Preachers.
4. Make collections, without giving an account of them.

From this basic issue, the controversy grew: but the main contentions of this party can be summarized as follows:

1. The President of the Conference must be elected for one year only, and not be eligible for re-election for several years to come. District Chairmen should be chosen locally

[17] The text certainly reads 'with': but one feels that Kilham meant 'without'.

THE NATURE OF EPISCOPÉ

and not by the Conference. This would maintain the parity of ministers, give the more talented brethren a chance to exercise their gifts without assuming permanent power.[18]

2. There must be no 'Travelling Bishops'.[19]

3. At every level, there must be representation of the people. Members should not be received or excluded, Leaders appointed or removed, in fact nothing of importance should be decided without consent of the people.

4. Circuit Quarterly Meetings and District Meetings should be composed of lay representatives as well as Itinerants.

5. Conference, too, should be a mixed assembly of Preachers and laymen.

6. It should not be left with the Assistant alone to call out men to travel. Kilham alleged that many unsuitable men had been enlisted through this method. All candidates should be approved by Quarterly and District Meetings consisting of both Preachers and laymen.

7. Stewards chosen by the people should handle all connexional moneys.

8. With regard to the stationing of the Preachers, at the Circuit Quarterly Meeting preceding Conference the Leaders and Stewards should 'declare the sense of the people concerning the Preacher'.[20]

Kilham believed that in the early Church, bishops were superintendents, chosen by the consent of ministers and people;[21] hence in Methodism 'every superintendent is the bishop of the circuit; his colleagues in full connexion are his presbyters'.[22] District Meetings represented the ancient Synods, and the Conference the great Councils of the

[18] In 1791, District Committees and their Chairmen were elected *ad hoc*; but in 1792, Chairmen were appointed by Conference and it was to this that the Kilhamites took exception.
[19] See Kilham's *Paul and Silas*, p. 16.
[20] Financial matters were also mentioned but are not relevant to our discussion.
[21] See Kilham's *Martin Luther* broadsheet, also his *Plain Account of the Methodist New Itinerancy*, p. 3 and *The Trial of Alexander Kilham before the Conference*, p. 10.
[22] Just what Bunting said, many years later; is that why he was accused of being a Kilhamite?

Church. He felt that it was quite wrong that in Methodism Chairmen should be chosen and appointed by Conference and imposed upon the Districts, because 'rejection of delegates from the people will, in time, produce a corrupt ministry'.[23] In other words, Kilham felt that oversight of the ministry by the ministry was not enough. Only oversight by the people or their representatives could guarantee a pure ministry. The Preachers, of course, disagreed!

With regard to ordination, the Kilhamites favoured the laying-on of hands and regretted its cessation in 1792; they thought it was a scriptural rite, but that it ought to be received once only and not three times as in the case of ordination of deacon, presbyter and bishop.

As for the sacraments, these were not a primary issue with the Kilhamites, though they strongly advocated administration wherever the people desired it. They thought the *Plan of Pacification* was hedged around with too many restrictions and that there were too many majorities to respect before the will of the people was necessarily observed.

This, then, was the scheme which stirred up so much trouble in the short space of eighteen months and ended with the expulsion of its champion from the Methodist Conference and the founding of the first important secession, The Methodist New Connexion. Some later Wesleyan historians are anxious to point out that Kilham was expelled, not for his ideas, but for his insolence and flouting of discipline. Professor W. R. Ward thinks he was expelled for political reasons.[24] Be that as it may, there can be no doubt that he left his mark on the parent body, for it was through his agitation that the rules were revised and *The Form of Discipline* compiled.

Why did Kilham fail? We suggest, for the following reasons:

1. His attacks on the Preachers were unjust and made without supporting evidence. He made many personal enemies.

[23] *Plain Account*, p. 6.
[24] See above, ch. 1, p. 15.

THE NATURE OF EPISCOPÉ

2. His criticism of Wesley was grossly misplaced. Wesley's followers were in no mood to see their late Father in God defamed, a mere five years after his death. Kilham's suggestion that Wesley's Sermons should be revised was radical enough, but when he said they should be revised *by the people*, it was the last straw! He then added insult to injury when he claimed that the forms of Church government among the Methodists were 'borne as a temporary evil' while Wesley was alive.[25]

3. A more serious reason for Kilham's failure was that his scheme would have reduced the Conference to 'a clearing house and court of registration'.[26] No wonder he was of the opinion that its business could be got through in a week! To the Wesleyan Preachers the Conference was the Pastoral Council of the Church; the collective episcopé of the Connexion, where ministers met in a common brotherhood. It took nearly a century for laymen to break into that preserve. In reply to Kilham's charge that the Conference was autocratic, the Preachers pointed out that its power was held only by mutual consent of Preachers and people and that it was restricted by such agreement as Chapel Deeds, Minutes of Conference and the Plan of Pacification. The power of Conference was neither usurped, nor wholly delegated by men, but,

> first given to them by God in common with all who are called by him to the work of the ministry ... it is a power inherent in themselves as ministers who have first formed themselves into a body.[27]

4. In Kilham's scheme, the minister was little more than a hired preacher, dependent upon the suffrage of the people. He begins with the maxim that all Christians are equal in the sight of God, therefore all Church Officers (including ministers) must be:

[25] *A Brief Statement of the Dispute at Nottingham* (1797), and *A Defence of the Conduct of the Conference*, p. 24.
[26] *L.Q.R.* October 1885, p. 154. The Methodist New Connexion did not embody Kilham's plans to the extreme; this was left to the more radical break-away movements of the next century. In fact, of all the splinter movements, the M.N.Cs were the nearest to the Old Body.
[27] *Circular to Members of the Connexion* from Manchester and Salford Trustees.

by the appointment and approbation of the people, and to be accountable to them for everything that concerns their office.

5. The time was not ripe for elective representation in Church courts, and as much as Kilham appealed to Paine and the measure of civil liberty already granted,[28] the shadow of the People's government in France still lay heavily across the country and the Wesleyans were in no mood to welcome anything that smacked of Republicanism.

6. Kilham would have the people appoint, and to some extent have power to dismiss, their Preachers. Joseph Benson, however, saw the dangers of this course. In his *Discipline of the Methodists Defended*[29] he pointed out that Societies would become divided for and against their pastor, a Preacher would be concerned about pleasing the people, especially the rich, who paid him. It would, in fact, destroy the itinerancy, for some Preachers would become so popular in one particular place that it would be impossible to move them.

So we see what the Wesleyans rejected during the six crucial years after Wesley's death. On the one hand, they would have nothing to do with a hierarchy of travelling bishops; on the other hand, they rejected the Republicanism of Kilham. What they did accept, a scheme produced as the result of the impact of both these advocated extremes, is contained in *The Form of Discipline* of 1797 and to this we must now turn.

---

[28] *Progress of Liberty*, p. 19; M.C.A. letters of John Pawson to Benson, 13th April, 1797, and to Atmore, 4th July, 1797. See *An Address to the Methodist Conference in Ireland* (1797), *Minutes* i. 404. In Huddersfield the M.N.Cs were called 'Tom Paine Methodists'—see Taylor, *Methodism and Politics*, p. 85; Ward, W. R., *The French Revolution and the English Churches*, pp. 66ff.
[29] p. 14.

CHAPTER THREE

THE FORM OF DISCIPLINE (1797)

THE Conference of 1797 reported that it had 'carefully revised the Rules drawn up and left us by our Venerable Father in the Gospel [and] collected together those Rules which we believe to be essential to the existence of Methodism, as well as others to which we have no objection'.[1] As a result, the 1797 *Form of Discipline* became the Magna Carta of Wesleyan Methodism,[2] as modified by the pressure of events during the six years after Wesley's death—the period during which, as Charles Welch expressed it, 'Wesley's autocracy was superseded by "a limited or restricted aristocracy"'.[3]

It is not our purpose to subject *The Form of Discipline* to detailed scrutiny, but only to note the chief constituents in the Wesleyan ecclesiastical system which expressed a certain conception of church and ministry. These are, (a) the supremacy of the Conference, (b) the status of District Chairmen, (c) the office of Circuit Superintendent, (d) the idea of the Pastoral Office, and (e) the role of the laity.[4]

The Supremacy of the Conference

In the first place, *The Form of Discipline* preserved the supremacy of the Conference which from the earliest days had always been the *dernier ressort*. Wesley's autocracy was something less than absolute. He constantly sought the advice of his Preachers and acted upon it as he thought fit. At the same time, to advise and not to rule was the purpose

---

[1] *Minutes*, i. 377.
[2] In this chapter, quotations from this document will be given as they appear in the *Minutes*, volume 1, 1862 edition—e.g. F.D. vii. 7.
[3] *The Wesleyan Polity*, p. 65.
[4] This chapter deals with points established in 1797; later we shall show how they were modified or maintained between 1797 and 1850.

of those early assemblies.⁵ As time went on, however, this annual gathering of Preachers gained prestige and came to possess an authority of its own. It is therefore no surprise to find that the government of the connexion was ultimately placed there and the Conference accorded a legal status. It became, in the words of Jabez Bunting, 'the living Wesley'.

However, as we have seen in the previous chapters, the authority of Conference was challenged from two directions. On the one hand, the Bristol Trustees claimed the right to accept or reject, at their own discretion, the Preachers whom the Conference appointed. This was a direct 'right wing' challenge to the authority of the Conference. On the other hand, the Kilhamites while accepting the authority of the Conference, revolted against its all-ministerial composition and clamoured for lay representation.⁶ This was a 'left-wing' revolt which was carried farther by the Protestant Methodists and other splinter groups in the next century. In the end, however, the right wing revolt taught the Preachers to confirm the supremacy of Conference against any local assumption of power; the latter controversy failed to establish that lay-representation was either desirable or necessary.

At the same time, neither of these movements was without its influence. Many of the concessions which appear in *The Form of Discipline* were due, directly or indirectly, to the agitations of 1791-7, but none undermined the supremacy of the Conference.⁷

The District Chairman

While the Conference decisively rejected the appointment of District Superintendents, episcopé at District level was essential. As the Conference could meet only annually,

⁵ Wesley's *Letters*, vi. 376.
⁶ The Methodism New Connexion, i.e. the body formed by the Kilhamite secession, unlike later secessions, invested their Conference with authority, though it was composed of ministers and laymen in equal numbers.
⁷ What added considerably to the authority of the Conference was the continuity given to it by the members of the Legal Hundred.

THE FORM OF DISCIPLINE (1797)

some measure of executive authority was plainly needed to maintain discipline and deal with emergencies between one Conference and the next. Furthermore, some intermediate authority was required to bridge the gap between the Conference and the Circuits. We have seen that, immediately after Wesley's death, District Committees were set up and that during the period 1791–7 the powers and duties of the District Chairmen gradually evolved until they were finally written into *The Form of Discipline*. It is with regulations that we are concerned here, for it was on the authority of the District Meeting and, consequently, on the strength of District episcopé, that one of the crises of Methodism turned in the first half of the nineteenth century.

District Committees were formed, says William Myles, 'to supply the want of Mr Wesley's general superintendence'.[8] His meaning is plain. The ordinary administration of the Connexion was settled by its Rules, confirmed by Conference and published in the *Minutes*. While John Wesley was alive, he saw to it that, between Conferences, the Preachers and local officers discharged their duties efficiently; if not, they were suspended or removed, pending the next Conference. In this way, Wesley exercised his 'general superintendence'; and it was just this that District Meetings were designed to supply.

At the same time, these District Committees developed into something more than *ad hoc* meetings to deal with 'critical cases' (the term used in 1791); they became a regularly held regional consistory to review District affairs and prepare for the Annual Conference.[9] Furthermore, if District Committees were intended to supply the lack of Wesley's general superintendence, it was highly necessary for them to be invested with authority corresponding to that held by Wesley. So it is not surprising that the District Chairman was, in fact, given considerable powers. Together with his brethren on the committee, he was 'res-

---

[8] *Chronological History* (Fourth edition), p. 211; see also Beecham, J., *Essay on the Constitution of Wesleyan Methodism* (henceforth quoted as E.C.W.M.) (Third edition, 1851), p. 39.
[9] F.D. xxv—*Minutes*, i. 692.

ponsible to the Conference for the execution of our laws, as far as his District is concerned'[10] and 'that no Chairman may have cause to complain of the want of power'[11] it was provided that any Chairman should be able to call to his aid, if he thought necessary, three of the nearest Superintendents with power to vote as any other member of the Committee.[12] In view of the fact that Conference had refused to appoint separated District Superintendents lest they wielded too much power,[13] this is a significant stipulation; evidently, they saw no harm in giving the Chairman all the power he needed. So the value of the *Form of Discipline* here is that it 'effectually provided for the maintenance and enforcement of discipline by the *collective pastorate of the District*'.[14]

In the normal course of affairs, where discipline was administered effectively by the superintendent and the leaders, the Chairman's duties were strictly limited. He had no authority to interfere with any circuit but his own.[15] Chairmen themselves, if charged with a misdemeanour, were to be tried by a District Court convened by the superintendent who raised the charge. If the chairman was found guilty, he was to be suspended until his case could be considered at the next Conference. Provision was also made for the trial of preachers accused of immorality and also for cases where 'there be a difference between two preachers'. In the last resort the President of the Conference could be called in to assist the Chairman, 'if applied to for that purpose by the Chairman of the District or by a majority of the Superintendents in that District'. Furthermore, in all these cases, any member of Society could be admitted as

[10] Ibid.
[11] *Minutes*, i. 395.
[12] Ibid.
[13] The 'power' element was evidently not the only reason for the rejection of Bishops. As we saw in the previous chapter, the rank and file of the Preachers did not like the idea of men without pastoral responsibility 'lording' it over them. It was the idea of 'separation' from ordinary circuit work, the creation of a distinct class of ministers that weighed most heavily against the Lichfield Scheme.
[14] *E.C.W.M.*, p. 71.
[15] *Minutes*, i. 691.

evidence into a District Meeting, provided the matter had first been heard in the Quarterly Meeting.

The success of this scheme lay in the mutual oversight of a body of ministers where the principle of parity was strictly observed. It did not call for the creation of another class of ministers without circuit responsibility or with life-appointments to office. It was a truly *collective* episcopé.[16]

Therefore, in a situation which called for efficient government between Conferences,[17] the *Form of Discipline* of 1797 supplied a real need.

The Circuit Superintendent

During Wesley's general superintendency, the Assistant (later called the Superintendent) was all-powerful in his circuit. In fact, the power wielded by the Assistant was sufficient to form one of the complaints of the Kilhamites against the system. We have just seen that, after Wesley's death, there was a need for some intermediary authority between the Conference and the Circuits and that this was supplied by the District Committees. It is of some significance, however, that when the word 'Assistant' was no longer meaningful, the new title of 'Superintendent' was not given to the District Chairman (to whom it might well have applied) but to the Assistant or head of the Circuit. This is all the more surprising when it is remembered that in America, where Methodism was organized under Wesley's orders, the titles 'Bishop' and 'Superintendent' (both offices are in operation) were bestowed upon District officers without pastoral charge. In other words, in America episcopé was exercised at *District* level, in Britain at *Circuit* level.[18]

Alexander Kilham took exception to the power of the

[16] There was a tendency for the Irish Conference to regard Dr Coke as their General Superintendent, but the Conference stifled that by ruling that all correspondence must be sent to them and not to the Doctor—*Minutes* i 254.

[17] Pawson complained that many weak and inexperienced superintendents lacked the support which only a consort of fellow-ministers could give—see many of his letters in the M.C.A.

[18] It is difficult to determine exactly when the word 'Superintendent' began to displace that of 'Assistant'. The Minutes of 1796 make the alteration quietly, but it had been in common use much earlier. See: Bradburn, S.,

Superintendent. He maintained that in the early days it was necessary to give the Assistant considerable authority to organize the Societies, to admit and dismiss Leaders, etc., but that in a mature organization like Methodism of 1795 the Assistant's powers ought to be held in consultation with his Leaders. *The Form of Discipline* went a long way to meet these objections and admitted that they had handed over to the people 'far the greatest part of the Superintendent's authority'.[19] It also went on to say that the authority of the District Meeting had been reduced to 'a bare negative in general'. This was somewhat overstating the case, for while some concessions had been made to the *vox populi*, both the Superintendent and the District Chairman retained considerable power.

While the District Chairman and his committee were 'responsible to the Conference for the execution of the laws', in the last resort it was the Circuit Superintendent who was the responsible official. The District machinery was created largely to enforce his authority if need be. It is true that the powers of the Superintendent, in terms of what he could do on his own, were curtailed from what they were in Wesley's day, but right through the *Form of Discipline* he is the 'episcopos'. He presides at the Quarterly Meeting, the Leaders' Meeting (though often he will delegate some of the work of the Leaders' Meeting to his colleagues) and Trustees' Meetings; in fact, nothing, apart from purely routine matters, can take place in the Circuit without his consent.[20] His prerogative to admit and dismiss members and officials became a violent storm centre in the next century.

The Superintendent was, therefore, the true episcopos. He was pastor pastorum;[21] the key man in the Connexion.

Methodism Set Forth and Defended, p. 42. Kilham, A., *Martin Luther*, p. 3. Myles, W., *Chronological History* (4th Edition), p. 90.
[19] *Minutes*, i. 394.
[20] *Minutes*, i 392.
[21] *Minutes*, i 678; in the long list which comprises 'The Peculiar Rules of a Superintendent', heading all others is, 'To see that the other Preachers behave well and want nothing. He should consider these (especially if they are young men) as his pupils, into whose behaviour and studies he should frequently inquire. . . .' Is this an echo of Wesley's Oxford days?

THE FORM OF DISCIPLINE (1797)

He had responsibility for things spiritual and temporal. Yet he was always subject to checks and balances—the lower courts curbed the despot, the higher supported the weak and inexperienced. Methodism of this post-Wesley period did not err when it placed the episcopé of the Connexion in the hands of its Circuit Superintendents.

The Pastoral Office

As Chapter Two of Part IV is devoted to this subject, we shall only note at this point the sowing of the seed from which the later harvest was reaped. The chief thing to determine at this stage is the conception of the ministry held by the Methodist Preachers at this time. *The Form of Discipline* did not use the phrase, 'The Pastoral Office', but written into it is a conception of the ministerial office which goes back to Wesley's 'Rules of a Helper', or even further back to the ideal Anglican curé.[22]

Basically, there must be outward simplicity in all that a Methodist minister said or did. There must be no ostentation. The Conference of 1793 had discarded many of the outward marks of the ministry; ordination had been dropped, clerical dress (gown and bands) was forbidden and Preachers were not to address one another as 'Reverend'.[23] These men were simply 'Preachers of the Gospel' and one of them, Jonathan Crowther (Sen.) naïvely affixed the letters 'P.G.' after his name! It is true that this state of affairs did not last, for through time 'Rev.' crept in and in 1836 ordination by the laying-on of hands was adopted by the Conference. Gowns and bands have never been officially sanctioned and it is only since the 1939–45 war that they have been in common use among Methodist ministers. Until almost the beginning of the present century, the Methodist Preacher, although more and more regarded by himself and by others as a minister, could

[22] See Kent, J., *The Age of Disunity*, p. 195—'John Wesley gave the Itinerants all the powers which he thought that a true minister should possess. . . . the underlying origin of this high doctrine of the ministry was the constitution of the Church of England as John Wesley understood it.'
[23] *Minutes*, i 696.

never be mistaken for either an Anglican clergyman or a Dissenting (Presbyterian) minister in the pulpit—or out of it, for that matter!

There was a close bond of unity among the Methodist Preachers which finds clear expression in the *Form of Discipline*. 'The Brotherhood of the Ministry' is a phrase without theological content, but it was not without either meaning or power with those Methodist Itinerants. Wesley's exhortation to his Preachers to keep together appears in every edition of the Minutes from 1753 to 1797. They were to 'act in all things, not according to your own will, but as a son in the Gospel and in union with your brethren'. 'As the Preachers are eminently one body, nothing should be done by any individual which would be prejudicial to the whole or to any part thereof. . . .' This unity fostered the Connexional spirit and gave a particular character to the Conference. This was more than an annual business meeting or a legal session. The testing of the candidates,[24] the trial of discipline cases, the reading of the stations, and above all the remembrance of those who had died[25] gave the Conference a character akin to the chapter meeting of a religious order. The Methodist Preachers were held together by a common doctrine and a common discipline[26] which, more than any other single factor, strengthened the determination to maintain an all-ministerial Conference.

It was this, the Preachers' conception of their own office, which Kilham did not grasp. He had no vision of The Pastoral Office. At that very first Conference of Wesley and his men, the question was asked and answered:

Q. What is the office of a minister?
A. To watch over the souls whom God commits to his charge, as he that must give account.
Q. What is the office of our Assistants?

---

[24] *Minutes*, i. 678.
[25] Obituary notices have appeared in the Minutes since 1778.
[26] In the Methodist Church today candidates for ordination are asked if they (a) Preach our doctrines, and (b) approve our discipline—Standing Order 718.

THE FORM OF DISCIPLINE (1797)

A. In the absence of the Minister to feed and guide, to teach and govern the flock.[27]

This was a responsibility which could not be shared with non-pastors; hence Conference had to be an all-ministerial assembly; and given the responsibility, it carried with it a corresponding authority.

> Methodism was, in the first instance, based upon the principle that God has placed the government of the Church in the hands of its Pastors ... in 1795 and 1797, the power of the Pastor was not taken away from him and given to others, or even shared with them ... all the privileges then conceded by the Conference were only so many fences and guards thrown around the Pastor, to prevent him from using his power injuriously ... by means of the District Committees and the right of appeal to the Conference, all cases of difficulty which cannot be settled in the ordinary way, nevertheless are determined by pastoral authority ... the final decision of extraordinary questions is not with the people, but rests with the collective pastorate.[28]

The Role of the Laity

Although the all-ministerial Conference gave Methodism of this period the character of a 'limited aristocracy', many concessions to the laity were written into the *Form of Discipline*. Some of these were the direct result of pressure exerted by the Kilhamite revolt, but others recognized the will of the people. The Conference address to the Methodist Societies in 1793 confessed, 'it is the people ... who have

---

[27] This undergoes slight modification in the *Form of Discipline*:
Q. What is the office of a Christian minister?
A. To watch over souls as he that must give account; to feed and guide the flock.
Noticeable for its absence is the phrase 'to teach and govern'. Prof. W. R. Ward doubts whether any of the changes brought about by the *Form of Discipline* were based on any particular doctrine of the ministry, though a later generation held that it preserved the Connexional principle and the authority of the Pastoral Office unabridged.—*op. cit.*, p. 38.

[28] Beecham, J., E.C.W.M., p. 116f. See also Crowther, J., *Christian Order* (1796), 'The minister that does not assert and maintain the authority with which he is officially invested by God himself, is unfaithful to him who put him in authority', p. 3.

forced us ...'. Where permission was given to a Society to have the sacraments, it was to be in response to the desires of the people as expressed through their representatives, the Leaders.[29] Other concessions include:

1. The Preachers must publish an annual report of the Yearly Collection and the affairs of Kingswood School.[30]
2. All outstanding bills for the upkeep of Preachers were to be approved and, if approved, met by the Circuit Quarterly Meeting.[31]
3. No circuit to be divided without the consent of the Quarterly Meeting.[32]
4. The Leaders Meeting to have power to declare any person unfit to be received into membership and after such a declaration, the Superintendent had no authority to over-ride it.[33]
5. No person to be expelled for immorality until the charge had been proved at a Leaders Meeting.[34]
6. The Leaders Meeting to have a voice in the choice of Leaders and Stewards.[35]
7. The Local Preachers Meeting to give approbation before anyone is received as a Local Preacher.[36]
8. If Conference pass a rule relative to Societies, and that rule be objected to in any Circuit, it will not be enforced in that circuit before the following Conference; if it be confirmed by the next Conference, it shall be binding on the whole Connexion.[37]
9. Instead of taking matters into their own hands as the Trustees of Bristol did in the case of Henry Moore, provision was made, through Circuit and District

[29] F. of D. xxvi. I. i.
[30] F. of D. xxix. 19. Kilham had alleged that there were moneys collected that could not be accounted for.
[31] F. of D. xxxiv. I. 3.
[32] F. of D. xxix. 9.
[33] F. of D. xxiv. III. 1.
[34] F. of D. xxxiv. III. 2.
[35] F. of D. xxiv. IV. 1.
[36] F. of D. xxvi, addenda 4.
[37] F. of D. xxxiv. VII.

THE FORM OF DISCIPLINE (1797)

machinery, for the removal of an offending Preacher, but only Conference had power to expel or suspend.[38]

10. All candidates for the ministry had to be approved by the March Quarterly Meeting. This gave the Societies an important part to play in the initial stages of a minister's career.[39] (This went far to meet the objections pointed out by Kilham, that unsuitable men were enlisted by the Preachers.)

In this way, a working compromise was achieved. The Conference always had the last word, but *vox populi* was not ignored, nor were the laity without a share in the government. The *Form of Discipline* ended with the words, 'Thus, brethren, we have given up the greatest part of our executive government into your hands, as represented in your different public meetings'.[40]

Thus we see Wesleyan Methodism as it was embodied in *The Form of Discipline* of 1797. The lessons of six years of dissension had been learned and the result summarized as follows:

1. Its Connexional character was preserved, and with it, the Itinerant System. No Society or Circuit was independent of the whole, of which the Conference was the supreme ruling body.
2. The authority of the Pastorate was maintained.
3. The District Meeting was empowered to give effective supervision between Conferences.
4. The laity were given participation in the affairs of the Connexion and the authority conferred on local meetings provided checks and limits to any undue assumption of power by an individual—be he Superintendent or District Chairman or President of the Conference.

The strength of the system lay in the fact that those who compiled it believed that it was in accordance with New Testament teaching, but this will be looked at in a later chapter.

[38] F. of D. xxix. 12.
[39] F. of D. III. 3.
[40] F. of D. xxiv. VII; the truth of this was much debated in later years.

CHAPTER FOUR

SUMMARY OF PART ONE

IT remains for us now to sum up this post-Wesley period by asking two questions. The first is, 'What (as far as can be ascertained) would appear to be Wesley's intentions for the government of the Connexion after his death?'; the second, 'Why, in fact, did Methodism veer towards a Presbyterian, rather than an episcopal or independent polity?'

Wesley's Intentions

The fact that both Trustees and Preachers, in so very different ways, claimed to be fulfilling the intentions of Wesley, at least suggests that those intentions were not clearly defined; and this is confirmed by the controversy between those who advocated the Lichfield Scheme and those who violently opposed it—both on the grounds that they were fulfilling Wesley's intentions. What, then, were those intentions? Can they be discerned? Let us set out the rival claims, together with whatever supporting evidence we can muster.

(a) *The first claim is that Wesley intended to establish a threefold order of ministers with District Bishops or Superintendents.*

In favour of this, there are the following considerations:
i. Wesley stated a preference for the threefold ministry and episcopal church government:

> As to my own judgement, I still believe 'the episcopal form of Church government to be both scriptural and apostolical': I mean, well agreeing with the practice and writings of the apostles ... but that it is prescribed in scripture I do not believe.[1]

---
[1] Letter to James Clark, 3rd July, 1756: *Letters*, iii. 182.

SUMMARY

ii. His ordination of Alexander Mather as Superintendent without sending him out of England.

iii. Most of the senior Preachers, Coke, Moore and Pawson, men who were nearest to Wesley in his later years, were sure that some form of episcopal government was in line with his intentions,[2] hence the Lichfield Scheme.

iv. The testimony of the American Church which, under Wesley's instructions, was organized on an episcopal basis. It is true that he scolded Asbury for using the title 'Bishop', but he raised no objection to the system which Coke and Asbury established. The Americans said that Wesley 'recommended the episcopal form' to them and consecrated Dr Coke as Bishop, 'that our episcopacy might descend from him'.[3] James Dixon believed that it was to the American Church that one should look for 'the real mind and sentiments' of Wesley.[4]

v. In *The Sunday Service of the Methodists*, compiled for the use of the Societies in Great Britain, Wesley retained 'The Form and Manner of Making and Ordaining of Superintendents, Elders and Deacons'.

(b) *The second claim is that Wesley favoured a Presbyterian Order.* In favour of this, it is urged:

i. The Trustees maintained that Wesley intended Methodism to keep to 'The Old Plan'[5] in which there was a strict parity of ministers.

ii. Wesley himself observed a strict parity among his Preachers, insisting that ordination or election to the Legal Hundred should not impair this.[6]

iii. The constitution of 1797 was the natural development of Wesley's own system in which the Assistant was directly responsible to him for the administration of discipline in the circuit. When Conference assumed the authority formerly exercised by Wesley, the next in authority was the Assistant,

[2] See Pawson's letter quoted in ch. 2, p. 43.
[3] *The Doctrines and Discipline of the Methodist Episcopal Church in America* (Tenth edition), 1798, p. 7.
[4] *Methodism, Its Origin, etc.* (1843), p. 127.
[5] See above, ch. 1, p. 20.
[6] *Minutes*, i. 242.

and when the District Chairman came upon the scene as an intermediary, it was not so much that he possessed power in and for himself, but that he was there to bolster the authority of the Assistant. He had no power to interfere in any circuit but his own, unless specially called in to do so. As we saw in chapter two, when the title 'Superintendent' did appear, it was not given to the District Chairman but to the Assistant.

iv. If Wesley had intended Methodism to be organized on an episcopal plan, he would have written it into the Deed of Declaration.

Can we now answer the question, 'What were Wesley's intentions?' We can offer nothing more than a personal judgement. We would suggest that in his heart of hearts, Wesley preferred episcopal government, and that the American Church represented his mind on the subject; but to organize Methodism *in England* on these lines was too much like setting up a rival establishment to the Church of England.

Why did Methodism adopt a Presbyterian Polity?

The answer to this question lies, I think, largely in the character of the Preachers—a factor much neglected by historians of this period; so it will be worth our while to look at them for a while—warts and all!

Personal feelings alone militated against raising any of them—be it one, six or sixty—to an office superior to the rest; on this the Lichfield Scheme and all like it, foundered. Just after Wesley's death Pawson was afraid that Mather would be 'ordering, settling things'. This was a natural reaction, for according to Kilham, Mather was 'considered as Prime Minister in our Israel' while Wesley lived[7]—and, of course, had not Mather been ordained by Wesley without being sent out of England?

Again, many of the senior Preachers were familiar with, and had leanings towards, Presbyterian Church order. Coke was the only episcopally ordained minister who took

[7] *Martin Luther* broadsheet, p. 4.

SUMMARY

an active part in the affairs of the Connexion, so that he and Mather would be the only two with unreserved leanings towards episcopal government; but they were a minority, kept very much in check after Wesley's death. They had no commission to British Methodism comparable to that which Wesley bestowed on Coke and Asbury for America.

John Pawson, who later favoured episcopal government and was a signatory to the Lichfield Scheme, was won over to that point of view rather than being a native partisan of it. In his earlier years he was stationed in Scotland and his letters reveal a strong attachment to Scottish practices, especially in their administration of the sacraments.[8] His later support for Lichfield and his plea for 'Bishops to be Bishops'[9] was due entirely to the pressing need for strong government.

Of the Preachers who broke away to lead the New Connexion, Kilham had extensive experience in Scotland, while William Thom was an Aberdonian.

William Thompson, the first President after Wesley, was an Irishman.[10] George Smith, the historian of Wesleyan Methodism,[11] says that the chief reason for his election to the Presidency was his genius for ecclesiastical polity. He had made a close study of Presbyterian Church government and it is known that he was the chief architect of *The Plan of Pacification*,[12] just as he was the chief opponent of the Lichfield Scheme.

Furthermore, let us admit that, except for one or two men like Joseph Benson, the general level of culture of those who were left to mould Methodism in this critical period was not exceptionally high. Adam Clarke, a massive scholar, had not yet come into his own. Jabez Bunting,

---

[8] M.C.A. letter to Atmore, 8th January, 1791.
[9] M.C.A. letter to Atmore, 13th December, 1793.
[10] See *The Methodist Magazine*, 1845, p. 120, *Memoir of Atmore*: 'Mr Thompson was a man of strong sense, a fertile genius, clear understanding, quick discernment and sound judgement. After the death of Mr Wesley, he took an active part in the affairs of the Connexion and the outlines of our present form of ecclesiastical government were arranged principally by him.'
[11] See his *History of Wesleyan Methodism*, ii. 191.
[12] See above, ch. 1, p. 35.

perhaps Methodism's greatest statesman of the nineteenth century, did not enter the ministry until 1799. Dr Coke stood out as a man of scholarship and action—'the only sixpenny thing in a penny bazaar'; but he lived a whirlwind sort of a life, often in Ireland, America or the Channel Islands and could be impulsive if not indiscreet at times. He was thought to be the power behind the throne while Wesley lived and of being personally ambitious after Wesley died. Physically he was of the smallest of men but in other ways much superior, intellectually and in powers of leadership, to his Methodist contemporaries.

Of the other Preachers whom Wesley ordained, Moore was an Irishman and Mather a Scotsman who had fought at Culloden. Moore thought highly of his ordination and bitterly regretted that his colleagues did not call upon him to establish a succession when laying-on of hands was adopted in 1836.[13] Mather was said to be 'lofty and supercilious'.[14] When he advocated episcopacy for Methodism (himself, after Wesley, the fount of such succession) he was mildly ridiculed by Pawson, 'We could not see how a Scotch Presbyterian Bishop could support the Church of England'.[15]

It is difficult to sort out the Preachers according to their allegiances in the various issues that were debated during these years. For instance, Joseph Benson was against Sacraments and Bishops, while Pawson was in favour of both; but both Benson and Pawson were against lay representation. Taylor was against lay representation, but in favour of sacraments and bishops. Kilham was in favour of sacraments and lay representation, but against bishops. This cross-allegiance made the formation of strong, clear-cut parties difficult, but it also meant that tension was much less than it might otherwise have been.

[13] See his letter to the President of the Conference dated August, 1837, printed in my *The Sacrament of the Lord's Supper in Early Methodism*, p. 161. Moore thought he was the only Preacher alive at the time who had been ordained by Wesley, but also alive were Matthew Lumb and James Bogie. See *infra*, Pt. IV, ch. 3, n. 24.
[14] Kilham: *Martin Luther* broadsheet, p. 5.
[15] M.C.A., letter to Atmore, 13th December, 1793.

SUMMARY

Surveying the Preachers as a whole, however, with all their built-in fears and tendencies, considering their modicum of scholarship, it is understandable that they were guided more by practical necessities than by theological niceties. Nor is it surprising that in the absence of any precise instructions from Wesley (apart from the Deed of Declaration and Wesley's alleged saying that 'as soon as I am dead, the Methodists will be a regular Presbyterian Church'[16]) the Methodism that emerged was as democratic as the age would allow and as Presbyterian as a quasi-allegiance to the Church of England made possible.

We can therefore conclude our survey of Methodism of the post-Wesley period by saying that it may not have fulfilled Wesley's ideal of an organized Church, for he did not look upon the organization which he founded as 'an organized Church'; but the Connexion which he bequeathed to his successors was not untrue to the foundation he laid. After all, *The Form of Discipline* (which crystallized Wesleyan Methodism of 1797) had to reckon with all kinds of factors—personal, political and religious—which did not exist in Wesley's day. The next stage in our study is to see how this Methodism of 1797 and after stood up to the pressures of the early nineteenth century.

---

[16] Bradburn, S., *Are the Methodists Dissenters?*, p. 19.

PART TWO

Interlude

1797–1827

CHAPTER ONE

MINOR SECESSIONS

WE now come to consider some of the secessions which, in their own way, throw light on the temper of the Wesleyan Connexion during the first quarter of the nineteenth century.

The Band-room Methodists

In 1803, in North Street, Manchester, a certain John Broadhurst started to hold meetings in what he called 'The Band-room' and it soon attracted a large number of his fellow Methodists.[1] In itself, this would seem to be harmless enough; today such enterprise would probably be encouraged. In Broadhurst's day, however, it was an innovation which, not being within the jurisdiction of the Leaders Meeting, was immediately frowned upon with suspicion. Private conclaves, however well-intended by their founders, might harbour discontent, even sedition! So the Circuit Superintendent, William Jenkins, dutifully wrote to Broadhurst[2] pointing out the irregularity of his procedure and informing him that his meeting must submit to the discipline of the Wesleyan constitution. Jenkins wrote as 'a minister of the Gospel who is called to watch over your soul as one who must give an account...': Broadhurst was told that it was his duty, 'to submit to them that rule over you in the Lord'. Strong stuff for 1803, but discernably the material out of which the doctrine of the Pastoral Office was later moulded. Broadhurst ignored the appeal and remained uneasily within the Wesleyan fold awaiting another opportunity to try his strength. He had not long to wait.

In December, 1805, Manchester Methodists decided to hold their Covenant Service on the first Sunday of the New

[1] An account of these activities will be found in the *London Quarterly Review*, October 1886, pp. 23ff. Ironically, the Broadhursts were present at the trial sermon of Jabez Bunting—see *Life of Bunting*, i. 97.
[2] M.C.A., Ms. letter.

Year, as being most convenient for the majority of the members. It was to be a united service, for the town and North Street Leaders agreed to close their 'Room' that Sunday afternoon. However, for some reason or other, an independent service was held at North Street, to which people who were not members of Society were admitted. Not only was this contrary to the local arrangements, but, more serious, it transgressed the Methodist rule that only members of Society, on production of their Class Tickets, could be admitted to such a service. When the Manchester Leaders met again they resolved that in future, whenever such a service was to be held in any of the three town chapels, the North Street room be closed, and that no person be admitted to such services in North Street without a Society ticket or a note from one of the travelling preachers. To mitigate any hardship occasioned by the latter part of the resolution, it was decided to allow notes to be issued by Leaders and that they be valid for six months. On all accounts, this was fair treatment to all who were familiar with Wesleyan procedure.

The North Street people, John Broadhurst among them, regarded this as a censure motion and after prolonged, but unsuccessful, negotiations, they withdrew under Broadhurst to revive the title of 'Band-room Methodists'.[3]

Not the least result of this controversy was that it produced a pamphlet of 36 pages which is of considerable significance in tracing Methodist thought about the church and ministry at this time. The full title is, *A Statement of Facts and Observations, relative to the late separation from the Methodist Society in Manchester: affectionately addressed to the members of that Body, by their Preachers and Leaders*. It is noteworthy that the third Preacher in the Manchester Circuit at that time was none other than Jabez Bunting, in the sixth year of his ministry. In spite of his subordinate position, his ideas which were to mature and be expounded

---

[3] In 1808 they had 16 congregations, all in Lancashire and Cheshire. In 1859 the biographer of Jabez Bunting reported that a remnant of them still existed, but most of them had joined the Primitive Methodists (i. 276).

with such authority in years to come are evident on every page; so this is (as far as we can tell) the earliest exposition of the Wesleyan doctrine of the Pastoral Office and, as such, is worthy of our closer attention.

The two principles on which the Manchester Preachers took their stand were the authority of the Leaders Meeting and the maintenance of the 'Closed Meeting'. The former need not detain us very long. The 1797 *Form of Discipline* had declared that the Leaders Meeting was the proper place for the consideration of all Society matters, but 'other formal meetings may be held, if they first receive the approbation of the Superintendent and the Leaders Meeting, provided also that the Superintendent, if he please, be present at every such meeting'.[4] The Band-room Methodists had broken this rule and the Preachers were only upholding the constitution.[5]

Of more significance for our purpose, however, is the fact that this dispute produced a vigorous defence of the 'Closed Meeting' and a condemnation of 'the promiscuous admission of all who choose to attend without distinction of motive or character'. The authors of the *Statement* declare that this 'promiscuous admission' had been practised at North Street and that it was a violation of our Lord's precept in Matthew 8:7 and Wesley's Sermon thereon.[6] They also maintained that it was 'contrary to the general current of scriptural history and example' and inconsistent with the 'nature, business and design of those religious meetings ... Society Meetings, Love Feasts, etc. ... which are for the communion of saints'. Finally they said it 'impedes the due administration of ecclesiastical discipline' and was contrary to Methodist usages, and rules.

[4] *Minutes*, i. 704.
[5] For a similar transgression of this rule the Leeds dissentients were charged —see below, Pt. 3, ch. 1.
[6] Sermon XXV. On the verse, 'Neither cast your pearls before swine', Wesley says, 'Talk not to them (i.e. impenitent wrong-doers) of the mysteries of the Kingdom. Tell not them of the exceeding great and precious promises which God hath given us in the Son of His love. What conception can they have of being made partakers of the divine nature, who do not even desire to escape the corruption that is in the world'— Sugden, *Standard Sermons of John Wesley*, i. 526.

There is a fine point of principle here; namely, that the Church should be separate from the 'world'. Says the *Statement*, 'the grand object of [our] discipline is to effect and maintain an open and visible separation between *the Church* and *the world*'. So the writers drew a clear distinction between meetings for propagating the Gospel to the outsider and meetings for committed Christians. The former consist mainly of preaching 'directed to mankind at large' the latter are 'Society Meetings' which imply penitence and faith.

The conception of 'purity' is here applied to the church or congregation, as distinct from individual piety. In another context we shall encounter the phrase, 'the purity of the ministry', but here the Manchester Preachers are contending for the purity of the Society, collectively as well as individually. A 'pure' Society in this context means one which is unadulterated with unbelieving or unconverted people. The authors of the *Statement* were afraid that 'promiscuous admissions' practised by North Street would adulterate an otherwise 'pure' Society. They say:

> If the doors of one of our private assemblies be thus thrown open to every invader, with what consistency can we refuse to wink at similar intrusions into all our Bands and Love Feasts and Sacraments? And then what will become of Christian purity and discipline, or what are we to do with many explicit declarations and precepts of the Word of God?

The *Statement* ends with a warning against revivalists who are generally 'censorious', 'wanting in humility', and who 'produce an agitation of the passions, rather than a permanent love to God'. The pith of the Wesleyan reply to the Band-room separatists was the belief that discipline should not be divorced from privileges:

> Such laxity . . . permits [men] to enjoy many of those outward privileges which belong to a Religious Society without submitting to its wholesome restraints and scriptural regulations. . . .

The Wesleyans were certainly closing their ranks.

The Church Methodists[7]

In 1823, a certain Mark Robinson of Hull, angry with the Conference for separating Beverley from the Hull Circuit, fell to criticizing the constitution of the Connexion, and was ultimately led to propound a solution of his own. In an effort to translate his ideas into practice, he took with him a small band of followers under the title of 'Church Methodists' and built a chapel at Cherry Burton, near Beverley, 'beyond which', says Gregory, 'it never spread and from which it soon vanished'.[8]

The two poles around which Robinson's scheme revolved represented a strange blend of 'The Old Plan' and the republicanism of Alexander Kilham. First of all, he assumed that the majority of the Methodists were alarmed at the growing rift between their church and the Church of England. He imagined that Methodists were out of sympathy with the celebration of the sacrament in their own chapels, as it implied a 'rival altar' to that of the Parish Church. Consequently, he believed that the only way to halt this trend was for Methodism to return to what he conceived to be original Methodism. In essence he advocated the same things as the Trustees did in 1794—namely, that the Itinerants remain Preachers and cease to regard themselves as ministers, and that members should attend the Parish Church for their sacramental services. Robinson was encouraged in his ideas by a similar movement in Ireland, where a group of contenders for the same ideals called themselves, 'Primitive Wesleyan Methodists'.[9] An apostle of this Irish movement helped Robinson to found his sect at Beverley.

Robinson's second principle was that Methodism, being a lay movement within the church, should admit laymen to

[7] For a full account see Smith's *History of W.M.*, iii. 73 and Gregory's *Scriptural Church Principles*, p. 189.
[8] Gregory, *op. cit.*, p. 190.
[9] See *The Proceedings of the Wesley Historical Society*, xxxiv, 73ff, article entitled, 'Church Methodists in Ireland' by Frederick Jeffery; also the same writer's W.H.S. Lecture (1973), 'Methodism and the Irish Problem', ch. 3.

the Conference. This does not call for any elaboration here, as Robinson produced no argument that had not been thought of by Kilham in 1797; so all that remains for us to do is to mention the issues on which Robinson challenged the constitution of the Wesleyans and how the Wesleyans replied in defence.

In the first place, Robinson contended that Article VII of the *Form of Discipline* promised liberty to the people, but did not grant it. This article laid down that if any new Conference legislation be objected to at the first Quarterly Meeting in any circuit, it should not be enforced in that circuit; but if the legislation be confirmed at the next Conference, it should be binding on the whole Connexion. Robinson contended that the 'first' Quarterly Meeting met too soon after Conference for any new legislation to be brought before it, and that the phrase 'in conjunction with the Preachers' was a subtle way of retaining power in the hands of the ministry. Furthermore, he said, it was still too easy for Conference to make unpopular legislation 'binding on the whole Connexion'.[10] To this, it was replied that as 'the first Quarterly Meeting' was not, as a rule, held until late September or early October, there was plenty of time for any circuit to have Conference resolutions before it. As for the phrase, 'in conjunction with the Preachers', this had no sinister meaning. It meant simply 'including the Preachers'. In the last resort, if new legislation were to be generally resisted in the circuits, Conference would not pass it, so that a certain power of veto resided in the Quarterly Meeting. The weakness of Robinson's argument lay in the fact that he was taking Article VII out of context and ignoring altogether the provisions of *The Plan of Pacification*.[11]

In urging that there should be a yearly meeting of representatives chosen by the Quarterly Meetings, Robinson's basic concern was, 'whether or not the rules by which our Societies are governed place the whole power in the hands of the Preachers, or whether the people have a

[10] Robinson, M., *Observations*, pp. 7ff.
[11] See Sandwith, H., *An Apology for Wesleyan Methodism*, p. 9.

reasonable share in the government'.[12] He also cited civil affairs and the rights of Englishmen to have a say in their government. Humphrey Sandwith replied to these points on the lines adopted by many later apologists when they had to parry this thrust. There is a difference (they argued) between the government of a State and that of a Church. As Sandwith said, 'Our rights as Englishmen form by no means a correct precedent for regulating our conduct as Methodists'.[13] Bunting, of course, held that the people were adequately represented at every level in official meetings and 'even at Conference, the temporal part of the business is conducted in committees of which respectable laymen are always some of the most active members'.[14]

The fact was that the emerging doctrine of the Pastoral Office was driving Methodists into defending a much more autocratic system of government than that which was current in civic affairs. While civil government was moving, albeit slowly and painfully, towards more democratic forms, the Wesleyans were maintaining a fundamentally authoritarian system which was to be sorely tried in 1849.

Replying to Robinson's plea for a representative Governing Assembly, Charles Welch attempted to show that true representation is impossible and that in the Methodist New Connexion, the natural home for all who thought as Robinson did on this matter, Lay Representation was impracticable. Many M.N.C. circuits sent only one representative to their Conference and that was the minister. Welch further contends that Lay Representation leads to 'the depression of ministerial energy and influence'. He concludes with the remarkable statement:

> A delegate and a minister are not equal men: the employment, character, consecration and piety of the latter are assumed as the greater; that it should be so, is the voice of reason and of God![15]

[12] Robinson, *op. cit.*, p. 37.
[13] *Op. cit.*, p. 26.
[14] M.C.A. letter, Jabez Bunting to Humphrey Sandwith, 10th February, 1825.
[15] Welch, C., *An Investigation of Mark Robinson's Observations*, p. 15.

The fact is that at this late date, thirty years after Kilham fought the same battle, the Wesleyans were not really interested in Lay Representation. Those who still had a conscience about it could join the New Connexion, and the Wesleyans did not need it for, as Watson pointed out, their system had its effective checks and balances. 'The power of the Preachers in their Circuits is in no instance more than the power of preserving and enforcing the established doctrines and rules of the Body', and in the Leaders Meeting they are restrained in admitting and expelling members. The duty of Conference is 'to overlook the whole system, and to preserve these known and accepted Laws and Rules in unimpaired and vigorous operation . . . Such are the general powers, checks and balances of the constitution of modern Methodism'.[16] This was an answer much more convincing than anything that was given to Kilham when he pleaded for Lay Representation in 1795.

This last serious attempt to get Methodism to return to its mother's womb provides us with an opportunity to review the relationship of the Wesleyans and the Church of England at the end of the first quarter of the nineteenth century. To begin with, there was a steady development of Church consciousness in Methodism. It was becoming a church in its own right, and to say that it ought to return to the fold of the Establishment was asking for the impossible. Furthermore, it was a reflection on the vigorous life and unmistakable ethos of Methodism itself, which was by now displaying all the marks, and dispensing all the services, of a true church. As James Everett remarked, 'Methodists evince by their morals, their tempers, their conversation and their devotional exercises that they actually constitute a part of Christ's church'.[17] Wesley had always insisted that the 'marks' of a true church are to be found in the holiness of its members; and Methodism sustained that by doctrine and discipline. Adam Clarke's paternal advice to an American Methodist was, '. . . keep your doctrines and your discipline. Preach the former without refining on

[16] *Methodist Magazine*, 1825, pp. 536–7.
[17] Everett, J., *Remarks on a Pamphlet*, p. 9.

them; observe the latter without bending it to circumstances.'[18]

This new upsurge of 'Church Methodism' had special significance in that it was met by a new generation of scholars, men who had been nurtured in a Methodism which had considerably matured in the previous thirty years. During the last decade of the nineteenth century, when the Kilhamite agitation was at its height, the Connexion was struggling, virtually leaderless, towards self-consciousness, striving to be as loyal as it could to the none-too-clear precedents set by Wesley. But in 1824 Mark Robinson had to deal with a Methodism which was much more sure of its principles and much more forceful in its expression of them. It could call upon able apologists like Dr Humphrey Sandwith and Charles Welch (two laymen) and, the ablest of them all, Richard Watson; and it is to Watson's article in *The Methodist Magazine* for 1825 that we now turn.[19]

This article was really a long and searching review of the teachings of the Church Methodists. Watson saw clearly and exposed incisively the impossibility of their position. To begin with Robinson was seeking to destroy the whole Wesleyan system because of a few alleged defects. The Preachers were accused of agitating for the sacraments in Methodist chapels. 'What if they are?' says Watson; they are agitating for the right things, for 'Methodism has renounced the dogma that diocesan episcopacy is the only legitimate form of church government.' Furthermore, Watson could argue from the principle that the Methodist Preachers were scriptural ministers. This was possible in 1825, but not in 1795. The stalwarts of 1795 had not quite reached that point in their thinking, for the idea of a

[18] *Methodist History*, July 1965, p. 23. See also Miles Martindale, *Methodism Defended*, who argues under three headings—doctrine, discipline and worship. Humphrey Sandwith described Wesleyan doctrine as 'Evangelical Arminianism', in distinction from that of the evangelical clergy of the Church of England which was, 'a high and rigid Calvinism... degenerated into antinomianism'—*Apology for Wesleyan Methodism*, p. 61.

[19] See pages 464–5. The article is anonymous, but it is included in the complete *Works of Richard Watson*, edited by Thomas Jackson.

Methodist *minister* was still to come. Watson, however, proclaimed it with authority and acceptance.

Watson's most telling argument was that Mark Robinson's brand of Methodism would have been as unacceptable to the Anglicans as it was to the Wesleyans. Robinson was asking Methodism to renounce its claim to be a church in its own right and direct its people to attend the Parish Church for the sacraments. This threw Watson back on the nature of the ministry and his reply was that when a man is *separated* (the operative word) he must have the right to administer the ordinances of the church to his people. This is 'ordination'—by whatever outward signs it is bestowed—in the New Testament sense of the word. To the multitudes whom Wesleyan Methodism had collected 'from the world', 'we are a church of Christ with all the institutions of such a Church, according to the scriptural model'.

Mark Robinson did not greatly trouble the Wesleyans. His movement is barely noticed by historians, but for us it is not without significance. It moved the parent body to clarify its position. It was the last stand of 'Church Methodism'. It provided an occasion for the Wesleyans to develop a little further their growing conception of 'The Pastoral Office'. They did not have long to wait before they could expound it in its fulness. In the meantime, we must look at three other secessions which did not originate as protests against the constitution (as with the M.N.C.s and the Church Methodists) but were more or less independent revivals, though they began under the leadership of one or more people who were Wesleyans. They merit our attention because they demonstrate the Wesleyan reaction to revivalism and its clash with ecclesiastical discipline.

The Tent Methodists

In 1814, George Pocock of Bristol began preaching from place to place in a tent, often accompanied by Methodist Local Preachers. The venture met with sufficient success for at least one person to devote his full time to the work. In 1820, however, the movement was bursting the confines of

Wesleyan discipline and an independent though small Connexion was formed bearing the title, 'The Tent Methodists'.[20]

The Tent Methodist secession represented the failure of a revival movement to find a home within the now highly disciplined Wesleyan Connexion. Methodism was not, nor ever had been, a loose federation of free-lance evangelists. It stipulated that if the Tent Methodist movement wished to remain in the Wesleyan fold only fully accredited Local Preachers must be employed. Pocock refused to give any such guarantee and continued to use men over whom the Conference had no control. In fact, he convened his own Board of Management which became known as 'The Friends of Tent Preaching'. The complete independence of this from the Conference is clearly indicated in Pocock's own words, 'The committee chosen that evening were as capable of deciding who were proper to be employed as Tent Preachers as the Conference itself'.[21] We cannot here follow the charges and counter-charges that went to make up this unholy wrangle; sufficient to note that Pocock refused to submit to Wesleyan discipline, built his own chapels and in the end was written off as 'ceased to meet'.

This secession did no damage to the Wesleyan cause, nor did it call forth any statement of policy or principle, but it did emphasize the fact that the Wesleyans would not sacrifice their laws for the sake of one man, or a group of men, however well-intentioned they might be.[22] This was Bunting's line all along from 1803 when he regretted that William Bramwell had not left the Connexion,[23] to 1835 when he was alleged to have said, 'It is no sin for a man to think our discipline wrong, provided that he quits us'.[24]

[20] An account of the rise of the movement is given in *The Rules of the Tent Methodists*.
[21] *A Correct Statement of Facts*, p. 5.
[22] *Op. cit.*, p. 11.
[23] M.C.A. letter to George Marsden, 13th December, 1803.
[24] Gregory, B., *Sidelights on the Conflicts of Methodism*, p. 193.

The Primitive Methodists

It is regrettable that we have no account of the origins of Primitive Methodism written from the Wesleyan point of view, or based on contemporary Wesleyan sources.[25] It is generally said that Hugh Bourne was expelled from the Wesleyans at Burslem because he celebrated the anniversary of the first Camp Meeting by holding another and that his expulsion took place at the Burslem Quarterly Meeting. But according to the Wesleyan constitution the expulsion of a member could take place only at a Leaders' Meeting or at a meeting of the Trustees and Leaders; the latter would apply to Bourne as he was a Trustee. The cause of Bourne's expulsion is more likely to be found in another quarter, especially if it is insisted upon that it took place at a Quarterly Meeting. According to a rule of 1803 any member taking out a licence to preach without the consent of the Quarterly Meeting shall cease to be a member. Now Bourne had procured such a licence at the Stafford Quarter Sessions. Furthermore, he rarely met in Class, he preached in his own circuit without the authority of the Superintendent minister and visited other circuits without the necessary invitation and authorization. It would thus appear that the Quarterly Meeting condemned Bourne for violating the Methodist rule on licences and that it was on this ground that his Superintendent withheld his ticket of membership.

This, of course, immensely widens the background and involves the attitude of the Wesleyans to preaching licences. They had always taken great pains to prevent indiscriminate application to the Quarter Sessions for licences to preach.[26] This explains why, initially, they

[25] An article in the L.Q.R. for October, 1886, attempted to do this, though without access to local circuit records: see the issue for October, 1886, pp. 21, 38.
[26] The rule of 1803 said, 'If any members of the Methodist Society apply to the Quarterly Sessions for a licence to preach, without being approved as a Preacher by the Quarterly Meeting ... such persons shall be expelled the Society'—*Minutes*, ii. 183. See also my article in *The Local Preachers Handbook*, No. 9, pp. 1ff; and M.C.A. 'Resolutions passed at a Meeting of the London Circuit, 1802, 30th December; Joseph Benson in the chair' (single sheet).

welcomed Lord Sidmouth's Bill to restrict unlicensed preachers. It was only when its real import was realized that they so violently opposed it. The Wesleyans were anxious to dissociate themselves from some of the less reputable types of revivalist preachers who were not unknown during the first quarter of the nineteenth century, and who were impatient of the ordered worship of the Wesleyans and spurned its discipline. Hence, when Hugh Bourne took out his licence without the concurrence of his Circuit Quarterly Meeting, there came the clash between the discipline of the Connexion and the fervour of the individual. From one point of view it may appear to be a quenching of the Spirit; on the other hand, the Superintendent was only doing his duty in dealing with a recalcitrant brother.

On a deeper level still, of course, this raises the question of the relationship of the Church in general and the Wesleyans in particular to Revivalism. It is not a new thing for the Church to be told that her sole mission is to preach for the conversion of sinners, forgetting that this is only part of her mission. In the early nineteenth century, Methodism was still an evangelizing body, but it was awakening to another role which was associated with its growing church consciousness. It was beginning to realize that what the evangelist did was only a beginning. As the writer in the *London Quarterly Review* said, converts must be trained to, '... go on to perfection. Conversion and Christian Perfection are the distinguishing doctrines which especially define the objects of the Methodist Church and both the evangelist and the "pastor and teacher" are necessary to their full expression.'[27] Bunting is reported to have said, 'I do not think we can be proved to be evangelists. Our proper office is pastors and teachers ... I believe that we are teachers to instruct and pastors to govern the people.'[28] This attitude to evangelists and evangelical movements goes far to explain why the Wesleyans acted as they did to men like Bourne and Clowes. As Professor

[27] See L.Q.R. Oct. 1886, pp. 21, 38.
[28] Gregory, B., *Sidelights*, p. 83.

W. R. Ward points out, the Wesleyan tight scheme of salvation left no room for a dynamic Society like the Primitive Methodists.[29]

We sometimes wonder whether or not a little more elasticity on the part of the Wesleyans would have retained men like Hugh Bourne and William Clowes of the Primitive Methodists, or William O'Bryan and James Thorne of the Bible Christians; but ardent evangelists like these had little in common with the growing ecclesiastical or clerical temperament of the Wesleyans. They would have been ill at ease with the doctrine of the Pastoral Office; they would have chafed under the discipline of the Wesleyan Conference. So it is probable that they would have left the Wesleyans—elasticity or not!

The Bible Christians

The Connexion known as 'The Bible Christians' originated in circumstances similar to those which gave rise to the Primitive Methodists; that is, it was not a dispute over the constitution, but the result of revivalist activities of a man who refused to submit to Wesleyan Discipline. This man was William O'Bryan. He had much more contact with the Wesleyan authorities than Bourne had, and many attempts were made to keep him within the Connexion, but when he laid claim to personal oversight of the Societies he had founded, the authorities had no other choice than to leave him to his own devices.[30]

The expulsion of Bourne and O'Bryan from the Wesleyan

---

[29] Ward, W. R., *Religion and Society in England*, p. 76. For a good example of Wesleyan sensitivity to extra-mural activities of its members, see my Ph.D. thesis for an account of 'The Community Preachers'.

It is not generally known that the Primitive Methodists suffered a secession. A group of societies in the Nottingham area revolted on a question of ministerial stipends and established themselves as 'The Original Methodists'. See a series of articles in *The Proceedings of the Wesley Historical Society*, vol. 35, pp. 116ff. by Donald Grundy and vol. 35, p. 57 by William Parkes. The Original Methodists exhibited Methodist Reform *ad extremum*.

[30] For a recent account of the early Bible Christians, see Shaw, T., *The Bible Christians*, W.H.S. Lecture for 1965.

fold cannot be dismissed simply as tyranny of the system over the individual. Methodism was a discipline imposed upon individuals and Societies. History had provided sufficient cases of undisciplined men founding, and then abandoning, Societies they had raised up. O'Bryan himself was guilty of this, leaving his followers to be nurtured by others. The root cause of O'Bryan's separation from the Wesleyans was that he was enrolling scores of people in his Societies as Methodists over whom the Wesleyans had no control. The Wesleyans rightly felt that no one should bear the title without submitting to the rules.

At the same time, it ought to be said that between the Primitive Methodists and the Bible Christians on the one hand and the Wesleyans on the other, there was never the diffidence that there was between the Reformers and the Old Connexion.[31]

Summary

It can thus be said that at the end of the first quarter of the nineteenth century, Methodism was a highly disciplined Body. It regarded the real church (as the word ἐκκλησία signifies) as a company of people 'called out of' the world.[32] Its ministry must be pure in doctrine and conduct. Piety was more important than culture,[33] so candidates were subject to strict examination and oversight. This oversight —or episcopé—was exercised over all the Itinerant Preachers and more than compensated for anything that appeared to be lacking in the formal reception of Probationers into the full ministry. As Joseph Sutcliffe said, 'The examination, the confession of faith, the vows of fidelity and the charge, in point of solemnity, cannot be exceeded by any ordination whatever'.[34]

The core of Methodism lay in its committed members, the men and women who met in Classes and Bands; but there was an increasing number of adherents who wor-

[31] See, Rigg, J. H., *Church Organisation*, p. 323; L.Q.R., July 1887, p. 337.
[32] Everett, James, *Remarks on a Pamphlet*, p. 9.
[33] Vipond, W., *Doctrine, Discipline, etc.*, p. 51.
[34] Sutcliffe, J., *Divine Mission* (1814), p. 47.

shipped at the chapels and supported Connexional Funds. There was a growth in both numbers and wealth which led some of the members to fear for the simplicity of worship, speech and dress which had been its traditional pride.[35] Class Meetings were in danger of formality and the Connexion as a whole was becoming refined and sophisticated. The writer (almost certainly James Everett) of *Wesleyan Centenary Takings* made the shrewd observation, 'When Richard Watson and Jabez Bunting appeared, a new era of Methodism commenced: the pulpit was more closely and correctly studied; taste and refinement were on the advance'.[36] It is not surprising, therefore, that there was a generation who could look back to 'the good old days' of greater simplicity with a certain degree of nostalgia.[37] Itinerants, now addressed as 'Reverend' (despite the unrescinded Minute of 1793) came out the worse in comparison with the self-sacrificing Local Preachers.[38] This produced the counter-effect of a vigorous defence of the full-time ministry in general and of the Wesleyan Pastoral Office in particular.[39]

Unfortunately, a certain 'smugness' can be detected in some of the writers of the period. Joseph Sutcliffe, for example, could write in a grandiose manner, 'Hence the sunshine of prosperity and the cornucopia of affluence have fallen to our lot, while the lowering clouds have burst in a thousand strokes of vengeance on the more daring and unbelieving continent'.[40]

The Kilhamites had left the fold, but the last word had not been heard of the liberalism which underlay his revolt.

[35] Miller, R., *An Affectionate Address*, p. 4. See also *Thoughts on Class Meetings*. For Class Meetings see an article in *The Proceedings of the Wesley Historical Society*, vol. 39, p. 12—'The Decline of the Class Meeting and the Problem of Church Membership in Nineteenth-century Wesleyan Methodism' by Henry D. Rack.
[36] Volume 1 (1840), p. 133.
[37] See two anonymous pamphlets, *Methodism in 1821* and *Reflections on the Present Position* (1824).
[38] Anon., *Lay Preaching Defended* (1820), p. 6. For an excellent modern study of the Local Preacher in Methodism see a Leeds M.A. thesis on the subject by Margaret Batty (1970).
[39] Martin, R., *A Serious Address* (1815).
[40] Sutcliffe, J., *The Divine Mission of Methodism*, p. 30.

MINOR SECESSIONS

Dissentients within the fold complained, with varying degrees of annoyance, of the autocracy of Conference, but they had not the courage of their convictions to join the New Connexion.[41] At the same time, it took more than an insistence upon the authority of the Pastoral Office[42] to prevent the upheavals which marked the second quarter of the nineteenth century. Before we deal with the first of these upheavals—the Leeds Organ Case—we must take a further look at the polity and temper of Wesleyan Methodism during this period.

---

[41] See an anonymous pamphlet, *An Exposition of the Proceedings of the Old Methodist Conference*.

[42] A reviewer of Watson's *Life of Wesley* wrote in the *Methodist Magazine* for 1831: 'A spirit of faction also has been permitted partially to rend our societies, the aim of which has been, on the one hand, to calumniate the Methodist ministry and weaken its moral influence on the community; and, on the other, to depress the pastoral authority below its scriptural elevation in the Church and effect a proportionate relaxation of godly discipline' (p. 399).

CHAPTER TWO

POLITY AND TEMPER

'THE Form of Discipline' gave Wesleyan Methodism a basic constitution. It represented a mutual agreement between Preachers and people, although for some it did not go far enough. Opposition to an all-ministerial Conference smouldered on[1] and during the first half of the nineteenth century the Connexion was beset by revolts which varied in intensity from murmuring discontent to secessions such as we have noted in the previous chapter. From 1797 to 1827 revolts against the constitution (as distinct from revivalist movements) were sporadic and local, but the Leeds Organ Case was the first of three major nineteenth-century secessions which will call for our careful consideration. At the same time, it is not easy to estimate the exact force of the reforming spirit before 1827. Kilham alleged that the Methodist people were enslaved by a ministerial autocracy and ready to rally *en masse* to his 'liberating' call. Methodist New Connexion membership figures, however, show nothing approaching a landslide. After three years they reported only 5,794 members, and by 1827 this figure had not been doubled. In the same period, the Wesleyans grew from 82,713 to 237,239. One would have thought it easier for a young Connexion of less than 6,000 to increase than an older one of over 82,000. In the meantime, the Wesleyan constitution was adapted to prevailing conditions and now we must see (so far as it refers to Church and Ministry) how it stood up to both internal and external pressures.

Admission of Members

At Society level, discipline was still strictly maintained. As

---

[1] See an anonymous pamphlet entitled, *Reflections on the Present System of Methodism* (1824); also, Douglas, J., *Methodism Condemned*—a violent attack on the Conference with Kilham as a martyr. It was answered in *The Condemner Condemned*.

in Wesley's day, the admission of new members was closely watched. Since so much turned upon the admission and expulsion of members during the turbulent events of 1835, it is necessary to quote in full the following account, which reflects the customs prevailing in 1810:

> In general, no person is admitted into Society, no, not so much as upon trial, except recommended by some person acquainted with them, and after meeting once or more in some class. The superintendent has power to admit *on trial* persons recommended by a leader with whom they have met, and to give notes of admittance or permission to Love Feasts, of his own mere authority. Yet in all doubtful cases, prudence directs him to consult such as are most likely to furnish him with the necessary information. But before any person receives a quarterly society ticket, our rules require that the case be mentioned at the Leaders Meeting, and that a majority of the Leaders present avowedly or tacitly agree; that is, that they do not object to such person's being admitted a member of the Society. Every person admitted into the Society is not only to conform to the rules . . . but is required to meet in the Class to which he or she belongs at every opportunity.[2]

The strict maintenance of discipline was a strong force for cohesion, and it gave 'the people called Methodists' an identity which encouraged them to be different from 'the vain world'. 'Come ye apart' was their motto, and carefully guarded membership of Society fostered this spirit.[3]

Candidates for the Ministry

In view of what was to happen in 1835, it is important that we take note of an increasing concern over the selection, training and reception of candidates for the ministry into Full Connexion. One of Kilham's complaints was that superintendents enlisted men of inferior quality and that there was no means of checking this undesirable inflow.

[2] Crowther, Jonathan, *The Methodist Manual*, p. 130.
[3] Conference even laid down the law for the dress of Preachers' wives—'Many of the wives of our Preachers dress like the vain women of the world. . . .' (*Minutes*, ii. 139). See also M.C.A. letter from John Pawson to Charles Atmore, 24th February, 1800; *Minutes* v. 60, 62.

Kilham was right and in due time the reform he demanded was granted; but one can sympathize with superintendents faced with a shortage of staff, or with Conference with vacant stations to fill.

In 1797 it was laid down that all candidates must be approved by the District Meeting, but Conference could still, in an emergency, call out young men straight from Circuit. They assumed the status of 'Preachers on Trial'.[4] In 1810, however, the approval of the Quarterly Meeting had to be obtained before this was done. In 1802, it was stipulated that every candidate must be examined before the District Meeting, 'respecting his experience, his knowledge of Divine things, his reading, his views of the doctrines of the Gospels and his regard for Methodism in general'.[5] Then he must spend four years 'On Trial', during which period he was not allowed to marry and at the end of which (if he was approved) he was received into Full Connexion. There was no imposition of hands in ordination, but a pledge was given by each candidate that he 'preached our doctrines and approved our discipline'; as a token that he did this, he was given a copy of the *Large Minutes* inscribed, 'as long as you freely consent to, and earnestly endeavour to walk by these rules we shall rejoice to acknowledge you as a fellow-labourer'. Methodist writers of this period, in replying to attacks on their ministry, made much of the attention which was paid to the training of candidates. Lack of imposition of hands in ordination was answered by the contention that Reception into Full Connexion was 'virtual ordination'.

In 1815 another item appeared. It was asked what could be done 'to promote the mental improvement of our Preachers'; the answer was that 'every Preacher on Trial is required to deliver to the Chairman of his District a list of books he has read since the preceding District Meeting....'[6]

[4] Thomas Jackson, President of the Conference in 1838 and 1849, and one of the Connexion's most celebrated editors, was brought into the ministry in this way. See Jackson, T., *Recollections of my Life and Times*, p. 71. See also Crowther, J., *The Methodist Manual*, p. 139.
[5] *Minutes*, ii. p. 140.
[6] *Minutes*, iv. 122.

The 'Book List' still remains a requirement for candidates for the Methodist ministry. In the same year it was decided to examine candidates orally on their knowledge of Wesley's Works—another feature which has survived, in spite of pressure to delete all references to Wesley's Works as a doctrinal standard at the negotiations for Methodist Union in 1932.[7]

Ministerial Discipline

Finally, the Conference of 1827 took what it called, 'additional securities re character, qualifications and scriptural orthodoxy of candidates for our ministry' which enjoined that the Chairmen of Districts should 'not only examine very minutely' all candidates, but also report to the District Meeting 'respecting their health, piety, moral character, ministerial abilities, knowledge and belief of our doctrines, attachment to our discipline and freedom from debt, as well as from all secular incumbrances'.[8]

Traditionally, all Preachers were received into Full Connexion at the Conference, and in 1807 it was ruled that no Preacher was to be admitted without attending Conference for examination. In 1808, however, some Preachers on Trial found it a great inconvenience to travel the distances involved, so it was decided that they be received at the District Meeting and regarded as 'virtually received into Full Connexion without attending Conference'[9] but this was not satisfactory and two years later the former practice returned and formal admission again took place 'only at our Conferences'[10]—and so it remains to this day.

During this period, the importance of the District Meeting increased considerably. It was virtually an 'interim Conference' maintaining discipline over the

[7] See an article by John Kent in *Institutionalism and Church Unity* (Ed: Ehrenstrom and Muelder). Compulsory reading of Wesley's Works is now reduced to his *Sermons* and *Notes on the New Testament*—see C.P.D. (1974) S.O.718.
[8] *Minutes*, vi. 280 (1827).
[9] *Minutes*, iii. 30 (1808).
[10] *Minutes*, iii. 155 (1810).

Connexion—subject always to its decisions being ratified by the next Conference. The characters of all Preachers in Full Connexion were examined, candidates and probationers considered, note taken of those who had resigned, died or superannuated. It was still, at this time, the duty of Conference to call each Preacher's name, although it had also been done at the District Meeting.[11] This was no mere formality. During this period there were two outstanding 'cases' illustrating the care with which Conference investigated the character and conduct of its Preachers. In 1806 there was the first dismissal of a Preacher for doctrinal error, when Joseph Cooke's two sermons, one on Justification by Faith and the other on The Witness of the Spirit, proved him to be at variance with Methodist orthodoxy. In 1808 no less a person than Samuel Bradburn was accused of casting unjust reflections on the character of Wesley, so Conference enquired into the matter. On giving a satisfactory explanation, Bradburn was acquitted.[12]

A *cause célèbre* was that of Daniel Isaac, who in 1816 wrote a book entitled *Ecclesiastical Claims* in which he attempted to justify the claims of the Methodist ministry against those of Rome and certain Anglicans. He defended the orthodox Wesleyan attitude to Apostolic Succession in such a way that, had he known where to stop, Conference would have applauded their champion; but when he proceeded to launch a general attack on all ministerial authority and to impugn the position held by Wesley and his successors with 'indelicate and irreverent, if not, profane'[13] language he was severely reprimanded.[14] The subsequent history of this book does not concern us here, but the case is of significance in that it affords another example of the close scrutiny which the Methodist Preachers as a body exercised over them-

[11] See Crowther, J., *A Methodist Manual*, pp. 156–7.
[12] See Jackson, T., *Recollections*, p. 111.
[13] See Smith, G., *History of Wesleyan Methodism*, iii. p. 7; also Everett, J., *The Polemic Divine*—note that in the third edition, written in 1849 after Everett had been expelled from the Wesleyan Conference, a bitter anti-Bunting strain enters. See also my article on Daniel Isaac in *The Proceedings of the Wesley Historical Society*, xxxvi. pp. 2ff.
[14] The judgement of Conference on Isaac is recorded in *Minutes*, iv. 237 (1816).

selves as individuals. It is also a reminder of the fact that a Wesleyan could go too far in his criticism of ministerial authority and of the Church of England.

We have dealt at length with this ministerial 'inquisition', for it is impossible to exaggerate the importance which Wesleyan ministers attached to it and the seriousness with which they conducted it. It was part and parcel of their idea of 'accountability' of the Pastoral Office and (to look ahead a little) it is vital to an understanding of the expulsions of 1849—how *The Times* failed to understand it! Writing many years later (in 1873 to be precise), Thomas Jackson said in his *Recollections*:

> I was particularly impressed with the conscientious fidelity which the Preachers manifested in the investigation of each other's characters, and their care to maintain the purity of the Body, so that 'the ministry' might not be 'blamed' and its purpose defeated. Anything even approaching to sin was visited with severe animadversion.

To which we can only add the word of Dr J. S. Simon, who said that when the Legal Hundred had to sit in judgement 'a giant's strength was used with a brother's tenderness'. It is no reflection on the sincerity of ministers in the other Methodist Connexions to say that, lacking a high conception of the Pastoral Office and without a separate ministerial session of Conference, they had nothing like this 'inquisition'. It was distinctively Wesleyan, a direct legacy from Wesley's conception of the ministry as a body, and of the individual within that body.

The Liverpool Minutes

The seriousness with which the Wesleyan minister regarded his calling, as distinct from any pretensions about the nature of the Pastoral Office, can be seen in what are generally known as 'The Liverpool Minutes'.

In 1820, the Conference met on Merseyside. The country was passing through a severe trade depression and Methodists everywhere were feeling the pinch. George III had died and the air was thick with discontent. There was even a threat of revolution. The Conference Pastoral Address reflected these disturbances, but there was a more serious matter to trouble the Fathers and Brethren—a decrease of nearly 5,000 members, the first decrease for 54 years. The shock drove the Preachers to re-examine their calling. After serious discussion, the famous 'Liverpool Minutes' were produced, 'of which', says Dr G. Smith, 'it is scarcely possible to speak too highly. In a manner equally clear, forcible and practical, they range over the whole course of a Christian minister's duty.'[15] It has been said that they 'present the ideal Methodist Preacher and his work as no-one else has attempted to depict them'.[16] They were undoubtedly the work of Jabez Bunting.

In thirty-one clauses they offer a reply to the question, 'What measures can we adopt for the increase of spiritual religion among our societies and congregations and for the extension of the work of God in our native country?' In essence, they sketch contemporary Methodist life and the place of the minister therein. His duties spring from a high conception of his office. He is to preach, 'all those leading and vital doctrines of the Gospel', to give himself wholly to the work and to guard against all occupations that have no connection with it. He is to 'covet earnestly the best gifts' and preach out of doors; to try new places wherever the opportunity occurs; to meet Classes and Bands, being careful to observe the rule about the showing of tickets; to encourage Prayer Meetings, Watchnight Services and Love Feasts, especially in country places; to establish weekly meetings for children and to be diligent in pastoral visitation. He is to be scrupulously careful in choosing new Leaders, to care for the back-slider and exhort attendance at the Lord's Supper. The Sabbath must be strictly observed and schedules filled in correctly and returned punctually! The loftiest paragraph we quote in full:

> Let us ourselves remember, and endeavour to impress upon our people, that we, as a Body, do not exist for the purposes of party; and that we are especially bound by the example of

[15] Smith, G., *History of Wesleyan Methodism*, iii. 49.
[16] Gregory, B., *Scriptural Church Principles*, p. 232.

our Founder, by the original principle on which our Societies are formed, and by our constant professions before the world, to avoid a narrow, bigoted and sectarian spirit, to abstain from needless and unprofitable disputes on minor subjects of theological controversy, and as far as we innocently can, to 'please all men for their good unto edification'. Let us, therefore, maintain towards all denominations of Christians who 'hold the Head', the kind and catholic spirit of primitive Methodism; and, according to the noble maxim of our Father in the Gospel, 'be the friends of all, the enemies of none'.[17]

The Conduct of Worship

Before we leave the subject of Wesleyan polity there is one other topic to which we must give our attention, as upon it a crucial issue turned in 1827—the conduct of worship and the introduction of organs into Methodist chapels. Worship in early Methodism was extremely simple, hymn-singing and preaching being the chief ingredients. Nightingale, a satirical critic of Methodism, pointed out that the one deficiency in a Methodist service was 'not having the scriptures read to the people'.[18] He was right, for scripture reading did not necessarily have a place in a Methodist service, except when it was held in Church hours, in which case the directions of *The Plan of Pacification* were applicable whereby 'The Preachers shall read . . . at least the lessons appointed by the Calendar'.[19] In 1809 the Conference felt the need for underlining this rule.

There was, however, another factor shaping Methodist worship. By the beginning of the second decade of the nineteenth century, Wesleyan Methodism was catering for a clientele who were not entirely satisfied with its primitive simplicity. While these people were not in membership with the Society, their desires could not be ignored. While they were not inclined to submit to the searching discipline of the Class Meeting, they attended Sunday services, subscribed to the funds and paid for sittings. They were

[17] *Minutes*, v. 149 (1820).
[18] Nightingale, J., *A Portraiture of Methodism*, pp. 251–2.
[19] *Minutes*, i. 693.

referred to as 'hearers', 'adherents' or 'members of the congregation'.[20] Of course, they raised a problem at Love Feasts and Sacramental services to which members only were admitted, but otherwise they were welcome. But it was from this circle that there came moves to 'improve' the Sunday worship, the chief of which was the installation of organs. This is yet another incident in the progress of Methodism from Society to Church. Dr J. S. Simon has admirably summarized the position:

> As long as Methodists were mere members of a private Society, worshipping in small buildings, they could fence their meetings and, to a considerable extent, impose their own terms on those attending them. By the year 1827, however, a policy of building huge chapels had been adopted. These buildings were much too large for the exclusive needs of the Society. They were intended to attract and accommodate those who, for various reasons, chose to worship in Methodist chapels. The middle passage between the position of mere 'Society' and a fully equipped 'Church' had to be made.[21]

With these factors in mind, we turn to the rules which governed the conduct of worship before 1827. The *Plan of Pacification* had laid it down that the introduction of the Sacraments into any Methodist chapel must have the approval of a majority of the Trustees on the one hand and of the Stewards and Leaders on the other. It is important to note this, for in the Leeds Organ Case a subtle point of argument turned on this regulation. The dissentients at Leeds argued that what applied to the Sacraments should apply to other elements in the worship of the Church, namely, the installation of an organ.

As for the conduct of worship, generally, the responsibility for seeing that all was done decently and in order lay fairly upon the shoulders of the minister:

[20] James Everett distinguishes between 'members of Society' and 'mere attenders on the public ordinances'—*Remarks on a Pamphlet* (1812), p. 11.
[21] *London Quarterly Review*, July 1888, p. 275. Another example of this passage from Society to Church—baptisms were to be done in public worship and administered only to children of members or adherents. *Minutes* iii. 292 (1812).

Let no Preacher, therefore, suffer his right to conduct every part of the worship of Almighty God, to be infringed upon, either by singers or others. But let him sacredly preserve and calmly maintain his authority; as he who sacrifices this, sacrifices not only Methodism, but the spirit and design of Christianity.[22]

Finance

Finance requires our attention only in so far as it has repercussions on polity. Early in the nineteenth century, the administration of Connexional Funds was greatly improved by the appointment of clerks and the admission of laymen to the committees. This was a notable advance, since Kilham had trenchantly attacked the way in which the Preachers handled the finances of the Connexion. Conference was at last taking itself seriously and the time was ripe for the advent of its greatest administrator, Jabez Bunting, whose early years in the ministry coincided with the nadir of Methodist finance.

Consider the position in the first decade of the nineteenth century. The country was poor and the populace uneasy.[23] Methodism was saddled with debt and without capable hands to pull it together. At the same time, wisely or otherwise, many large chapels were built with money advanced by the wealthier people of the Connexion. Once a chapel was built, it was the duty of the Trustees to see that the fabric and furnishings were kept in order and that it was put to no uses contrary to those laid down in the Conference Deed. This Deed regulated the doctrine preached from the pulpit so that the Trustees, in partnership with the minister, were responsible, in a way not shared by the Leaders, for the maintenance of Methodist doctrine and discipline.

[22] *Minutes*, ii. 290 (1805).
[23] M.C.A. letter from John Pawson to Charles Atmore, 8th May, 1800, where Pawson speaks of riots at Leeds which prevented the holding of a market. He says Methodists were so straitened and the cost of provisions so high that only a few Preachers should go to Conference; only so could they ease the burden of hospitality.

The Laity

It was this power given to Trustees which, more than any other single factor, led to the ascendency of laymen in Methodism. As few chapels were opened free of debt, the men who held the purse-strings to pay the piper could often call the tune. We have seen something of the power of Trustees in the Portland Chapel controversy of 1794. They were sincere men who shouldered considerable responsibility and sought to discharge it faithfully, and it is not surprising that such men, throughout the Connexion, should increasingly make their influence felt. It is true that they were never able to breach the walls of the all-ministerial Conference, but their voices were heard in District Committees and they were doubtless a power behind the throne. Bunting, a cleric of clerics if ever there was one, nevertheless saw the value of this lay participation and encouraged it.

In 1801, the Conference decided that Circuit Stewards should attend the District Meeting to 'advise on financial matters'[24] and in 1803 the first mixed committee was formed. This marked the beginning of a new chapter in the financial affairs of the Connexion and shows, in a way, that the power of the laity in the early nineteenth century has been rather underrated. It was real and it was effective; else why were the revolts of Kilham and others not more successful? Was it because, in relation to the laity, the autocracy of Conference was by no means so commanding as is often supposed; that the laity, with money behind them, were subtly in command?

Be that as it may, there is no doubt that Methodist Connexionalism was greatly strengthened by the setting up of Committees of Management. In 1810 Conference tackled its chapel debts and a concerted effort was made by the whole Connexion; co-operation between the wealthy and not-so-wealthy did much to strengthen the Connexional spirit. A loose federation of independent chapels could never

---

[24] Strangely, there is no mention of this in the Minutes. It is referred to in the *Methodist Magazine* for December, 1801.

have achieved such results. Nor could it have been achieved without a partnership of ministry and laity which is not as fully recognized as it ought to be. The Wesleyan doctrine of the Pastoral Office precluded laymen from taking a share in the pastoral oversight of the flock,[25] but at least they were not without a say in determining the context in which that oversight was exercised.

---

[25] Class Leaders were, up to a point, co-pastors, but their role did not extend beyond the Leaders Meeting, and they were not really recognized as co-pastors—see below, Pt. IV, Ch. 2.

PART THREE

The Clash

1827–49

CHAPTER ONE

THE LEEDS ORGAN CASE

THE installation of an organ in Leeds Brunswick Church was the occasion, but not the root cause, of the first of three major nineteenth-century secessions from Wesleyan Methodism. It is not necessary for us to give a detailed account of events, for these have been chronicled by the historians;[1] our concern is with their significance as far as they affected attitudes to church and ministry.

At the same time, a brief indication should be given of what the celebrated 'Leeds Organ Case' was all about. On 9th September, 1825, Leeds Brunswick Church was opened for public worship. It was the largest of its kind so far and the great congregation it attracted prompted the Trustees to turn their mind to an organ. Early in 1827, following the procedure laid down by the Conference in 1820, they applied to the District Meeting for permission to proceed. Meanwhile, the Leaders and Local Preachers, claiming to represent the rank and file members, denied that an organ was necessary and expressed this opinion to the District Meeting. By 13 votes to 7 the District Meeting concluded that, 'it is not desirable to grant the required permission to place an organ in Brunswick Chapel'. But the Trustees did not let the matter rest there; they transferred the debate to the Conference. Conference reversed the decision of the District and granted permission to the Trustees to go ahead with the organ. This at once raised cries of 'tyranny' and a turbulent autumn ensued.

Clandestine (therefore illegal) meetings were held, until the ringleader, a Local Preacher named Matthew Johnson, was suspended by the Leeds (East) Superintendent, who was also the Chairman of the Leeds District. Things became

---

[1] See the histories of Smith and Stevens, articles in the *London Quarterly Review* (referred to in the text) and in the *Proceedings of the Wesley Historical Society*, volumes xxxv, xxxvii and xxxix.

so difficult that in December he took advantage of the *Form of Discipline* and called a special District Meeting to consider the case. Conference officials came down from London, and after several days spent in hearing evidence they severely castigated the 'rebels' and upheld the decision of the Superintendent in his suspension of Johnson.

Johnson and his sympathizers were all the time organizing themselves for retaliation and, if necessary, secession; so when the ensuing Conference upheld the decision of the Special District Meeting, separation became inevitable and the dissentients re-grouped under the banner of 'The Protestant Methodists'. It has been said that the Brunswick organ cost Leeds Methodism a thousand pounds and a thousand members.

We propose to treat the case under headings which indicate the chronological development of the points at issue. These are: (a) the initial dispute over the organ, (b) the constitutional issue, and (c) rival conceptions of the ministry as held by the Protestant Methodists and the Wesleyans.

The Organ

It is often alleged that if the dispute over the organ had not arisen, the dissentients would have found another excuse for challenging the constitution; that the organ was a pretext for the expression of a deep, smouldering discontent on the part of a forceful minority within the Connexion.[2] Before the organ was mooted, there were observers who confidently predicted that a storm would break, but were frankly surprised when it came from that quarter. They expected it to blow up over the supervision of Sunday Schools,[3] which had grown up quickly in Leeds, staffed mainly by Methodists, but running quite independent of the organization and discipline of the Church. It was claimed that without

[2] Address of the President of the Conference to the Leeds Methodists, December, 1827; M.C.A. letters from Bunting to Entwisle, 22nd December, 1827, Galland to Bunting, 4th and 25th January, 1828; Ward, W. R., *Religion and Society in England*, pp. 135ff.
[3] Anon., *Sound Thoughts for Sound People*, p. 8.

the controlling chairmanship of a minister, teachers' meetings degenerated into unholy rows and became hotbeds of disaffection. To the displeasure of the Sunday School officials the ministers decided to bring these schools under the control of the local circuit and rules were laid down for their administration. The teaching of writing was abolished as a 'profane subject for the Sabbath'—again to the displeasure of the Sunday School workers. Further friction developed in an otherwise worthy movement, the Leeds Prayer Leaders, when a similar effort was made to bring them into circuit organization. Yet a third source of disaffection lay in a decision to divide the large Leeds Circuit into two. This was a wise move since the circuit covered the whole of the city and a wide area around, but it aggravated tempers and ulterior motives were imputed.[4] The spread of this discontent was facilitated by the lamentable lack of ministerial oversight. With only four ministers for over 5,000 members disaffection spread unchecked and ministers had no means of winning the confidence of the people or establishing any authority among them—especially those on the perimeter of their rounds. Erroneous and slanderous gossip about the ministers or the constitution went largely unanswered and undefended.[5]

The proposal to install the Brunswick organ therefore provided a rallying point for much misinformed discontent. Organs were identified with popery; they belonged to the sphere of ordered, liturgical worship. To nineteenth-century Methodists they were 'identified with the service of the Church of England'[6] and the manoeuvres of the Bruns-

---

[4] See *Proceedings of the Conference*, p. 11—speech of Isaac Turton.

[5] See Anon., *Sound Thoughts for Sound People*, p. 5. It is not impossible that the Leeds troubles had some connection, in origin and temper, with the Inghamite Societies which were strong in Yorkshire.

[6] *Address of the London South Circuit*, p. 32. '. . . and are, in general demanded by what is termed the Church party among us.' Note the reversal of roles —in 1794, the 'church' party were those who were for simplicity of Methodist worship, leaving the Church of England to supply the type of worship associated with organs. But the quotation given above shows that even the Church party were by now (1828) expecting to find this more sophisticated type of worship within Methodism, hence the need for organs.

wick Trustees stirred memories of Bristol in 1794. The overt objection to the organ was just along those lines—that it would destroy 'that primitive simplicity of worship which has been so long and so signally owned of God',[7] that it would 'introduce novelties which would almost unavoidably produce formality and conformity to the world with all their baneful consequences'.[8] The fact is, we are here face to face with the old problem of 'society or church' in a new form. In the Brunswick community there were, on the one hand, Methodists of the old stock who met in Class and were satisfied with the simple, spontaneous type of worship. They customarily held a Society Meeting after Sunday evening service and this meeting, says Joseph Entwisle, was 'a visible and marked line of distinction between the Society and the Congregation'.[9] Those whom Entwisle refers to as 'the Congregation' were people who, while appreciating the simplicity of Methodist worship, welcomed anything that added decorum and beauty to the service. Some of them were sympathetic to the liturgy; others, not so disposed, nevertheless appreciated the value of an organ and supported the efforts of the Trustees to get one. They were not necessarily members of Class, but they were seat-holders and contributed to the finances of the Church. It was they whom the Conference had in mind when it tried to justify its action in granting permission to install the organ by saying that it must cater for all who come within its buildings for worship.

Hence, in its initial stages, the Leeds Organ Case represented a tension between the 'Society' element, whose spokesmen were the Leaders and Local Preachers favouring simplicity and spontaneity, and the 'Church' element, whose spokesmen were the Trustees wishing to see Methodism providing that fuller diet of worship which an organ would encourage. Methodism was still painfully emerging from 'Society' to 'Church'.

[7] Barr, John, *A Statement of Facts*, p. 1.
[8] Ibid., p. 1.
[9] *Memoirs*, p. 376.

THE LEEDS ORGAN CASE

The Constitution

(a) *The Organ Rule of 1820*

From a dispute about an organ, the contest soon moved on to another plane[10]—an argument about the constitution; from the desirability of an organ itself to the way in which it was granted; and it all turned on the celebrated Organ Law of 1820. It reads:

> We think that in some of the larger chapels, where some instrumental music may be deemed expedient in order to guide the congregational singing, organs may be allowed by special consent of the Conference; but every application for such consent shall be first made at the District Meeting: and if it obtain their sanction, shall be transferred to a committee at the Conference who shall report their opinion as to the propriety of acceding to the request, and also as to the restrictions with which the permission to erect an organ ought, in that particular case, to be accompanied.[11]

On the face of it, this was straightforward enough, and no doubt served well in ninety-nine cases out of a hundred. Leeds, however, with all its built-in tensions, was the hundredth, in which it did not work. It was full of ambiguities which were exploited to the full by both sides. For one thing, it did not specify who was the appropriate body to present the application—Trustees or Leaders. This particular ambiguity would have mattered little where Trustees and Leaders were of one mind, but it had serious consequences in Leeds where the two bodies were in opposite camps. Another ambiguity (and the most serious one for our study) was that while it ruled what should be done if the District Meeting gave its consent, it said nothing about what should be done if (as in the Leeds Case) the District Meeting refused its sanction—was that the end of the matter; had the District Meeting the power of veto, or did the last word remain with the Conference?

The argument went to and fro with considerable heat.

[10] See M.C.A. letter from Edmund Grindrod to John Bowers, 29th December, 1828.
[11] *Minutes*, v. 145.

The Preachers argued that the last word must always lie with the Conference. The dissentients argued that the rule clearly implied that if the District Meeting was not able to give its consent, the case went no further—at least for a year. As John Barr said, 'Where there is no sanction from the District Meeting, there can be no legal application to Conference'.[12] Three questions are raised here, all of them complicated by events—the function of the District Meeting, the authority of the Conference, and the interpretation of the *Form of Discipline*.

(b) *The Function and Power of the District Meeting*

As we saw in a previous chapter, District Meetings were instituted 'to take the place of Wesley's general superintendence in the intervals between one Conference and the next',[13] but the events of 1827 raised three issues. The first was whether the decisions of a District Meeting could be overruled by Conference; the second was whether a District Meeting had power to judge and pass sentence on a Local Preacher; the third was whether the Special District Meeting of December 1827 was constitutionally convened and whether it had exceeded its powers. Consider these:

i. Could the District Meeting be overruled by the Conference? The dissentients took the Organ Rule to mean that if the District Meeting did not sanction an application, the case proceeded no further and that the Conference was not entitled to consider a case which the District had turned down. This was a sensible interpretation of an ambiguous rule. But apart from the *right* of Conference to overrule the District, there can be little doubt that in the Leeds case, it was *unwise* to do so. The proposal had been rejected by the Leaders by 60 votes to 1; by the District by 13 votes to 7; and approved by the Trustees by the narrow margin of 8 to 6 with 1 neutral.

However, it is not with the wisdom of the Conference we have to deal, but with its rights; and the question is, 'Wherein lay the *right* of the Conference to overrule the

[12] *A Statement of Facts*, p. 32.
[13] See above, Part I, ch. 3.

decision of the District Meeting?' The basic reason was that Conference had the last word in everything; that the District Meeting was only a committee of Conference and in allowing the trustees the right to appeal it acknowledged this fact.[14] It was further argued that the organ application would have been considered by Conference in the normal way when the District Minutes were reviewed.[15] In whatever way one may interpret the 1820 rule, one must admit that the last thing Conference would do would be to hand over its responsibility to the District Meeting.[16]

ii. The second question was, 'Had the District Meeting the authority to pronounce judgement on anyone other than a minister; in particular, on a Local Preacher?' The point was that Edmund Grindrod, superintendent of the Leeds East Circuit, had suspended Matthew Johnson for holding 'illegal' meetings, and the Special District Meeting had upheld his action. The challenge came not from Leeds, but from Southwark; and so the issue was now not local, but connexional; not the organ, but the constitution. The Southwark dissentients alleged that the Special District Meeting had usurped the power of the superintendent and the local church courts and had assumed the right of making laws for the connexion and devising new tests and declarations. As to the other point, the dissentients claimed that the trial of a Local Preacher should take place in a Circuit Local Preachers Meeting, and that of a private member in a Leaders Meeting; that a District Meeting or the Conference had no right to do either.[17]

iii. The third query related to the Special District Meeting convened by the superintendent of the Leeds East Circuit in accordance with the provisions of the *Form of Discipline*, which read:

[14] John Barr, a leading dissentient, argued that the 1820 rule contained no right of appeal—see his *Vindication of a Statement*, p. 30.
[15] *Minutes*, i. 249.
[16] Galland, T., *Letter II from a Minister in Leeds*, p. 12.
[17] *Address of the London South Circuit*, p. 13. James Bromley saw the danger and wrote and told Bunting so—see M.C.A. letter dated 17th July, 1828. He also saw the futility of the Declaration which the Leeds Preachers drew up. He said to Bunting, 'But oh! above all things avoid legislating under injured feelings'.

The Chairman, in all cases which, in his judgement, cannot be settled in the ordinary District Meetings, shall have authority to summons three of the nearest superintendents to be incorporated with the District Committee, who shall have equal authority to vote and settle everything till the Conference.[18]

The dissentients claimed that the Special District Meeting of 4th December, 1827 contravened these rules, so they refused to recognize it or to appear before it. They did so on the following grounds: In the first place, they said it was illegally constituted in that there was no provision in the rules for the importation of Jabez Bunting and Richard Watson; that the presence of these two Conference men meant that Conference was less than impartial and its status as a court of appeal jeopardized. Secondly, the dissentients questioned the contention of the ministers that the powers of the District Meeting were absolute during the interval between one Conference and the next. Thirdly, they maintained that the District Meeting could deal only with ministerial cases; therefore, so far as ministers were concerned, there was no 'extra-ordinary emergency' in Leeds to warrant a special meeting at District level. Finally, and this was basic, the dissentients believed that the District Meeting had no right to meddle with circuit affairs.

Undoubtedly, this special District Meeting raised crucial issues and we cannot but sympathize with the Leeds Superintendent and others who were acting with no clear precedents to guide them. They were creating precedents which were being challenged as they emerged. It was a testing time for that confidence between ministers and people without which no church can exist; but the dissentients felt that a new element was creeping into Methodism —'tyranny from the top'! Probably they were right, but whether they protested for the right reason and in the right way is another question. Another writer, reflecting on events nearly thirty years later, wrote of that Special District Meeting as 'a new court in Methodism' and 'the

[18] *Minutes*, i. 692.

THE LEEDS ORGAN CASE

initiation of a system to which resort was to be had . . . for the prompt punishment of disobedience and as a terror to be held over refractory circuits'.[19] The revolt revolved around the right of Conference to 'interfere' in circuit affairs and this brings us back to the fundamental issues of Connexionalism versus Independency, episcopé and the like.

(c) The Authority of the Conference

The Leeds dissentients were often wrong in their diagnosis of trouble, but they were right when they said, 'The dispute in which we are now engaged is not merely whether our simple mode of worship shall be altered by the introduction of organs, the liturgy, etc., but whether the Conference shall possess supreme and absolute sway over the Methodist Societies'.[20] Clearly, by the autumn of 1828 the question of the installation of an organ was no longer the centre of controversy; the crux of the matter was the authority of Conference.

Ever since the death of Wesley, the Preachers had maintained that the Conference was the final and supreme court of appeal; but the dissentients saw it only as 'a secret assembly, governing all, and amenable to none, in which the governed have neither voice nor representative'.[21] The reply came from Richard Watson who pointed out that Conference was a 'common governing body'[22] guarding the rights of ministers and people alike. It was foolish for a member to disparage the right of Conference to 'interfere' in a local dispute for it was the 'common authority' to which both sides could appeal.[23] This would have been impossible in a system of Independency, and it was a form of Independency that the Southwark dissentients would have imposed upon Wesleyan Methodism. As it stood, it

[19] *The United Methodist Free Churches Magazine*, 1863, p. 290; the writer is thought to be Matthew Johnson.
[20] *An Appeal to the Members of the Wesleyan Methodist Societies*, p. 7.
[21] Churchman, *A Letter to the Rev. I. Keeling*, p. 10. On Conference as a court of appeal, see Keeling, I., *A Reply to 'A Statement of Facts'*, p. 20.
[22] Watson, R., *An Affectionate Address*, p. 6.
[23] *Address to the Methodists of Leeds*, p. 6.

was a viable combination of local and connexional jurisdiction. In ordinary cases, the local courts operated, but provision was made for critical cases; as, for example, when the local courts were powerless or unwilling to act. Then, Conference acted; whether the subject were minister, local official or ordinary member. This was not priestly despotism, but paternal oversight.[24] In the Leeds case, the Trustees had as much right to 'protection' as the allegedly 'priest-ridden' people.[25] Leaders, and all others, have every right to petition Conference, but not to rule it. The dissentients had nothing to fear, for there were checks and balances at every level of administration, from the Conference to the Society. As far as the Conference is concerned, it was composed of ministers who, on their return to circuit, had to give an account to the people upon whom they were dependent in the last resort for their livelihood. One preacher remarked, 'I had rather a little too much power remained in Conference where we have so many checks, than be given to those who love liberty so well as to keep it to themselves'.[26]

(d) The Form of Discipline

The Form of Discipline (1797) and *The Plan of Pacification* (1795)—always printed together—were regarded as a compact between Preachers and people, made in good faith and expected to be honoured in the spirit as well as in the letter. They were a product of that period, immediately after the death of Wesley, when Methodism was in the process of fixing the seat of authority in the connexion and resolving the differences between those who wished to keep Methodism 'societary' and those who saw that it must develop as a church. *The Plan of Pacification* was a compromise on the Sacraments; *The Form of Discipline* amounted to a working agreement between the Preachers with their all-ministerial Conference and those who felt that the people ought to share in the government of the Connexion.

[24] See *Report of a Special District Meeting*, p. 9.
[25] See *Address to the Methodists of Leeds*, p. 6.
[26] Church Methodist, *A Letter to a Churchman*, p. 11.

THE LEEDS ORGAN CASE

Together, the *Plan* and the *Discipline* formed the foundation of Methodist polity and, on the whole, with mutual confidence between ministers and people, it worked well. It is true that the Preachers did not surrender their all-ministerial Conference and that there were still radicals for whom the *Discipline* did not go far enough. They agitated for more lay control and it was clear that they would be satisfied with nothing less than a mixed Conference or even circuit independency. They were the moving spirits behind the secessions of 1827, 1834 and 1849.

When the Leeds case highlighted the question of authority both sides appealed to the *Plan* and the *Discipline*. The points of contention were (a) Did the *Plan* legislate for organs? (b) Did the *Discipline* transfer any authority from the Conference to the local courts? (c) Did the Discipline transfer the right of expulsion from the Superintendent to the Leaders Meeting? and (d) What authority had the 'Miscellaneous Regulations'? Consider each of these in turn.

(a) *The Plan of Pacification* required joint agreement between the Trustees (on the one hand) and the Stewards and Leaders (on the other hand) before Conference would grant permission to administer the Lord's Supper in any church. It was on this analogy that the Superintendent of the Leeds East Circuit brought the organ issue before his Leaders Meeting. The dissentients held that he was right in doing this;[27] the Conference said he was wrong, for organs were not mentioned in the *Plan*,[28] and censured the Superintendent for what he did,[29] saying that while the Leaders may express their opinion they had no right to interfere authoritatively. Be that as it may, the question remains whether Conference would have acted with more wisdom had they paid more heed to the wishes of the Leaders.

(b) On the second point, the dissentients argued that both the *Plan* and the *Discipline* transferred considerable authority from the Conference to the local courts. They quoted such phrases as:

[27] Barr, J., *A Statement of Facts*, p. 7.
[28] Keeling, I., *A Reply to 'A Statement of Facts'*, p. 17.
[29] Stephens, J., *An Address to the Methodists at Leeds*, p. 14.

We have given up the greatest part of our executive government into your hands as represented in your different public meetings.

The whole management of our temporal concerns may now be truly said to be invested in the Quarterly Meetings, the District Meetings having nothing left them but a negative.

We have given up to you far the greatest part of the Superintendent's authority.[30]

From these general statements, the dissentients drew two conclusions. The first was that the organ question should have been decided entirely within the courts of the local church, and that the District Meeting and the Conference had exceeded their authority in pronouncing judgement on it. The second conclusion was that the people were 'priest ridden' by the all-ministerial District Meeting and Conference.

Richard Watson replied to all this. He argued that the Conference conceded no more than a check upon the Preachers. It did not give minister and leader an equal share in power and authority. Pastors had a responsibility, but to make the discharge of that responsibility dependent upon the co-ordinate authority of themselves and Leaders would destroy the benefits of Connexionalism. It would also deny to both Preacher and people an impartial and common court of appeal. As Watson said, '... certain powers are inseparable from the duties of the ministry and cannot be transferred, or put into commission with those who have not this calling.'[31] This is the doctrine of the Pastoral Office pure and undefiled! The *Discipline*, continued Watson, guarded the powers of the ministry, but in no case did it abolish them or transfer them to others.

(c) As the question of the expulsion of members arose in an intense form in the Warrenite affair, we shall postpone consideration of that issue to the next chapter.

(d) The fourth point deals with the force of a group of rules in the 1797 Minutes headed 'Miscellaneous Regulations'. The Conference of that year addressed a 'Letter to

[30] *Minutes*, i. 393–4 (1797).
[31] Watson, *op. cit.*, p. 10.

the Methodist Societies' in which it introduced to the people the terms of the new arrangements, later to be known as *The Form of Discipline*. Following the letter, we find certain 'Sundry Miscellaneous Regulations', beginning, 'With respect to Districts', and it was upon their authority that the Special District Meeting was convened. Watson justified the action in his *Affectionate Address*, but the dissentients held that the Conference party had sheltered under the Miscellaneous Regulations to override the rights of the local courts. Furthermore, they alleged that the Miscellaneous Regulations were drawn up after the 'Letter' had been forwarded to the Societies and therefore could not have the force of the rules commended in the Letter.[32] This was an attempt to divide the *Discipline* into two parts, one of which gave liberty to the people as agreed by both Preachers and people; the other, either an afterthought or an appendix, applying only to Preachers without in any way anulling the liberty granted in the other part.

The Conference of 1829, in replying to these contentions, stood by the *Form of Discipline* as a whole,[33] i.e. including the Miscellaneous Regulations; it could do no other. So with this official pronouncement the celebrated Leeds Organ Case ends. It does not fall to our lot to trace the fortunes of the dissentients as they organized themselves as 'The Protestant Methodists'.

The Ministry

In 1828 the controversy, which began with the Brunswick organ and continued as a dispute on the constitution, moved finally into a discussion on the conception of the ministry. As we have seen, the peculiar Wesleyan doctrine of the Pastoral Office was now emerging. The *point d'appui* was the allegation by the dissentients that the people were 'priest ridden', and that the Preachers were 'lording it over God's heritage';[34] they accordingly advocated the equality

[32] *Circular to Wesleyan Methodists*, pp. 11, 23.
[33] *Minutes*, vi. (1829), pp. 512-13.
[34] Johnson, M., *A Reply to False Statements*, p. 9.

of minister and laymen, together sharing in the government of the church. It was this stand which brought forth the first considered statement on the Pastoral Office. It came from the pen of Richard Watson, under the title of an *Affectionate Address* (1829). Watson's outline of the duties and responsibility of a Wesleyan minister make interesting reading. He is:

... to preach the Gospel.
... to collect all who profess to have received his message into communion with the church of Christ; this being an obligatory ordinance of God.
... to watch over all such with pastoral care, in order to their spiritual advancement in knowledge and grace.
... to reprove and rebuke the careless, the obstinate and unruly, with all 'longsuffering and doctrine'.
... to separate immoral and unruly persons from the flock, after due admonition.
... to show leniency and forbearance, in this exercise of discipline, in hopeful cases.
... to provide for the perpetuation of the ministry, by encouraging those who may give evidence of a fitness and a call to preach the Gospel.
... to appoint subordinate agents to assist him in various departments of his work, when it swells beyond the limits of his personal exertions.
... to guard the doctrine of all subordinate teachers, as well as their conduct.
... to visit all offenders, in this respect, according to the merits of the case.
... to excite the people by his exhortations to such liberalities in the proper support of their own religious institutions, in providing for the poor and sick, and in other branches of religious charity, as the Gospel requires, generally, but 'in this grace also'.

All these duties are inherent in the very office of a Christian pastor; and all the *powers* necessary to fulfil them do therefore of right, inalienable right, belong to his office; and this, whatever form of church government he may minister under, though it should be that of Independency.

The essence of this was responsibility with authority; yet

authority subject to checks, counsels and restraints. The Wesleyan constitution did not transfer ministerial authority to those who are not of that office. This was the answer to those who claimed that the minister had no special authority which was not already inherent in the Leaders. Watson also made the point that the checks provided for in the *Discipline* were not designed to obstruct the use of ministerial authority for the running of the church. For instance, the minister must take counsel with his Leaders in the admitting of members, but *he is the person admitting*. He must have the consent of the Leaders before a person can be expelled, but *he is the person expelling*. The concurrence of the laity is required before a man is admitted into the ministry, but *he and his brethren are the parties ordaining*.

This high doctrine of the ministry was, naturally, challenged by the dissentients from the start.[35] Their idea of the office of a minister is seen in the constitution of the Protestant Methodist connexion. Assuming a connexion of twenty circuits, their Annual Assembly would consist of twenty Presiding Elders, twenty Preachers, (perhaps Elders), twenty Leaders, two additional persons from every circuit with over a thousand members and three Itinerants; the last named sitting only with permission of the Missionary Committee. 'A Careful Observer' was right when he pointed out that this system places the ministers 'lowest in the scale of influence and authority and condemns them to be treated with the utmost jealousy and suspicion'.[36] This represented the ideas and beliefs of the dissentients pressed to their logical conclusion.

Conclusion

The significance of the Leeds Organ Case lies in the fact that it was the first real upsurge of radical Methodism.[37] From the point of view of the 'establishment', it had its regrettable

[35] Ashton, J., *Reply to 'An Affectionate Address'*, p. 79.
[36] Careful Observer, *Sound Thoughts for Sound People*, p. 14.
[37] For political implications see the writings of E. R. Taylor, R. F. Wearmouth, Maldwyn Edwards, E. P. Thompson.

moments. Bunting, in later years, had grave misgivings[38] and it is significant that 'not one of the speakers who had been in the ministry during Wesley's lifetime approved of the way in which it had been handled'.[39] There was too much vindictiveness behind the scenes—on both sides[40]—and it is clear that the Conference party intended their actions to be a warning to others. It certainly brought to the fore the giant Wesleyan protagonists, Richard Watson, John Beecham and William Vevers. Unfortunately, Watson died in 1833, but Beecham and Vevers lived to fight another day.

It was, let us not forget, an age in which it was sincerely believed that the ministry could not survive without absolute authority, unshared with laymen.[41]

---

[38] Gregory, B., *Sidelights*, p. 97; Life of Bunting, ii. 235.
[39] Gregory, *op. cit.*, p. 59; a perusal of a ms account of the 1828 Conference bears this out (M.C.A.).
[40] M.C.A. letters—Bunting to Matthew Tobias, 23rd February, 1829, in which the writer says that the thousand or so members lost to Leeds dissentients 'are very little missed'; Grindrod to Bunting, 28th November, 1827, 'we shall so dispose of the Leeds business as to read a useful and lasting lesson to the whole connexion'. Gregory (*Sidelights*, p. 72) was surprised that Bunting, who had been so popular in Yorkshire, should be reported as saying, 'The Yorkshire Methodists, with all their excellencies, need teaching a lesson'. See also *Address to Methodists of Leeds*, p. 18.
[41] Entwisle, *Memoirs*, p. 355.

CHAPTER TWO

THE WARRENITE SECESSION

IN 1834–5 the controversy associated with the name of Dr Samuel Warren gave birth to the third secession from Wesleyan Methodism. It was akin to the Leeds Organ Case in that it was another revolt of the radicals and another episode in the progress of the Wesleyans from Society to Church.[1] The story begins with the Conference of 1833 when a committee was appointed to look into the matter of 'the better education of our Junior Preachers'.[2] One of the members of that committee was Dr Samuel Warren. After a discussion about the various ways in which young ministers could be helped, it was unanimously agreed that the most satisfactory solution would be to establish a 'Theological Institution' and the committee suggested to Conference that it be done immediately with Dr Bunting as President. After the committee dispersed, Dr Warren turned sour. He objected to the Institution as such and to Dr Bunting as President. He was, of course, fully entitled to change his mind if he so wished. Unfortunately, he decided to fight a pamphleteering war. Had he confined his controversy to the courts of the church of which he was a distinguished member, it would probably have taken a normal course; but when he began to denigrate his fellow-ministers, he was rightly arraigned before a Special District Meeting, which suspended him from his station as superintendent of the Manchester Circuit.

Dr Warren then challenged the Wesleyan constitution in a court of law, but on losing his case, he was carried from

---

[1] For full accounts of the Warrenite secession, see:
Smith, G., *History of Methodism*, iii. 231–321;
Stevens, A., *History of Methodism*, iii. 356ff;
Townsend, Workman and Eayrs: *New History of Methodism*, i. 427, 517;
London Quarterly Review, 1890–2, for a series of articles, published anonymously, but J. H. Rigg in *Church Organisation*, p. 299, says they were by Dr J. S. Simon.

[2] *Minutes*, vii (1833), p. 298: see also *Statement of the Preachers*.

one issue to another. He found himself at the head of a reforming party which adopted the title of 'The Grand Central Association' (later, 'The Wesleyan Methodist Association'), but within a short time he extricated himself from its clutches and found refuge in the Established Church.

The Warren affair had a place in two streams of development in Wesleyan Methodism. It was, as we have said, an incident in the progress of Methodism from Society to Church. Just as the Leeds Organ Case was inspired by those who sought to 'improve' Methodist worship, so the Warrenite controversy began as an attempt to 'improve' the standard of ministerial education. In the early days, Methodist worship was unsophisticated and largely spontaneous, for the Preachers were evangelists with a simple Gospel message. Neither organs nor college training were necessary. Therefore, just as the anti-organ party at Leeds argued that the instrument would destroy the pristine simplicity of the services, so the anti-institution men of 1835 contended that college training would 'spoil' the Preachers by damping their ardour. Both controversies, then, have to be reckoned as part of the price paid by Methodism in emerging from the simplicity of a Society to the fuller obligations of a Church.

In the second place, the Warrenite controversy was another phase in the increasing pressure of Liberalism upon the growing Conservatism of the Wesleyan hierarchy. We saw how the Leeds affair began with a dispute over an instrument, developed into disaffection with the constitution and ended with a fundamental divergence on the concept of the ministry. The Warren affair progressed on similar lines; beginning as a protest against the Theological Institution, it developed into a lawsuit on the seat of power. A letter, dated 4th December, 1834, from James Everett to Dr Warren is worth quoting:

> We are borne away from one thing to another—from the Institution to the Constitution.... It was a most lamentable circumstance that any person should have been allowed to avail themselves of an opportunity of hanging other grievances

and objections . . . upon the one which was first urged, and of thus changing the leading features of the controversy.[3]

These shrewd words of the rebel-to-be, Everett, would have applied with equal propriety to the Leeds case, for underlying both eruptions were the same forces of liberalism, utilizing whatever pretext came to hand to further their cause. Seen in terms of the Wesleyan constitution, the challenge was fundamentally the same in 1828 and 1835— to the supremacy of the Conference, to the authority of the District Meeting and to the right of superintendents over admission and expulsion of members. The earlier contest was waged within the courts of the church; Dr Warren went to the civil courts. There was, however, one abiding result of the Doctor's action, for the legality of the Wesleyan Constitution as set out in *The Form of Discipline* was placed beyond any shadow of doubt.

The Wesleyans were destined to suffer yet one more disruption. As far as numbers were concerned, it was the severest of all and in terms of internal stress it was the most painful of all; but for the development of the doctrine of church and ministry it was of much less significance than the Warren affair of 1835. The Chancery suit virtually settled the issue.

The Training of the Ministry

For Wesley's early preachers little formal training was necessary, for he supervised their studies, and that was sufficient for their needs; but a very different situation faced their descendants of 1835. To the zeal of the evangelist must now be added a training in theology. The Preacher was now also a Pastor and teacher, ministering to people who were taking advantage of the increasing opportunities

[3] Chew, *Life of James Everett*, p. 297: see also *Statement of the Preachers on the Case of Dr Warren* (November 1834), p. 13. *The Christian Advocate*, a mischievous anti-conference publication, in its issue of 27th April, 1835, carried an article running to over 3,000 lines, but less than 60 had any references to the Institution—see *Dr Warren and the Association Unmasked*. See also *Work for Dr Warren*, p. 6, 'scarcely a word was heard on the subject of the Institution'.

for education.[4] Methodism was itself a force for improvement, and congregations did not take kindly to ill-educated preachers. Hence the call, from certain quarters, for some form of ministerial training.[5]

The need for some kind of training for the Preachers had been acknowledged since the early days. At the first Conference (1744) the question was asked, 'Can we have a seminary for labourers?' and the answer was, 'If God spare us until another Conference'.[6] In 1745 the matter was raised again and shelved until 'God gives us a proper tutor'.[7] Meanwhile, Wesley was educating his preachers by personal contact and through his *Christian Library*; some of them he sent for a short spell to Kingswood School.[8] After his death, the care of the young preachers was frequently before Conference. It became the duty of the District Chairman to see that each probationer in his District produced a Book List and was examined orally at the District Meeting. In 1804 a plan for the intellectual improvement of the junior preachers was proposed by Adam Clarke and other preachers stationed in London, but it did not meet with much encouragement.[9] In 1823 a powerful group of preachers—John Gaulter, Jabez Bunting, Thomas Jackson and Richard Watson—prepared a report but, again, nothing came of it. Others, equally influential men in the Connexion,[10] strongly advocated the establishment of an academy, but it was not until 1833 that Con-

---

[4] See *Learning and Piety United*, p. 14; *The Methodist Magazine* (1831), p. 383.
[5] *Learning and Piety United*, p. 22f—the writer of this anonymous pamphlet is believed to be John Hughes. See also M.C.A. letters—E. Gibbons to James Sigston, May 1st, 1813 and Joseph Sutcliffe to Jabez Bunting, December 26th, 1828.
[6] John Bennet's *Minutes*, p. 17. Ms. in Methodist Archives.
[7] *Op. cit.*, p. 27.
[8] Adam Clarke and Jeremiah Brettell are examples—see Vevers, W., *An Appeal to the Wesleyan Societies*, p. 15 and *Proposals for the formation of a Literary and Theological Institution* (probably by Dr Hannah), p. 12. For Wesley's rebuttal of the charge that he employed illiterate preachers, see his letter to Dr Thomas Rutherford, March 28th, 1768—*Letters*, v. 359.
[9] Jackson, Thomas, *Recollections*, p. 80; *Observations on . . . a Plan of Instruction*—an official Conference document, 1807.
[10] Edmondson, J., *Essay on the Christian Ministry*, pp. vi, vii; letter of Adam Clarke in Crowther, J., *Defence of the Wesleyan Theological Institution*, p. 24.

ference took the matter seriously, and when they did the objections which were raised against it revealed both the anxieties of the people and the popular image of what a minister is and ought to be.[11] It is instructive to note what those objections were.

1. In the first place it was said to be 'at variance with the plans and proceedings of the venerable Founder of Methodism'.[12] In spite of the known attitude of Wesley and the decisions of his early Conferences, this was advanced as a serious argument, even by Dr Warren.[13] He argued that while there were many brilliant scholars in the ranks of the Methodist ministry, basically the Methodist Preacher should remain untrained and that Providence would always provide sufficient men of the academic type to meet the needs of the Church.

2. Secondly, there was an ingrained fear of losing what Dr Warren called, 'our primitive simplicity'.[14] The pioneer Itinerants were honoured as men who 'roughed it'; rightly or wrongly, there was a fear lest college-trained men, 'losing their simplicity and zeal . . . should acquire delicate habits by no means consistent with the toils and privations to which they may afterwards be exposed'.[15] Or, as Dr Warren, in more picturesque language expressed it, 'The men thus raised up are indigenous to the soil and climate in which they are reared. Instead of being improved by the salubrious fumes of a hot-house Institution, they would degenerate and become worthless, if not even noxious. . . .'[16] A more balanced attitude is that of Wesley, the scholar-saint, who never set piety against learning, and while his Itinerants were mostly unlettered men, gave them such education as they had time and ability to assimilate.

[11] The Methodist New Connexion had taken up the challenge with much less reluctance—see Crowther, J., *A Defence of the Wesleyan Theological Institution*, p. 25. The American Episcopal Church had long had a 'college' for ministerial training.
[12] *Proposals for a Theological Institution*, p. 9.
[13] Warren, S., *Remarks on the . . . Theological Institution*, p. 14.
[14] '. . . to preserve the simplicity and piety of the Body from degenerating into outward show and lifeless formality'—Warren, S., *op. cit.*, p. 28.
[15] *Proposals for a Theological Institution*, p. 14.
[16] Warren, S., *op. cit.*, p. 16.

Jonathan Crowther (sen.) ably summed up the attitude of reasonable men in Methodism when he said, 'It is not a pre-requisite for admission as a Preacher among us that a man be what is termed a *scholar*. Yet the Methodists neither despise nor neglect learning.'[17]

3. There was a third, and more serious objection; that academic considerations would become more important than the inward call. Wesley, and indeed the Methodists since his time, knew enough of the university-trained clergyman whose moral life was, to say the least, open to question. He had commented severely on such men, for on their shoulders must lie much of the blame for the cleavage between Methodism and the Church of England. So one can understand the fears of those who saw the danger if ever Methodism substituted learning for piety; namely, that the wrong type of candidate should be admitted on the grounds of academic attainments alone.

4. Finally, there were several minor and largely personal objections to the Institution. Dr Warren argued, for instance, that the Institution had not the support of the people, and he overstated his case with a personal attack on Bunting and his friends. He denounced 'the coalition of a few or the ascendency of an individual'.[18] At the same time, it was widely thought at the time that if he had been given a post on the staff of the Institution he would have forgiven much that he censured in Bunting.[19]

So the Theological Institution was founded and Methodists were learning to link piety and learning. Understandably so, for many of them had had their fill of well-meaning but unschooled preachers who did more harm than good; and they were coming to the conclusion

---

[17] Crowther, J., *Observations and Arguments*, p. 2, see also the same writer's *Portraiture of Methodism*.
[18] Warren, S., *op. cit.*, p. 29.
[19] 'I once observed to a very sensible lady, a near relation of his (Dr Warren) that for several years he maintained a highly respectable character in the Connexion, and that had he persevered as he began, there can be no doubt that he would have been made the President of the Conference. "Had he believed that", said she, "he would never have turned agitator".'—Jackson, *Recollections of my own Life and Times*, p. 277.

that piety, however sincere, was not enough in the office of a Christian minister.[20]

On the whole, the Connexion welcomed an educated ministry; so much so that by 1847 circuits were asking for 'Institution men'![21] The Wesleyan conception of the ministry was undergoing a change. The minister was to be more than an evangelist; he was to be also Pastor and Teacher.

The Rules of 1797

(a) The Law of Expulsion

As the Warrenite controversy moved from the Institution to the Constitution, 'the transactions of Leeds', as one writer says, 'were neither forgiven nor forgotten'.[22] The establishment of the Theological Institution 'without consulting the authorized meetings' was regarded as evidence that 'the Conference had well-nigh engrossed the whole power of the Connexion in their hands'. They appealed to the people to claim the right which had been granted to them in 1797 but filched from them by Conference since: namely:

> The law of 1797 provided that no officer or member should be expelled but by a majority of a Leaders meeting . . . but this Magna Carta of your rights has been treacherously taken away.[23]

The issue was crucial. It was more than just a question of 'Did the *Form of Discipline* actually say that?' for if it did, then a re-consideration of the duties and the nature of the office of a Wesleyan minister would be called for. To the

[20] Anon., *Learning and Piety United*, p. 6, 'We have sufficient proof how little good has been done in general by men who neither read nor study. . . .' Remember Wesley's comment on preachers who bawl the Gospel!
[21] Woolmer, T., *An Answer to some Complaints*, p. 28. Strong support for the Institution was forthcoming from Overseas—see, e.g. Minutes of St. Christopher's Synod for September, 1836, p. 17 (I owe this reference to the Rev. Donald C. Henry).
[22] *An Address to the Delegates representing the Wesleyan Methodist Association in Manchester*, p. 3.
[23] Ibid., p. 4.

Wesleyans, the responsibilities of the Pastoral Office must, to be effective, carry certain powers; included in those powers, and inherited from John Wesley, was the right to admit and expel members of Society. The dissentients claimed that in 1797 this power had been transferred to the Leaders Meeting. The Conference contended that, while the *Form of Discipline* set certain checks to the authority of the superintendent, it did not rob him of this power, which was inherent in his office as Pastor. We must, therefore, examine the rules as printed in the *Form of Discipline*, together with the claims made for them by the Warrenites and, finally, the authority accorded them by the Chancellor in his verdict of March, 1835. It is a complicated story.

Prior to 1797, the rules and regulations of Methodism were contained in successive editions of *The Large Minutes*,[24] together with Wesley's *Nature, Design and General Rules of the Methodist Societies*, published in 1743. The Conference of 1797 decided to revise all these rules and publish them in a convenient form.[25] This was done, and the result appeared as the well-known *Form of Discipline*. It is easily identified by the misprint, 1779 for 1797, on the title page. Here the following rules appeared:

> ... a superintendent ought also to visit the classes quarterly ... to take in or put out the society or the bands.... At the Conference of 1797 it was agreed that no person shall be expelled from the Society for immorality till such immorality be proved at a Leaders Meeting. (Section V. II. 2; the last sentence repeated in the 'Leeds Regulations', III. 2.)[26]

No person shall be appointed a leader or steward, or be removed from his office, but in conjunction with the Leaders Meeting; the nomination to be in the Superintendent and the approbation or disapprobation in the Leaders Meeting (Leeds Regulations, IV. 1).

As to the exclusion of members from the Society, the far

---

[24] See *Minutes*, i. 444ff for a tabular view of the editions of 1753-7, 1763, 1770, 1772, 1780, 1789.
[25] *Minutes*, i. 392.
[26] 'The Leeds Regulations' are a set of rules which were sent to the Societies at the close of the Leeds Conference in 1797, and later incorporated in the *Form of Discipline*—see *Minutes*, i. 390ff and 703ff.

greater number exclude themselves by utterly forsaking us; but with respect to others, let the rules of the Society be carefully attended to and the Leaders be consulted on such occasions and the crime proved to their satisfaction (Section VI. 4).

We particularly notice that nothing is said about expulsions for other reasons, such as infringement of rules, which was to cause so much trouble in years to come. In any case, as they stood the Rules were ambiguous. They could mean *either* that in cases other than immorality, expulsion was (as always since Wesley's time) in the hands of the superintendent alone; *or* that all cases of expulsion must be determined by the Leaders Meeting.

But to proceed with Conference decisions. The Conference also decided that a smaller collection of rules relating to local officers and meetings should be published. What was that collection? The dissentients claimed that it was a pamphlet of 12 pages—some editions had 18 pages—published in 1798 and entitled *The Nature, Design and General Rules of the Methodist Societies, established by the Rev. John Wesley*.[27] We shall refer to this as 'The 1798 paraphrase'. This contained one crucial sentence, '*Neither can any member of the Society be excluded but by a majority at a Leaders Meeting*'. At the trial of Dr Warren, the Conference party argued that this was an unauthorized and inaccurate paraphrase of what was said in *The Form of Discipline* and that the promised 'smaller collection' or 'summary' did not appear until 1804, in which the rule read, 'No person must be expelled from the Society for any breach of our rules, or even for manifest immorality, till such fact or crime has

[27] It may be appropriate at this point to clear up a confusion over titles. Wesley's *Rules* of 1743 bore the same title as the disputed pamphlet of 1798, *The Nature, Design and General Rules of the Methodist Societies*, and this led many people to assume that the latter was a reprint of Wesley and thus carried his sanction. This misconception was reinforced by the fact that the opening paragraphs of both publications were identical. On the second page, however, the 1798 book leaves Wesley and goes its own way, paraphrasing the *Form of Discipline*, not accurately, but in the light of current usage. There were several reprints of the 1804 pamphlet; we have examined those of 1808, 1809, 1810 and 1813.

been proved at a Leaders Meeting'. This still left the *act* of expulsion with the superintendent.

Now for the point at issue, taking the case of the dissentients first, and following Robert Eckett's *An Exposition of the Laws of Conference Methodism* (1846) as our guide. He argued:

i. That the laws, as well as the usages, of Methodism were that no person should be expelled without the consent of a majority of the Leaders Meeting—for any cause whatever.

ii. That although this transferred the power of expulsion from the superintendent to the Leaders Meeting and that, consequently, as the Minutes said, 'by far the greatest part of his authority was given up', much of that authority still remained and was duly recognized.

iii. That the Conference party could hardly dismiss the 1798 paraphrase as 'unauthorized', for it bore the imprints of the Conference Office and the Connexional Book Steward. If it was inaccurate it should have been recalled, corrected or repudiated by the Conference.

Eckett therefore concluded that in 1797 Conference gave the Leaders Meeting power to decide all cases of expulsion and that this power was never disputed until 1828 when the District Meeting confirmed the superintendent's expulsion of the Leeds dissentients without the consent of the appropriate meeting. He also suggested that the theory of the superintendent's sole right of expulsion gained ground only after the Leeds Organ Case in 1828; so that, when the next rebellion came in 1835, it was written into the laws that even a person acquitted by the Leaders could be expelled by a superintendent.

The Conference party, on the other hand, argued that while the verdict of guilty or not guilty had to be decided in the Leaders Meeting (the jury, as it were) the superintendent alone could award the penalty. Dr J. S. Simon, writing in 1892, says that the Regulations of 1797 did no more than limit the superintendent's power of expulsion to certain specified cases and that his right to admit and exclude still remained where Wesley placed them, in the hands of the Pastorate. In support of this, he produced two

THE WARRENITE SECESSION

pieces of evidence. First of all, he pointed out that in 1797 there were two parties bringing pressure to bear upon the Preachers and their actions confirm the stand which the Conference took. On the one hand there were the Trustees, and there is no sign that they ever urged the Preachers to surrender any of their disciplinary powers. On the other hand, there were the Kilhamites and they withdrew because the Preachers would not relinquish their authority. The second piece of evidence Dr Simon produced was that the *Form of Discipline* explicitly stated that the superintendent is 'to take in or put out of the Society'. Other regulations may check the superintendent's authority, but they do not abolish it or transfer it to the Leaders Meeting.[28]

To these two points must be added the fact that when the new rules were made in 1835, there were living at least three prominent ministers who were present at the Conference of 1797 and each of them had been called to the work by Wesley. They were James Wood, Joseph Entwisle and Richard Reece. Surely they would have protested if 1835 had betrayed 1797. No one, in fact, in the 1835 Conference rose to protest that the new rules were out of accord with the accepted practice of the Connexion.[29] On the contrary, James Wood said, 'On the law of the Conference of 1797 respecting the expulsion of members, I do affirm, I never had but one opinion, namely, that the *fact* was with the Leaders Meeting, but the *sentence* was with the superintendent'.[30]

At the same time, this defence of the official interpretation

[28] *London Quarterly Review*, April 1892, pp. 103-11.
[29] The 1835 rule regarding expulsions reads: 'If a majority of the Leaders ... should be "satisfied" that sufficient proof is adduced to establish the fact of a wilful and habitual negligence, or of the violation of some scriptural or Methodistical rule, and shall give a verdict to that effect, then the Leaders Meeting has discharged *its whole part* of the painful duty to be performed, and the case is left in the hands of the Superintendent. On *him* devolves, in his pastoral character, as the person whose peculiar call and province it is to 'watch over that soul' as one that 'must give an account' the sole right or duty of deciding on the measures to be adopted towards the offender, in consequence of the verdict thus pronounced'— *Minutes*, vii. pp. 579–80.
[30] Quoted in *Remarks in reply to certain caluminous Mis-statements*, p. 2.

of the rules still leaves two questions unanswered. The first is, How did the Book Steward in 1798 come to paraphrase as he did? Even if his paraphrase could be regarded as a false interpretation of the official rule, it must have had some foundation in current usage. The second question is, Why did the 1798 paraphrase come virtually to supersede the *Form of Discipline* to such an extent that (a) in 1828 John Beecham had never seen a copy of the latter,[31] and (b) the 1798 paraphrase was actually accepted as authentic?

We can only conclude that while the *Form of Discipline* did in theory leave the power of expulsion with the superintendent, in actual practice he always acted in consultation with his Leaders Meeting. This, we suggest, was the situation when the paraphrase of 1798 was made. Through the years of calm, this arrangement was a viable compromise.[32] It meant that while the authority of the Pastor was not removed, it was never rigorously asserted. When it was asserted in 1828, it came as a 'new thing in Israel'. This also explains the testimony of such Preachers as James Wood quoted above. It also explains why the Preachers could claim that the power of expulsion lay with the Pastorate alone, and the dissentients that it had been transferred to the Leaders Meeting. The former was the letter of the law, the latter was the 'use and wont'. The tragedy was that there was no one at the helm with vision and tact to steer the ship safely between the two.

At this distance in time, one can see both sides. The dissentients could hardly be blamed for accepting the 1798 paraphrase as official, for it not only carried the official imprint, it also reflected common practice. On the other hand, the Conference was anxious not to make the Leaders Meeting both judge and jury, thereby destroying any connexional uniformity in meeting out justice. It was even more anxious to keep the final verdict out of the hands of local courts, which would doubtless include people who

---

[31] See Beecham, J., *Essay on Constitution of Wesleyan Methodism*, third edition, p. 62.

[32] This is evident from the quotation from Jonathan Crowther's *Methodist Manual* (1810), quoted on p. 89 of Part II, ch. 2 above.

were known to, and were perhaps relatives of, the accused. They could hardly be expected to produce an impartial judgement. Saddest of all, false motives were alleged, and the dissentients accused the legislators of 1797 of 'deceptions practised on our people'.[33] Fortunately, the Lord Chancellor judged those legislators more impartially. He said that they were 'not professional persons, accustomed to prepare for all the exigencies likely to happen, but simple, straightforward, intelligent men who had in view only the exigencies of the moment'.[34] In that judgement we, too, are happy to rest.

As a postscript to this rather involved, but highly necessary discussion of the law of expulsion, it ought to be said that the Lord Chancellor upheld the *Form of Discipline*, famous as 'Exhibit F' at the trial, and so confirmed the pastoral authority of Wesleyan ministers. The allegations that the Preachers had assumed unwarranted powers, and that an oppressed people had been lulled by ignorance into a neglect of their rights, were shown to be false. So Dr Warren and his sympathizers went off (as the Leeds dissentients did before them) to form a Connexion after their own liking. Their rule relating to the expulsion of members read:

> That no private member shall be subjected to Church censure, suspension from privileges, or exclusion from Society without the consent of the majority of the Leaders or Society Meeting.

(b) *Article VII of the Leeds Regulations*

A further complaint of the Warrenites was that, in establishing the Institution, the Conference had broken Article VII of the Leeds Regulations, which provided that if any new rule for the Societies at large be objected to by any Circuit, it be not applied in that Circuit until the next Conference.[35] The reply was that the Institution did not affect the 'Societies at large', and that no appeal for funds

[33] Allin, T., *Letters to John Maclean*, p. 48.
[34] *Dr Warren's Chancery Suit*, p. 3.
[35] *Minutes*, i. 704.

was being made to the people. Furthermore, it was stressed that the training of the ministry was a matter for ministers alone.[36]

(c) The District Meeting

One other challenge came to the *Form of Discipline*, and that was with regard to the authority of the District Meeting. This was yet another stage in the campaign (the immediate predecessor being the Leeds Organ Case) to transfer authority from the minister to the people.

The place and authority of the District Meeting has already claimed much of our attention. We have seen that it was part of the effort to organize Methodism after Wesley's death. Its authority was defined in 1797 only after prolonged consultation with the Kilhamites (on the one hand) and the Trustees (on the other). In our consideration of the Leeds Organ Case, we saw that one of the points of contention was the right of the District Meeting to try persons other than Itinerants; another was the legality of the Special District Meeting. In the Warrenite controversy, the authority of the District Meeting was again challenged, and one cannot but say that the Chancellor's verdict is welcome as a settlement of the issue.

Dr Warren challenged the right of the Special District Meeting to bring him to trial. The Plan of Pacification gave to Trustees, Leaders and Stewards (in association with the ministers of the District) the right to summon a District Meeting for the purpose of trying a minister who may be believed by a majority of his Leaders or Trustees to be 'immoral, erroneous in doctrine, deficient in abilities' and a few other infringements of the rules; but no suspension was permitted without a trial. Dr Warren asked the Court of Chancery to declare that he had been illegally suspended by the Trustees of Oldham Street Chapel, Manchester,

[36] See *A Declaration of Methodist Preachers* (1834): Regulations which relate to the improved preparation of candidates for the ministry belong exclusively to the ministry *already* existing. St Paul's Epistles to Timothy prove this to be a scriptural principle. They who are already in the office of the ministry are to commit the deposit 'to faithful men, able to teach others'. Of that ability they are to be the final judges....

and that the District Meeting which tried him was an illegal court. We have not the space to review the proceedings before the Chancellor's court, but this was done thoroughly by Dr J. S. Simon in the *London Quarterly Review* for October, 1890. It is sufficient for us to say that Warren's case was not upheld, either by the Vice-Chancellor or by the Lord Chancellor. Both of these judges confirmed the authority of the District Meeting to try and, if necessary, to suspend a Preacher. This authority had not been taken away (as Dr Warren contended) by the Plan of Pacification.[37]

With this judgement on the authority of the District Meeting, there also stood a similar verdict on the Conference with its power over both Preachers and people, a power which, as his corporate successor, had been bestowed by Wesley himself. This power had been limited, so far as the people were concerned, and safeguarded and checked so far as the Preachers were concerned, by the Plan of Pacification. The would-be reformers in 1827 and 1835 argued that by the Plan of Pacification the power of the Conference over the Preachers was retained, but the people were free from its control. The judgement of the Vice-Chancellor proved this to be a mistaken inference. He under-pinned the authority of both Conference and District Meeting as together wielding the power originally possessed by John Wesley. In the words of J. S. Simon, Lord Lyndhurst 'affirmed that the Conference was the fount and origin of law; that it was the interpreter of its own laws and that the rules it passed were binding on both Preachers and Societies'.[38]

Before we leave this consideration of the law suit, one further result must not be overlooked. It established once and for all the legality of the *Form of Discipline*. It finally disposed of the claims of those versions on which Dr Warren and his friends based their arguments. It established the identity of the basic rules of the Connexion and gave

[37] *Dr Warren's Chancery Suit*, p. 15.
[38] *London Quarterly Review*, October 1890, p. 67. See also, Smith, G., *History of Wesleyan Methodism*, iii. 277.

them the backing of the law: and we must remember that these laws were more than a set of legal enactments. They expressed the very ethos of Wesleyan Methodism. It is of interest to note that after the Judgement of 1835, the *Form of Discipline* replaced Wesley's *Large Minutes* as the volume which was presented to ministers at their ordination. It was inscribed:

> As long as you freely consent to, and earnestly endeavour to walk by these rules, we shall rejoice to acknowledge you as a fellow labourer.

The Secessions

We have now reached a point where we can usefully compare the aims and the constitutions of the various secessions which we have noticed so far; for the Warrenite revolt was really the last of its kind. It is true that a still greater storm was to burst upon the Connexion in 1849, a disruption that made 1827 and 1835 appear, in comparison, a mere ripple. It is also true that 1849 was but another episode in the upsurge of liberalism, but its expression was different, in that it was not primarily a revolt against the constitution, nor did it found a Connexion with principles any different from those of the Protestant Methodists in 1827 or the Wesleyan Methodist Association on 1835. The Warrenites were the last would-be reformers of the Wesleyan constitution, and their body, the Wesleyan Methodist Association, represented the climax of Methodist reform. So we pause here to consider the principles of Free Methodism in general.

Dr J. S. Simon once remarked that each agitation in Wesleyan Methodism, 'revealed a special tendency and illustrated a definite principle in the realm of ecclesiastical affairs'.[39] A brief resumé of what we have seen to be the principles of the three major secessions will show this to be true.

The revolt under Alexander Kilham in 1796 was part of

[39] *London Quarterly Review*, October 1893, p. 48.

the understandable reaction after the death of Wesley, when his controlling hand was removed and it was not certain who would take the helm. Conference became his corporate successor, but it could not inherit his unquestioned authority. A new system had to evolve. When it did take shape, Conference was shorn of much of Wesley's autocracy and was hedged with limitations which Wesley would have scorned. There was an attempt to introduce some form of local independency, but it was not successful, and in the final constitution the Conference remained the supreme authority. Even in the Methodist New Connexion, the Conference was supreme. More successful was the process of fashioning the parent body on Presbyterian lines, but this went only so far, as we shall see in a later chapter. The Kilhamites contended for lay representation at every level of administration. Some of the later reformers alleged that immediately after the death of Wesley there was an invasion of 'the rights of the people' by the Preachers. This is not true, for the agitation in 1794–5 was not 'Preachers versus people', but 'Preachers and people versus Trustees'. The Conference was acting on behalf of the people in pressing for the administration of the sacraments in Methodist chapels.[40]

The Leeds Organ Case was wholly a lay revolt. No Itinerant Preacher joined the Protestant Methodists. It was a revolt against the Pastoral Office and the growing clericalism of the Conference. It stood for full local independence with no interference from either District Meeting or Conference. As a reforming movement, it was not widespread or numerically large; in fact, it was the upsurge of a discontent which more or less smouldered on until it found another pretext and further compatriots to swell its ranks.

This further support came with the Warrenite agitation, and at the inaugural meeting of the delegates at Manchester in April 1835, the Protestant Methodists made themselves heard in no uncertain manner. In fact, they were more extreme than the Warrenites and only a compromise kept

[40] Rigg, J. H., *The Principles of Wesleyan Methodism*, p. 14.

them together to form the Wesleyan Methodist Association. While the Leeds Organ outbreak commanded no ministerial support, the Wesleyan Methodist Association enrolled three Wesleyan ministers among its founder members. There were Samuel Warren (suspended by, and later expelled from, the Wesleyans), Robert Emmett (a supernumerary minister) and a Mr Lamb from Ireland. Let it be said that the meeting in April, 1835, was convened to consider reforms which, if adopted by the Wesleyans, would have satisfied the reformers; it was not called to form a new Connexion of Methodism—that was to come later when the impossibility of Conference accepting the reforms was realized.

In the meantime, what did the Warrenites stand for? First of all, they tried to prove that the Wesleyan constitution was alien to the intentions and heritage of the *Form of Discipline*. When the Vice-Chancellor and the Lord Chancellor proved them to be wrong, they then set out to fashion a reformed Connexion to their own liking. There was a sharp cleavage between the Protestant Methodists and the Warrenites over the question of lay delegation to Conference. The former said they would be satisfied with nothing less than a mixed Conference (as with the Methodist New Connexion); the latter would have retained the ministerial Conference, but with lay observers and ballot voting—a strange combination!

It was clear that the Warrenites did not press for lay representation, especially on the lines of the Methodist New Connexion, for a mixed Conference could still possess more authority than they wished any Conference to have. They did not want an authoritative Conference at all—mixed or ministerial—they wanted authority to reside in the local courts,[41] which amounted to Independency, not Methodist Connexionalism. It was the destruction, not the reform, of Wesleyan Methodism. No wonder Dr Warren had to confess that he could not accomplish his aims without abolishing Wesleyanism or reducing it to a state of

[41] See *The Corrected Report of the Meeting of Wesleyan Delegates at Manchester, April 20–23, 1835*, p. 21.

ruin. On the debit side, of course, it meant that Conference would no longer be a court of appeal, but that was a price which the reformers were willing to pay.

In the end, these movements would have the combined effects of lowering the status of the ministry, of breaking up circuits into independent units and of reducing the Conference to a mere Stationing Committee. Fundamentally, of course, they were revolts against the Pastoral Office.[42]

The Conference Rules of 1835

Just as the Kilhamite revolt prompted the Conference to compile the *Form of Discipline* in 1797, so the Warrenite secession led it, in 1835, to revise its rules. The result was a code which we must now examine, so far as it bears upon the subject of Church and ministry. One difference between 1797 and 1835, however, should be noted; in 1795 the Conference conferred with its adversaries, the Trustees, so that the resulting *Form of Discipline* was an amicable settlement. In 1835 the Conference refused to have any dealings with its opponents, the so-called 'Delegates', for it was evident that the latter were not appointed by any official body but were members of the self-appointed 'Grand Central Association'. Yet Conference never closed the door to 'any parties supposing themselves aggrieved',

---

[42] Two additional comments on this section:
 1. Mr David Gowland, in *Rochdale Politics and Methodist Schism* (Publication of the Lancashire and Cheshire Branch of the Wesley Historical Society—1965) has said, 'the newly-formed Association was not an experiment in democratic church government. Instead, the 1835 secession was basically a question of power transferred from a compact ministerial body to an equally close-knit group of laymen. The Wesleyan and Associationist structures of government remained almost identical except in so far as the latter impinged on the Wesleyan doctrine of the ministry. The real transformation lay in the reversal of roles.'
 2. A strange contrast should be noted between the attitude of the reformers in 1796 and that of those of 1836 with regard to the training of the ministry. The Kilhamites were all in favour of the development of Methodism into a church in its own right, and they advocated an educated ministry. The Warrenites were against the Institution and its work. This explains the strange remark of Jonathan Crowther (sen.): 'I always suspected Mr Bunting of being secretly inclined to Kilhamitism, but now I am confirmed, he is a Kilhamite!—*Work for Dr Warren*, p. 32.

provided their approach was 'in a peaceful and Christian spirit' and through the recognized channels.[43]

The results of the deliberations of the Conference are set out in 'The Special Address of the Conference to the Wesleyan Methodist Societies in Great Britain'. It is arranged in four sections:

    I. Financial Affairs.
    II. Expulsion of Members.
    III. Meetings for communication with the Conference by Memorial, on subjects of local concern, or on general laws of the Connexion.
    IV. Proposed revision and classification of our rules in general.

Section I need not detain us; but section II, dealing with the expulsion of members touched upon a live subject in 1835 and, as we shall see, in 1849. The rule relating to the expulsion of members seems to have evolved as follows.

    i. In the beginning, Wesley had supreme power to exclude.

    ii. His Assistants (later called 'Circuit Superintendents') also possessed power to exclude, but always subject to the over-riding judgement of Wesley.

    iii. In 1791, the power possessed by Assistants (i.e. Superintendents) became subject to the District Committee and Conference.

    iv. In 1794, the Superintendent and his colleagues were to 'consult the stewards and Leaders' before they expelled a member.

    v. In 1797, no member was to be expelled for immorality until such immorality had been 'proved at a Leaders Meeting'. With this the 1835 rules agreed, but added that, having done this, the Leaders Meeting 'has discharged *its whole part* of the painful duty to be performed and the case is left in the hands of the Superintendent'. This is followed by a stout re-affirmation of the duties inherent in the Pastoral Office:

[43] *Minutes*, vii (1835), p. 562.

On him (i.e. the Superintendent) devolves, in his pastoral character, as the person whose peculiar call and province is to 'watch over that soul' as one that 'must give an account', the sole right and duty of deciding on the measures to be adopted towards the offender, in consequence of the verdict thus pronounced. . . . The power of determining the sentence to be passed on an offender, thus uniformly and from the beginning reserved to our Superintendents, the Conference believes to be essential to the Scriptural Duties and Functions of the Pastoral Office.

vi. Having said this, however, the 1835 regulations agreed to 'adopt . . . additional guards and securities for our people, for the proper exercise of the powers confided to the Superintendents in cases of expulsion'. In the main, these provided for (a) a delay in pronouncing the sentence and (b) an appeal to the Minor District Meeting. As the former was dealt with above, only the latter calls for comment here. Appeal to a Minor District Meeting was something new and, of course, a decided gain to the laity. Hitherto, a member who felt unjustly expelled could appeal to the District Meeting as officially constituted, but in the new regulations, he may choose any two ministers of the District to which he belonged as his nominees on the Minor District Meeting.

If this Minor District Meeting did not satisfy him, he could still appeal to a Special District Meeting, if he so wished. The 1835 regulations modified the constitution of this Special District Meeting, which had caused so much distress at Leeds. Hitherto, the Chairman had authority to summon 'three of the nearest Superintendents', but there was no provision for the aggrieved party to call anyone. In 1835, both parties could summon 'any two Preachers from any District without restriction as to contiguity', and the four Preachers thus summoned would have full power to vote. This was a distinct advantage, and one can only regret that such provisions were not in force when the inflammatory District Meeting met in Leeds in 1827.

We can summarize the whole position with regard to the expulsion of members, as the rules of 1835 left it:

i. No sentence was to be pronounced at the same meeting as that on which the trial took place.

ii. In difficult cases, no expulsion was to take place without advice being sought from 'judicious and experienced members of Society'.

iii. All cases of expulsion to be considered by ministerial colleagues before sentence pronounced.

iv. The right of appeal to the District Meeting and the Conference by both member and superintendent, if either felt that the findings of the Leaders Meeting were 'notoriously contrary to facts'.

The purpose of these new safeguards was to protect the people from unjust or rash expulsion. The section ended with a plea:

> ... the Conference exhorts all superintendents to exercise, in connexion with a holy firmness, the moderation and mercy of the Gospel: bearing long and dealing tenderly, though faithfully, with the weak, the ill-informed and the mis-led. ...

Section III sought to deal with the problem of communication. It is one which besets all highly-organized bureaucracies, and in the case of Wesleyan Methodism, it was one of communication between Conference and people. The Wesleyans had always been suspicious of 'extra-mural' meetings of their people, and it was on the charge of convening or attending such activities that both the Leeds and the Warrenite dissentients were expelled.[44] At the same time, the Wesleyans had jealously maintained the character of the Conference as a court of appeal for all the Methodist people, but the procedure was either too vague or cumbersome that it had not proved to be the safety-valve for discontent that it was meant to be.

In order to open up a line of communication between Conference and any discontent which may be found in the

[44] In the *Form of Discipline*, the rule for 'other formal meetings' read, 'In order to be as tender as possible, consistently with what we believe to be essential to the welfare of our Societies, we allow that other formal meetings may be held, if they first receive the approbation of the Superintendent and the Leaders or Quarterly Meeting; provided also, that the Superintendent, if he please, be present at every such meeting'— *Minutes*, i. 704.

THE WARRENITE SECESSION

Circuits, the Conference decided that, after the June Quarterly Meeting the Superintendent should see if there was any desire for amending the rules. If there was, he was then to call a meeting (of a well-defined constitution) not less than seven, or not more than ten days after the Quarterly Meeting. All memorials must be confined to, 'such changes only as are consistent with the essential principles of Wesleyan Methodism and within the pale of our established constitution'. They also changed the rule about 'other meetings' to read:

> The Superintendent, or, in the case of his unavoidable absence, some other Travelling Preacher appointed by him, shall always preside at the meeting.

It was probably too much to expect that these amendments would satisfy the liberals. Certainly, they soon rose to the attack. Their main target was the rule which dealt with memorials to Conference, and this they criticized from three directions:

i. The rule of 1797 left the time of holding any 'other formal meeting' to the circumstances of the case; the new rule, however, restricted it to only three days in the year—between the seventh and the tenth day after the June Quarterly Meeting.

ii. The constitution of such meetings, under the new rule, was too limited. The 1797 rule left such a matter open, and presumably any number could attend.

iii. In 1797, the superintendent could be present 'if he please'; in 1835, he must 'always preside'.

iv. The 1835 rule enacted that any memorial to Conference must bear the signature of all who voted for it. This was regarded as a subtle method of detecting agitators, and inimical to free expression of opinion. It was felt that anyone who objected to Conference proceedings would become a marked man.[45]

v. The 1835 rules gave added strength to the Pastoral Office, or as W. B. Carter, a Wesleyan Class Leader of Birmingham, expressed it, 'the despotism of a separated

[45] *A Brief Exposition of the Conference Law of 1835*, p. 6.

order'. He also argued that it 'denuded the local courts of ... free action', imposed further authority upon the superintendent 'as a right inherent in the divine constitution of the pastoral office', and so destroyed the 'conjoint authority' which 'lay at the basis of constitutional Methodism'.[46]

Can nothing, however, be said in favour of the 1835 rules? Yes:

i. They at least removed special meetings from the whims and discretion of the superintendent and placed the issue firmly with the Conference.

ii. The constitution of the special meeting was a 'fair and sufficient representation of the piety, intelligence and Connexional property of the circuit'.[47]

iii. It must be remembered that in 1835 the constitution of the Quarterly Meeting was still undefined and in many circuits it consisted of only ministers and stewards. As late as 1850, some senior ministers maintained that this was the proper constitution of the Quarterly Meeting.[48] So the special meeting for airing grievances was far in advance of anything that had been devised hitherto for getting a general consensus of opinion at circuit level.

iv. It is true that members of the special meeting were nominees of the superintendent, but they were elected by a free vote of the Leaders; and, after all, superintendents were honourable men who knew their people.

v. The enquiry asked whether the Societies were satisfied with the existing rules of Methodism; the stewards were therefore collectively best able to convey a fair sense of the feelings of the people.

vi. Fixed periods, within which meetings must be held, were not unknown in Methodism. The time for holding both District Meetings and the Conference were thus defined.

vii. Conference believed that the most reliable information and expression of opinion came not from pressure

[46] Carter, W. B., *Methodism, Past and Present*, pp. 62, 67.
[47] Rigg, J. H., *The Principles of Wesleyan Methodism*, p. 32.
[48] *Op. cit.*, p. 33.

THE WARRENITE SECESSION

groups or agitators, but from the collective judgement of an officially constituted meeting.

viii. Conference rightly insisted that 'the fundamental principles of Methodism must not be tampered with'. Basic principles which had characterized Methodism since its inception had to be safeguarded, or it would cease to be Methodism. Since 1797 changes had been made, but they had not robbed the system of its identity. Some of the reforms desired in 1828 and 1835 would have resulted in something other than 'Wesleyan Methodism'. This can be verified by a comparison of the constitution of the United Methodist Free Churches with that of the parent body, and it was just that difference between the two that delayed ultimate union. When union came the compromise was such that one wonders how far the result is really Methodism as it was understood by the Wesleyans of our period. Certainly, the Wesleyan conception of the Pastoral Office disappeared and an amorphous doctrine of the 'Priesthood of all Believers' took its place.

Conclusion

For an assessment of the rules of 1835, we would concur with Dr George Smith, that they were 'too limited and too late'. Had they come in 1828 instead of 1835, they would not only have been a boon to Methodism, they would have aligned the Connexion with the general pattern of reform as it was showing itself in the repeal of the Test and Corporation Acts (1828) and the Reform Bill (1832). As it was, the impression was given that Wesleyan Methodism was reactionary and anxious. 'It protested too much!' A system more assured of the confidence of its people, more persuaded that the rank and file of its members were marching with it, would have taken these things in its stride and a negotiated settlement would have been possible. To anticipate the next revolt, it could be said that the controversy over the Fly-sheets points to the same conclusion. A self-confident body would have either ignored the Fly-sheets or answered them; but the Wesleyans, in self-defence, resorted to too many 'Declarations' to make one happy. It would be too much to suggest that those who signed did so under duress, but it could at least be said that by refusing to sign, they laid themselves open to suspicion. As Dr Benjamin Gregory said, 'Signatures under pressure of Declarations drawn up by someone else are invalid and misleading, but signature under penalty is worthless altogether....'[49] Wesleyan Methodism ought not to have deemed it necessary to resort to such doubtful tests of allegiance, and it was not enough to fall back on the authority of the Pastoral Office. Not everyone—least of all the Dissentients—accepted its premises; how could they agree to the conclusions?

---

[49] See Gregory, B., *Sidelights, etc.*, pp. 262-4. In the Conference of 1839, the Rev. Joseph Cusworth's election to the Legal Hundred was queried by someone asking whether he had signed the Declaration of 1835. Dr Beaumont at once rose in righteous indignation. 'I protest', he said, 'against any brother being held up as unsound because he had not signed a composition drawn up by certain brethren stationed in London....' Beaumont himself had not signed the Declaration!

CHAPTER THREE

THE FLY-SHEET CONTROVERSY

THE year 1849 was one of the climactic dates in Wesleyan Methodism for it saw the beginning of the severest upheaval the Connexion had ever known. In comparison the previous revolts were mere preludes. Preludes, indeed, they were; for the events of 1849-52 were the final eruption of forces which underlay all previous secessions. Fortunately, it was the last upheaval!

Yet nothing very new in the way of constitutional reform came out of it. It did not even produce a new denomination. The Reformers advised their sympathizers to stay within the Wesleyan fold and work for reform from within. It was only when they found this to be impossible that they joined forces with the Wesleyan Methodist Association in 1856 to form The United Methodist Free Churches.[1] Yet the movement is significant for our study of Church and ministry in that it emphasized, as none of the previous clashes did, the principles held by the contending parties. So we now turn to the events of 1849 with its principles and repercussions.[2]

The incidents were almost stark in their simplicity. In 1846, 1847 and again in 1848, anonymous Fly-sheets were circulated among Wesleyan ministers. No printer's name appeared and, so as to conceal further the identity of the author, they were mailed from different centres. The avowed object of these tracts was to expose alleged maladministration of Conference affairs, but it was done with an invective which amounted to slander.

It was impossible to identify with absolute certainty the

[1] The eight years which held nothing but protest gave the Reformers a rather negative look. See *An Address to the Methodist Societies from the Wesleyan Delegates in London* (1850), p. 6; and Taylor, E. R., *Methodism and Politics*, p. 188f.
[2] The literature on this subject is prolific. In the Methodist Archives there is a collection of nearly 600 pamphlets, in addition to articles, leaders, etc., which appeared in the magazines and newspapers of the time.

145

author of the Fly-sheets, though everyone had more than a suspicion that James Everett was behind them; in fact, John Kent has said that if he did not write them, he must have been green with envy of the person who did. Accordingly, at the Conference of 1849, every minister was asked, 'Are you the author, or are you connected with the authorship of the Fly-sheets?' Three men refused to answer and, after much deliberation, were expelled from the Connexion. They immediately began to travel up and down the country airing their grievances and spreading disaffection. The Conference reacted with yet another Declaration, and anyone who sympathized with the expelled ministers became a marked man or even expelled from the Connexion. It is said to have cost the Wesleyans one hundred thousand members. Efforts at mediation failed. The doctrine of the Pastoral Office was re-affirmed and Conference maintained a remarkable self-composure even when *The Times*, with the British Press in general, turned against them.

W. B. Carter, whom we have already met in the previous chapter, a Birmingham layman, moderate and a leader of the Mediation Committee, deplored the intransigence which underlay, and was expressed by, the resort to the Pastoral Office. He was quite willing to accept the divine institution of the ministry and the responsibility of ministers to their Lord and Master, but he rejected the claim of ministers 'to an exclusive government of the church by virtue of rights inherent in their office'.[3] His committee, 'The Mediation Committee', based on Birmingham and drawing many members from Yorkshire, regretted that the Conference did not devise 'some comprehensive and healing measure'. It appealed to them to make 'some effort to bring back the banished ones into the house'.[4] Daniel Walton recommended that the Conference debates be open to the public and believed that too many people assumed that Methodism was incapable of improvement. He pleaded with Conference in such terms as, 'treat your erring brethren kindly. Listen to their representations. Count them not as rebels

[3] *Methodism Past and Present*, p. 74.
[4] Heeley and Harris: *Address of the Mediation Committee*, p. 19.

and aliens.'[5] But all this was of no avail and we now turn to examine the contending positions.

The Methodist Reformers

The Fly-sheets made their attack on three fronts—Location, Centralization and Secularization—and in varying degrees these were the watchwords of all Methodist Reformers.

(a) Location

This was succinctly expressed in *An Address to the Protestant Evangelical Churches* (p. 3) which attacked 'certain officials who have been promoted to office and have been stationed in London for ten, twenty and, in some cases even thirty consecutive years'. Fly-sheet No. 1 believed that this was contrary to the Apostolic pattern and to the spirit and practice of Methodism; that it was inimical to a fair distribution of ministerial talent and an injustice to those who travel large circuits in all weathers. Fundamentally, 'location' was seen to be a blow at the root of itinerancy and a possible prelude to a 'settled ministry', alien to the spirit of Methodism. Furthermore, it was believed to have a disastrous effect upon the person 'located' in that it diverted him from his original designation as a Methodist itinerant preacher and, more often than not, it tended to damp the spirit of his calling. Above all, there was the suspicion that a 'located' cabal in London could be a potential centre for intrigue and ambition. The Reformers were, in fact, more than suspicious; they actually imputed intrigue and ambition to the Conference officials in general and to Jabez Bunting in particular.[6]

(b) Centralization

Location, the Reformers alleged, gave rise to centralization. It was, in a way, to be expected that an expanding body like Methodism should need an efficient administration and this demanded centralization. One cannot but

[5] *Counsels of Peace*, p. 31.
[6] See *The Wesleyan Review* (a Reform publication), vol. ii, p. 477.

feel that the Reformers were less than realistic about this. They rightly saw the dangers, but with public transport still slow and uncomfortable, it was natural for the main committees, together with Conference officials, to be centred on London. The Connexion could not have been maintained with secretaries operating from distant parts of the country.

The Reformers were on firmer ground when they underlined the dangers of centralization. In particular they thought that the London District assumed an unwarranted authority over the rest of the Connexion. There was, of course, much history behind this. With Wesley's house and chapel at City Road, London was the natural metropolis of the Connexion, and more than once the London Preachers were asked to give a lead to the provinces.[7] In 1803 the London Preachers used to meet on a Saturday morning, 'to fix the plans... and to give advice to any Preachers from the country who choose to apply for it'.[8] Occasionally London had over-stepped the mark and assumed a superiority which was resented by others. In the Warren case it had issued tests and assumed a right to catechize the Connexion. In some communications with the Free Church of Scotland, it had even acted prematurely of Conference sanction.[9] All this bore the stamp of a 'Conference within a Conference' with undefined power; and undefined power is more dangerous than power that is defined and controlled. When the Fly-sheets accused the Conference officials of receiving extravagant salaries, of paying enormous prices for property and of encouraging ostentation, they were on more controversial and delicate ground.

(c) Secularization

More could be said for this charge. When a minister is withdrawn from pastoral work and placed in an administrative post, he is liable to become 'secularised in thought,

---

[7] See *Minutes*, ii. 347 (1806) and iii. 222 (1811).
[8] See *Life of Jabez Bunting*, i. 169.
[9] Conference did officially communicate with the Free Church of Scotland —see *Minutes* 1843, p. 555 and 1844, p. 92.

affections, desires, purposes and habits'.[10] The Reformers felt that administrative posts such as that held by Dr Bunting were alien to the calling of a Methodist Preacher. 'We ask', said the Fly-sheets, 'by what authority the Wesleyan Church requires any man to desecrate his talents . . . as to fix himself in offices that war against his ministerial calling.'[11] In his book on the early correspondence of Jabez Bunting, Professor W. R. Ward says much the same about him, 'The immense administrative burden which he (Bunting) gradually shouldered channelled his creative energies in another direction; his books went unread, his sermon writing dried up, his ability to carry his congregation eventually declined . . .' (p. 15). So the Reformers were not far wrong; but when they indulged in personal abuse, they defeated their own purposes. Honest criticism of the administration would have deserved a hearing and an equally honest reply; but slander was an offence against the fellowship of the ministry and it was that which laid Everett and other Reformers open to censure.

(d) The Divine Right of the Pastoral Office

Initially, the Fly-sheets criticized the administration, but it was not long before the controversy moved to an attack on the Wesleyan conception of the Pastoral Office as expounded by Richard Watson, Alfred Barrett, John Beecham and Jabez Bunting. A pamphlet entitled *A Fraternal Address of the Third London (Reformed) Circuit* clearly held that the real cause of the conflict was the claim which the ministers made, 'of having received authority by Divine Right to rule the Church and exclude from Church fellowship whom they choose without the concurrence of the laity' (p. 1). W. B. Carter felt that the doctrine of the Pastoral Office was pretentious in that it rested not on qualifications but on divine right, and that the danger lay in the liability of the 'Collective Pastorate' doing what an individual pastor would not, or dare not, do. It was not even based on expediency. If it could be shown that it was

[10] The Fly Sheets, p. 32.
[11] Ibid., p. 33.

necessary for the well-being of the church it might have had a chance of acceptance, but based, as it was, on divine right, it carried a claim to power greater than it could bear. Furthermore, they argued that it was 'not sustainable by plain, scriptural interpretation'.[12]

The Reform movement was, in essence, a revolt against 'the keys'; against the allegedly divine prerogative to receive into and expel from the Church. The Wesleyan Reformers did not object to a full-time ministry; what they did object to was the self-bestowed power of the Wesleyan ministers.[13]

(e) Further Points from the Reformers

i. They did not press for lay-representation in Conference, as other Free Methodists did, though in the end union with the Wesleyan Methodist Association compelled them to accept it.[14] What they did object to was an all-ministerial Conference sitting behind closed doors and exercising what to them seemed like irresponsible power.[15] Robert Eckett, an extreme Reformer, thought that the Fly-sheets did not go far enough, for they 'were not aiming at the introduction of any really valuable or important change in the system of Methodism, or to obtain for the laity any relaxation of the oppressive parts ... but merely to turn Dr Bunting and others out of office'.[16] For Eckett, more than a change of administration was needed. He wanted a liberalizing of the whole polity of the Connexion to 'obtain for the people their rights'. This was quite true; the supporters of the Fly-sheets admitted that what they wanted was 'Reform, not Revolution; Restoration, not Destruction ...'.[17]

ii. The Reformers rather naïvely compared the Methodism of their age with the Methodism of 1797 or earlier;

[12] Heeley and Harris: *op. cit.*, p. 18.
[13] See *The Wesleyan Review*, vol. II (1851), p. 101, also *The Wesleyan Reformer* for January 1851, p. 11.
[14] *Misrepresentations and Falsehoods*, p. 44.
[15] *An Address to the Methodist Societies from Wesleyan Delegates*, p. 3.
[16] *Methodist Reform*, p. 5.
[17] *The Wesleyan Review*, Vol. II, p. 45.

they ignored the fact of development. George Southern, for example, pointed out that Wesley did not form a church, and lamented that the constitution of Methodism as he knew it was different from what it was under Wesley.[18] Of course, Wesley did not found a new church and equally 'of course' Methodism in 1850 was different from Methodism in 1797; Southern failed to see that in the very nature of Wesley's legacy, this was bound to be so. What the Reformers did not see was that in one respect at least 1850 was the *same* as 1797 and earlier—namely the Itinerants were 'examined one by one'.

iii. Some of the Reformers placed a strange interpretation on what the Conference of 1851 regarded as the three great principles of Wesleyan Methodism, namely, The Integrity of the Pastoral Office, The Connexional Principle and The Authority of District Committees.[19] 'The Integrity of the Pastoral Office' was interpreted as 'the sole right of Preachers to admit and put out of Societies and to administer all other Church government to the exclusion of the entire people and all other church officers'. 'The Connexional Principle' was regarded as 'the supreme power of Conference over every member, Society, Circuit and District, to make laws for them and govern them'. Southern denied that these were essential to a Church or even essentially Wesleyan. According to his perverted interpretation, probably they were not, but the Wesleyans thought of them differently.

iv. As in the case of all the other secessions, the Methodist Reformers' principles were most clearly displayed in the organization of their own brand of Methodism. A glance at the *Proposed Basis of Union* between the Reformers and the Wesleyan Methodist Association gives some idea of their views of the ministry. As might be expected, they gave every church the right to govern itself, to admit and expel members, to choose its own officers (including the minister) and no superior court at either District or Connexional level had any power of veto. While they believed in the propriety

[18] *A Few Thoughts*, p. 32.
[19] See *Minutes*, xi. (1851), pp. 677-78.

of a separated ministry supported by the people, entire separation to the work was not regarded as essential to the 'efficient discharge of such services as preaching the Gospel, Baptism and the Supper of the Lord'.

Conference Methodism

When the expelled ministers crusaded in self-defence, the burden of their speeches was that they had been expelled, (a) for refusing to incriminate themselves, (b) without a trial, and (c) by a court which was at once accuser, jury and judge—in short, by principles which would never have been tolerated in the common justice of the land.

The fact was that James Everett (to take his case alone) was asked, along with other ministers of the Connexion, to confirm or deny complicity in the Fly-sheets. This he refused to do—not without some verbal fencing with the President. He alleged that he was expelled on suspicion, rather than on evidence or proof of guilt. Conference apologists argued that he was not expelled for even suspicion, but for contumacy. The case for the Conference turns on two points, (a) the right of Conference to put 'a brotherly question', and (b) the difference between the Conference and a civil court of justice. Consider these.

(a) The right of Conference to put 'a brotherly question'

Basically, Conference had traditionally exercised a right to examine the Preachers one by one 'without any disguise or reserve'.[20] The ministerial session of Conference still has that right. But apart from this, one must understand the nature of the Methodist Conference and the relationship to it of every minister in the Connexion. On a collective form, it is the supreme episcopé of the ministry, Wesley's corporate successor; so let us go back to the fount and origin of this unique ecclesiastical body.

We begin with Wesley's first conference, 1744, when questions were asked concerning every Itinerant, e.g. 'Do you walk closely with God?' 'Do you read the books we

[20] See *Minutes*, i. 127 (1777), vii. 549-50 (1835) and xi. 281 (1849).

THE FLY-SHEET CONTROVERSY

advise?', etc. Throughout the development of Methodism, this right of enquiry was never relaxed, for in this way, the ministry was kept under constant scrutiny.[21] Personal piety, knowledge of the scriptures, soundness of faith, purity of morals—all these came up for examination. These annual examinations were conducted both in the District Meeting and in the Conference.[22] Only thus could Conference fulfil its task and trust of appointing ministers of approved piety and orthodoxy to the chapels under its charge. Only thus could the Societies, to whom their ministers came as complete strangers, be sure that there was unity in doctrine and discipline. As Thomas Jackson, wrote,

> ... these objects could never be obtained were it not for the kind fidelity with which the Methodist Preachers watch over each other, and the care which is taken by the Conference that men whom it appoints understand the Gospel of God and are imbued with its spirit.[23]

Wesleyan ministers stood in a near and peculiar relation to one another, and they voluntarily submitted to this close scrutiny by their fellows. At the Conference of 1744, Wesley was conscious of this when he spoke of 'the close union between those whom God is pleased to use as instruments in this glorious work'. The same Conference asked, 'What can be done in order to a closer union of our helpers with each other?' and part of the answer was, 'Let them speak freely to each other'.[24] It was in this tradition that Thomas Jackson, a century later, wrote, 'ministers who sustain a relation to each other so intimate, peculiar and delicate, must act towards each other with perfect openness and candour, otherwise their very union will rather be a bane than an advantage'.[25] It is only against this back-

---

[21] See Jackon, Thomas, *The Wesleyan Conference* where he quotes instances from the Conferences of 1746, 1766, 1770, 1777, 1791, 1802, 1804, 1805, 1807, 1812, 1815, 1821, 1827 and 1835.
[22] In fact, the principle of 'free and unreserved communication' applied to every member of Society as they met in class—see Smith, G., *Wesleyan Ministers and their Slanderers*, p. 4.
[23] Jackson, *op. cit.*, p. 22.
[24] *Minutes*, i. 556.
[25] *Op. cit.*, p. 26; see also *The Proceedings of the Conference*, p. 5.

ground of the unquestioned right of Conference to examine its members that the expulsions of 1849 can be understood. The failure of the press—both secular and religious—to grasp this, goes far to account for their almost unanimous condemnation of the Wesleyan Conference—though it does not exonerate them.

We have had many occasions to note the unity of the Wesleyan ministry, which was maintained largely by reason of its closely-knit Connexionalism and Wesley's insistence upon their always acting in concert with each other; but never was this unity so clearly manifest as in 1849. The Reformers may have attributed it to fear of acting independently; they may have thought that the rank and file were intimidated, but the unanimity with which the Conference voted on the expulsions is, to say the least, impressive. Among the four hundred or so ministers who made up the Conference, was there no champion to rise up in defence of Everett? There does not appear to have been even the semblance of an 'Everett Party'. We are told that, 'the whole Conference rose *en masse*, and decided that the man who refused to answer the question put to him from the chair must cease to be a Wesleyan minister'.[26] It is reported that only two hands were raised in Everett's favour.[27] Everett was condemned, not for writing the Fly-sheets (that was never proved) but for betraying the confidence of his fellow-ministers. The suspects were 'only required to abstain from what no Methodist ministers ever had the right of doing and must necessarily be mischievous if allowed'.[28] Their refusal was a breach of the ties which united the ministers of the Connexion.[29]

[26] Smith, G., *Wesleyan Ministers and their Slanderers*, p. 15.
[27] Gregory, B., *Sidelights*, p. 456.
[28] Hargreaves, *Misrepresentations and Falsehoods of the Fly-sheets Exposed*, p. 30.
[29] Benjamin Gregory recalls two interesting precedents to 'the Brotherly Question':
(a) Alexander Kilham was asked if he acknowledged a certain pamphlet and answered, 'I do'.
(b) Jabez Bunting refused to reply to a question, implying criticism, which was put to him by the Conference and said, 'I will not be catechised', threatening to leave the assembly. One is surprised Everett did not recall this incident, though perhaps he was not aware of it. *Sidelights*, p. 554f.

THE FLY-SHEET CONTROVERSY

(b) *The Conference not a civil court of justice*

Apart from the fact that a voluntary society has the right to make its own rules and in accordance with those rules to admit and expel members, the proceedings of the Wesleyan Conference were quite different from those of a civil court of law. For one thing, the manner of dealing with members who have been unfaithful, or who have impaired the family spirit, must of necessity be different from that of a civil court as it tries the society offender and the criminal.[30]

Further, the Wesleyan Conference shares with professional bodies the right to test its own members for unprofessional conduct and, when necessary, to expel those whom it judges to be transgressors.[31]

The condemnation of the Wesleyan Conference by the press was entirely due to the mistake of comparing the methods of the Conference (which they did not know or understand) with those of civil courts (which were well-known). *The Times* likened the Conference to the Star Chamber, though of 'the usual practice of the Conference' it confessed 'we know next to nothing'.[32] Bunting's reply to *The Times* was, 'You forget that we are a religious and not a secular society. We guard against those terms and usages which would assimilate us to the House of Commons or any other secular assembly.'[33] We now proceed to assess the significance of the conflict.

The Significance of 1849

(a) *Political Undertones*

Undoubtedly, the upheaval of 1849 was but another phase of the conflict which was already troubling political and social relationships. We are not saying that what was done in Wesleyan Methodism had political motives or objectives; but the spirit of the age was now finding expression in the religious world. As Professor Gordon Rupp once said, 'a European-wide tension met inside

[30] Hargreaves, *op. cit.*, pp. 5, 23.
[31] Hargreaves, *op. cit.*, p. 26.
[32] See Macdonald, G. B., *A Candid Reply re Conference Proceedings*, p. 21.
[33] Quoted by Rupp in *Ideas and Beliefs of the Victorians*, p. 110.

Methodism'.[34] The conservatism of the Conference clashed with the radicalism of which Everett and Eckett were the chief representatives. It was actually said that the divine mission of Conference was to guard against the inroads of reform;[35] accordingly, reformers, as such, represented 'the united forces of political and ecclesiastical radicalism'. On the other hand, the Reformers believed that the Conference was 'under the direction of a powerful party devoted to Toryism',[36] proof of which was to be seen in official opposition to Lord John Russell's Bill for relief from Church rates and to the Education Bill.

(b) *The witch-hunt against Reform*

One of the saddest aspects of the aftermath of the expulsions was the witch-hunt after reform. Any individual sympathetic to the expelled ministers was ruthlessly expelled from Society. Superintendents withheld Class Books from Leaders and tickets from members. When these superintendents sought the guidance of Conference officials they were advised to act firmly.[37] If Benjamin Gregory is to be trusted, 'some of the finest and most flourishing circuits in Methodism . . . were all but wrecked'.[38] Of the 100,000 members lost by the Wesleyans, only 41,000 were gathered in by the United Methodists Free Churches in 1857; 'a mournful minority of those who had been by three successive agitations detached from the parent stem'.[39]

(c) *The attitude of the Conference*

It is not difficult for us, at this distance in time, to see where the Conference erred and to say what it should have

[34] Rupp, E. G., *op. cit.*, p. 110.
[35] Zeta, *The Wesleyan Conference*, pp. 5f. and 17.
[36] Cropp, J., *Objections to Modern Methodism*, p. 21.
[37] M.C.A. correspondence of John Beecham during his year of Presidency, 1850–1; e.g. William Bacon to Beecham, 25th September, 1850 and Beecham's reply 30th September, 1850, Robert Day to Beecham, 14th December, 1850 and Beecham's reply 14th December, 1850, Amos Learoyd to Beecham, 28th November, 1850 and Beecham's reply 3rd December, 1850—and many others.
[38] *Wesleyan Methodist Polity and History*, p. 227.
[39] Ibid., p. 230.

THE FLY-SHEET CONTROVERSY

done. Before the century was out, Benjamin Gregory was already pointing out where Conference went wrong and drew up a formidable list of its mistakes.[40] We might say that it ought either to have ignored the Fly-sheets or answered them. Had they been the work of an outsider they could easily have been ignored, but it was difficult to turn a blind eye to what all knew to be the work of one of the brethren in the ministry. Not that they did go unanswered. Joseph Hargreaves, a minister of considerable repute, replied to all the accusations and proved many of them to be false; but there is no effective reply to slander.

So Conference stood firm—too firm, some would say. Its three principles were re-affirmed, and there was no relaxation of the high doctrine of the Pastoral Office. The Minutes here are worth quoting:

> The Conference regards itself as being bound by the principles set forth in the New Testament, and by the sacred trust transmitted to it by Mr Wesley and his co-adjutors, to maintain the PASTORAL OFFICE in unimpaired integrity; and, consequently, bound to uphold the SPIRITUAL AUTHORITY which is appropriate to that office and necessary to the execution of the duties which Christ has made imperative on all those who sustain it.[41]

The same Conference told the Methodist people, 'We hold the Pastoral Crook with steady and unfaltering hand'. The Free Methodists interpreted this as sheer high-handedness. They thought that the Wesleyans would have fared much better had they trusted more to the natural relationship between pastor and people. They maintained that there had been sufficient good-will to sustain ministerial authority, but once this conception of the Pastoral Office was codified the affection of the people was undermined.[42]

The underlying fault of the Wesleyans was lack of flexibility. There was too much of the spirit of, 'if you don't

[40] *Sidelights*, p. 546ff.
[41] *Minutes*, xi (1851), p. 678, a passage which includes the sentence, 'Our contest has been for the very existence of the Pastoral Office'. See also *The Wesleyan Vindicator*, 1850, p. 88.
[42] *An Appeal to the Evidence*, pp. 35–6.

like us, leave us!'[43] Charitableness was not one of their outstanding virtues[44] nor was contrition much in evidence. They regarded the Reformers as 'the erring and the fallen' for whom prayers should be offered that 'God may give them repentance'.[45] Connexionalism was legitimate if it bound Methodism together 'by means of a common ministry'[46] but when Societies or individuals discovered that it could foster unity for common action, the boot was on the other foot! One has, of course, to remember that those were days when Trade Unions were struggling to be born and Wesleyan Methodism was certainly not in the *avant garde*.

(d) The 1852 Committee

What were the positive results, if any, of this upheaval? The constitution was not re-written as the Reformers would have wished, but such modifications as were made were of lasting benefit to the Connexion. The revision was carried out by a strong contingent of ministers and laymen, although the Reformers objected that the right type of layman (i.e. with Reform sympathies) was not there.

In 1851, Conference appointed a committee of ministers who later conferred with a large band of laymen, 'to examine the principal suggestions contained in the memorials and other communications and report on the same to the next Conference'.[47] Accordingly in 1852 the

[43] See M.C.A. letter from Bunting to Humphrey Sandwith, 10th February, 1825 (an early expression of the idea!).
[44] This was seen, for example, in their refusal to initiate a fund for disabled Local Preachers from the proceeds of the Centenary Fund. When the Local Preachers Mutual Aid Association was formed, Samuel Jackson wrote a most uncharitable article in *The Wesleyan Vindicator* (1851, pp. 217ff). Fortunately, his fears proved groundless and the movement grew. See my article in *The Local Preachers Handbook*, No. 9, pp. 15ff.
[45] *Minutes*, xi. (1851), p. 697.
[46] Ibid., p. 696.
[47] For a full account of this committee, see *The Wesleyan Vindicator* or *The Watchman*. *The Wesleyan Vindicator* (1852) pp. 33-104 reports the speeches of Thomas Jackson, William Arthur and others which are valuable expositions of Wesleyan polity. For the attitude of the Reformers, always critical and often derisive, see *The Wesleyan Reformer* (1852), pp. 33ff, 50ff, 86ff.

conclusions of this large, mixed committee were presented to the Conference. With very few modifications, they were accepted and can be summarized as follows:

1. The constitution of the Quarterly Meeting was defined.[48]

2. A 'Special Circuit Meeting', consisting of twelve members, chosen by the Quarterly Meeting was set up 'for re-trying an accused member or local officer'. If a Superintendent felt himself 'obstructed in his pastoral duties by the prevalence of a factious spirit', he could summon this special meeting with the Chairman of the District presiding. If the accused was convicted, the sentence remained with the Superintendent in consultation with his colleagues and the Chairman. Both the accused and the superintendent had a right of appeal to the District Meeting and to the Conference.

3. The Law of 1797 enacted that a Trustee should be tried by a joint meeting of Leaders and Trustees. This was explained as applying only 'to the Trustees of the chapel with which the Society is connected', bearing in mind that the accused could be a Trustee of more than one chapel, to summon all his co-trustees would reduce the Leaders of his own Society to a small minority.

4. The right of appeal from local church meetings to the Conference was re-affirmed. This was to prevent the isolation of local Societies, to preserve the Connexional spirit, and to protect individual members 'from the undue pressure of local partialities, prejudice and irritation'.

5. The method whereby circuits could memorialize the Conference 'on Connexional subjects' was simplified and extended. The separate meeting to follow the June Quarterly Meeting was abolished and the right to deal with memorials was given to the June Quarterly Meeting itself. Ten days notice, however, had to be given to the

[48] Until 1852 the constitution of the Q.M. was undefined. See a letter from Charles Haigh of Bradford (Wilts.) to Bunting, 19th December 1836, asking for a ruling on who is eligible to attend the Q.M. He says, 'whoever is disposed to come and eat a good dinner has a right to vote....' Bunting replies, 'Let all come who have been accustomed to come and leave the results to God' (M.C.A.).

superintendent. Furthermore, no memorials were allowed which would undermine the fundamental doctrine or discipline of the Connexion[49] or would mean the interference of one circuit with the affairs of another.

These suggestions were confirmed by the Conference of 1853 and the upheaval of 1849 was followed by a period of consolidation and peace so that in 1877 the admission of laymen to the Conference was achieved as a bloodless revolution.

---

[49] It greatly annoyed the Reformers that the three basic principles of 1851 were not to be discussed. See *The Wesleyan Reformer* (1852), p. 103.

PART FOUR

Church and Ministry

CHAPTER ONE

THE RESULTANT POLITY

WE must now gather up the various strands in our study of the polity of Wesleyan Methodism and give an account of the resultant structure. The ecclesiastical polity of Wesleyan Methodism was hammered out on the anvil of dissension. We have seen that, in each of the four disruptions, certain principles had to be defended, but when the conflict was over, modifications had to be made. Against the pressures of liberalism the Wesleyans gradually produced an ecclesiastical system which was unique. The last and greatest modification to Wesleyanism lay ahead (outside our period), and that was the admission of laymen to the Conference. This means that our concern is with what we might call 'Classical Wesleyanism', with the all-ministerial Conference supreme and the doctrine of the Pastoral Office proclaimed in its fulness. The dilution of this doctrine had not yet begun; that process lay ahead as the Wesleyans drew nearer to the Free Churches and the prospect of union with the Free Methodists called for a compromise. This nineteenth-century 'Classical Wesleyanism' is now largely forgotten, but we claim that it is well worth consideration.

We begin our study of the polity of Wesleyan Methodism with an account of its structure, then consider its nature in comparison with Independency and Presbyterianism, and finally attempt an assessment.

Structure

(a) *The Supremacy of Conference*

After Wesley's death the Conference inherited his power, but not his prestige. The former was bestowed, the latter had to be won, and this was not achieved without conflict. However, in the face of every challenge, the supremacy of Conference was maintained. The Preachers realized that this was the king-pin of the whole structure, that if the authority of Conference were undermined, the Connexion would disintegrate into a loose conglomeration of independent societies and, as was the tendency with such societies, ultimately disappear altogether.[1]

The Preachers based the authority of Conference on divine origin;[2] as the corporate pastorate it was no more self-appointed than were the individual pastors who composed it. It was said that the Preachers 'usurped an undue degree of power, claiming and exercising too great a share in the direction of temporal concerns', to which it was replied:

> The power of Conference is neither 'usurped' nor wholly 'delegated' by men, but first given to them by God in common with all who are by Him called to the work of the ministry—Acts 20:28, 1 Thess. 5:12, 13, 1 Tim. 5:17-19, Heb. 13:7, 17.[3]

Furthermore, continues the statement, the power of the Conference is derived from internal consent in that the individuals who compose it have voluntarily bound themselves to abide by the collective judgement of the assembly.

When Conference moved into the third period of its development—called by Welch, 'a limited or restricted aristocracy'—it became subject to checks and balances. At times it wielded its power severely. In the Leeds Organ Case, for instance, Conference asserted itself as the supreme legislative and executive body of the Connexion with a right, through its District Committees, to interfere in the internal affairs of a circuit. After the Warrenite affair, the Lord Chancellor confirmed that Conference was legally the highest court in the Connexion and from its decisions on spiritual matters there was no appeal.[4] The Free Methodists, of course, regarded this as tyranny and in need of reform, but the Wesleyans felt that if discipline was to have

---

[1] M.C.A. letter from Samuel Bradburn to Richard Rodda, December 1791, 'The Conference must be the *dernier ressort* of power'.
[2] Barrett, A., *The Pastoral Office*, p. 220.
[3] M.C.A. broadsheet: *To Members of the Methodist Connexion*, Manchester, 1796.
[4] Vevers, W., *A Defence of the Discipline of Methodism*, p. 45.

any meaning at all, it must be applied impartially through the Connexion. The Reformers would have made the local societies their own judge and jury; the Wesleyans saw the need for one supreme Connexional court of appeal—the Conference. Wesleyan apologists denied that it was tyrannical; in fact, they demonstrated that, in view of the dependence of Conference upon the voluntary support of the people, it would be against its own interests to oppress anyone. Far from being tyrannical, it was, indeed it must be, paternal.[5]

By 1852 the power of Conference had been hedged by healthy checks and balances, some of which had been introduced after the Warrenite secession, which (belated as they were) represented an attempt to make it more responsive to local opinion. Unfortunately the Conference was too large and lasted too long. It drew too many ministers from their circuits for three weeks every year. Gradually this disability was remedied, but it is worthwhile noting that at one time the holding of provincial conferences was seriously considered. The idea was that these regional conferences should be held annually and a General Conference every two or three years. As early as 1809 this was mooted at the Sheffield District Meeting[6] and from time to time given an airing in a semi-public way. It is said that Jabez Bunting favoured such a scheme in his younger days, but as he grew older he saw the difficulty of re-casting so important an assembly, especially in its legal aspects, so as not to reduce its efficiency by meeting only every two or three years.[7] More important, he saw the value of the Conference as a focal point for Methodist opinion and affection. It was more than a supreme assembly for discipline and legislation; it was 'the mother of us all'; remove it and 'the people called Methodists' would cease to be a people![8]

[5] Vevers, op. cit., p. 45.
[6] Life of Jabez Bunting, i. 332.
[7] Bunting's reasons against biennial conferences are set out in a manuscript in his handwriting in the M.C.A.
[8] The official Conference was, of course, the Legal Hundred, whose ratification of all measures was necessary before they could become

Methodism can boast of many peculiarities, but nothing is more indigenous to the Connexion than the *Minutes of Conference*.[9] Through time this annual volume has developed into a large handbook of general reference, but throughout its career it has been the official means of communication between the Conference and the people. W. H. Rule once said, 'Our *Minutes of Conference* are exactly similar to the πρακτικον, "collection of acts" of an old synod; and are with us as good, to all intents and purposes, as were ever the decrees and canons of an oecumenical council to the clergy thereto submissive'.[10] Not least important in the *Minutes* is the 'Annual Address' or 'Pastoral Letter' to the Societies. Here the 'paternal nature' of the Conference is supremely displayed. We know of nothing quite like it in any other Church except it be the Papal encyclicals and the Synodical epistles of the early Church. Year by year the Conference sends greetings to its people, summarizing decisions made and, in a singularly successful way, conveys something of the spirit in which those decisions were reached. Down the years these Pastoral Letters give, as perhaps nothing else does, an insight into how Methodists were thinking, the temper and the judgements of the Conference, its reaction to contemporary events and its conception of the Christian life as Methodists ought to practise it—altogether a unique source of information for the student of Methodism. One of the tenderest of all Pastoral Addresses was that of 1793, written to commend the decisions of Conference on the

---

legally binding; although the Legal Hundred never refused to confirm what the larger conference approved. At first any Preacher in Full Connexion could attend Conference: later attendance was restricted to those who had received permission from the District Meeting; finally, numbers were limited to so many per District.

[9] See *Proceedings of the Wesley Historical Society*, xxxi, pp. 155ff for an article by Wesley F. Swift on the *Minutes of Conference*. While this article dealt only with the Wesleyan Minutes, it should be remembered that every branch of Methodism produced its Conference Minutes, very much alike in style and format.

The official record of the acts of the Conference is the *Journal*, large manuscript volumes housed at the Methodist Church Archives in London. They are highly confidential, as they record discipline cases.

[10] *Wesleyan Methodism*, p. 80.

THE RESULTANT POLITY

Sacraments; but the regular practice of addressing a letter to the Societies did not begin until 1819. It was published in the *Minutes* and in the *Magazine*, with the instruction that it was to be read 'forthwith in all our congregations'. A later development was to send an Address to the Irish Conference, subsequently extended to other autonomous Conferences. We feel sure that Methodism has not realized the potentialities of this Annual Address to knit the Connexion in goodwill and to bring the spirit and decisions of the Conference to the rank and file of Church members.

Finally, something must be said about Conference as the collective Pastorate. Richard Watson once said that the power of the Conference is only, 'the power which is essentially vested in each minister by the very duties which he is under Scriptural obligation to perform'.[11] As such a non-pastor could have no place in it. Once Conference is made a mixed assembly, the function of a collective Pastorate is destroyed and it becomes something quite different, a legislative rather than an episcopal body.[12] As the collective Pastorate, it watched over its individual pastors and the doctrines they preached; it admitted and expelled pastors, authorized their ordination and superintended their training.

Between Conferences power was vested in the President, who was elected annually by his fellow-ministers. He had authority to supply vacancies, to sanction changes and to assist at any District Meeting or Circuit Quarterly Meeting should the need arise. He was thus a person of considerable authority.

So the Conference, in addition to being the supreme legislative body of the Connexion was the guardian of its doctrine and discipline—the collective *episcopos*.

---

[11] *An Affectionate Address*, p. 6.
[12] The word 'episcopal' is used here in the sense of episcopé exercised over the whole Connexion. The Wesleyans, after 1878, preserved it in the Ministerial or Pastoral session which met independently of the Representative Session.

(b) *The Oversight of Districts*

The struggle to establish the authority and define the powers of District Meetings took place, as we have seen, in 1827, only to be followed by a further testing time in 1835. Originally intended to supply the lack of effective supervision and to deal with any emergency that might arise between Conferences, the District Meetings developed into useful regional assemblies of ministers. They also did much work in preparing for Conference.

At the same time, the District Meeting has never been easy to fit into the economy of Methodism. On the one hand, Conference is the supreme legislative body and the Circuit Superintendent the person responsible for seeing that its regulations are observed in the Societies. Between the Conference and the Circuits come the District Meetings as, in effect, little more than advisory bodies acting in cases of emergency on behalf of the Conference to whom account will have to be given. A District Chairman had no right of entry into a circuit unless invited by the superintendent or commanded to do so by the Conference. He was appointed not by suffrage of the District, but by the Conference, and he was 'made responsible for the execution of all the laws of Methodism so far as his District is concerned'.[13] He was to enquire as to whether Methodist discipline was observed in his District, to examine candidates for the ministry and act as *pastor pastorum* to all the ministers in Full Connexion.

Minor District Meetings were instituted to deal with discipline cases, and the Financial District Committee 'for the arrangement and settlement of the financial affairs of the District but with no ecclesiastical functions whatever'.[14]

It is important for us to notice how these District Committees gradually enlisted the services of laymen and therefore, as 'Committees of Conference' (as they were officially styled), gave laymen an effective share in the management of connexional affairs. In fact, the development of these committees proceeded *pari passu* with a gradual shedding of responsibilities by Conference. As a matter of necessity,

[13] Grindrod's *Compendium*, p. 124.
[14] Peirce, *Ecclesiastical Polity*, p. 399 (Third edition).

THE RESULTANT POLITY

Conference had to off-load some of its administrative work on to the Districts. A significant step was taken as early as 1801, when Conference decreed that every circuit steward should be invited to the Annual District Meeting 'during the settling of everything relating to the finances of the District'.[15] This was the beginning of lay co-operation, and it meant that the laity had a real say in such items as finance, the division and re-organization of circuits, the erection of chapels, ministers' houses and allowances.

Ministers' allowances provide an excellent example of Connexionalism at work.[16] Ministers were paid a basic allowance, plus certain sums for wife and children. The varying sizes of ministers' families and the varying resources of circuits often created problems and embarrassments for both parties. An attempt was made to 'place the more costly families in well-to-do circuits and the ministers with the smallest families in the poorer circuits',[17] but this was soon abandoned as impracticable. Separate allowances were tried for wives[18] and children, but this was dropped so far as wives were concerned, but 'children's allowances' survive to this day. In 1818 the problem was solved by each District making itself responsible for the Preachers' children within its boundaries.

Other funds were similarly placed under District Committees composed of equal numbers of ministers and laymen, and in this arrangement Jabez Bunting played a conspicuous part. District Meetings grew in prestige and usefulness, so that in 1820 it was decided to hold two per annum—one in September and the other (as usual) just before Conference. This led to the most important mixed committee of all, the Departmental Committee of Review, which met annually in the Conference town just prior to

[15] This is not recorded in the *Minutes*, but mentioned in the *Methodist Magazine* for December, 1801, p. 552.
[16] M.C.A. Letter of Jabez Bunting, Macclesfield, 11th August, 1802, giving details of amounts paid to ministers at the beginning of the nineteenth century.
[17] Rigg, J. H., *The District Synod in Methodism*, p. 13.
[18] *Minutes*, 1801, p. 96 mentions, 'The Preachers' Wives' salaries' and 'The Preachers' Children's Salaries'—from printed accounts it would appear that wives received £12 p.a. and children £4 p.a.

Conference itself. Its purpose was to summarize the work of the Departments in preparation for Conference. This Committee thus became, 'the central annual rendezvous of the Connexional forces from all parts of the country and of the Mission Field. They were seasons of rejoicing, of mutual encouragement, of festivity, public and social.'[19] Not every District was represented every year, but a selection was made from those Districts nearest to the Conference town. In 1835, the Home Mission Committee added laymen from every District in England.[20]

Thus, gradually, the principle of District Representation came to be recognized and while Conference was still an all-ministerial assembly, many decisions and much responsibility fell to the laymen of the connexion.

(c) The Authority of the Superintendent

The Circuit Superintendent, originally Wesley's 'Assistant', was undoubtedly the key man in Wesleyan Methodism. The Wesleyans took episcopacy into their system by settling the role and title of the episcopos at Circuit and not at District level. The Methodist diocese is the Circuit, not the District; and the episcopos is the Superintendent, not the Chairman of the District. The analogy between the District Chairman and the Anglican Diocesan Bishop is more apparent than real. Alexander Kilham was shrewd enough to observe that the Circuit Superintendent is the real Bishop in Methodism.[21] W. H. Rule styled him as ὁ τῆς χώρας ἐπίσκοπος—'local bishop' or 'superintendent of the neighbourhood'.[22] The Superintendent's authority to admit or expel members was the storm centre in 1835 and again in 1849, but it was maintained, albeit with increasing checks and safeguards against its abuse.

It was Bunting, however, who did more than anyone else to establish the authority of the Superintendent. Benjamin Gregory thought that Bunting's first recorded pronounce-

[19] Rigg, J. H., *op. cit.*, p. 19.
[20] In 1861 this was extended to other committees.
[21] 'Martin Luther' tract, p. 3: 'Every Superintendent is Bishop of the Circuit. His colleagues in Full Connexion are his Presbyters. . . .'
[22] *Wesleyan Methodism*, p. 68.

ment of his fundamental church principles was occasioned by the Leeds Organ Case in 1826. This is probably true of his first *recorded* word on the subject, but in Part II, chapter 1 we saw reason to believe that the mind of Bunting was behind the Manchester Statement of 1806. What Gregory said of 1826 was true of 1806, namely, '[Bunting] makes the supreme authority of the Pastorate the one essential principle of ecclesiastical polity, which, being secured, all other things were mere details and matters of expediency and easiest working. In Dr Bunting's view the Superintendent of the Circuit is "The Angel of the Church".'[23]

An interesting incident, which well illustrates Bunting's position, occurred during his term as President of the Conference. He was called upon to deal with a breach of the Methodist rule that 'the Superintendent only, aided by his colleagues, is to make the Circuit Plan'. To the delinquent Superintendent, he wrote:

> The Superintendent in our economy is the man directly responsible to God and to the Conference and to the Connexion for every department of Methodistical service in the Circuit placed under his care. Having the whole responsibility, he must have correspondent authority; and that necessarily implies that the supreme direction of the whole work must be vested in his hands, checked and guarded indeed, but still sufficiently strong to answer the purposes of a good and efficient government. He is the father of the family and must have paternal rule over the whole household. He is the general-in-chief and must judge of the disposal of all his troops.[24]

To Bunting, plan-making was a question of leadership and he defended the Wesleyan system on three grounds. First, it protected the people, especially those in the smaller Societies, against 'an incompetent and unsatisfactory supply of their pulpits'; second, in the interests of peace and harmony among the Local Preachers themselves who could not but be the victims of 'local prejudices and partialities

---

[23] Gregory, B., *Sidelights*, p. 496. See also the famous 'Liverpool Minutes', now acknowledged to be the work of Bunting, 1820.
[24] *Life of Jabez Bunting*, ii. 252.

and animosities'; third, courtesy demanded that the Superintendent should seek the wishes of the local brethren before the plan is made, but, 'the final power of planning we must retain....' He once said, 'Travelling Preachers are more than members; they are all present as the Pastors and Ministers of the people. The Superintendent is the chief pastor, the others are his helpers and fellow-labourers in the ministerial and pastoral care.'[25] Again, at the Conference of 1835 he said, 'Consult your stewards, but the Superintendent, as the angel of the church is responsible after all'.[26]

Bunting's ideas about 'The Angel of the Church' were formulated more precisely by Alfred Barrett, who observed that in the Church at Ephesus the charge was not addressed to the Elders but to the Angel, as the one who 'appears invested with the chief responsibility'. He believes this to be evidence of 'the willing subordination of the body of Elders in a church to one of their number as their head and chief administrator'. He regards the angel as 'an actual and human servant of Christ in the Christian sanctuary', on the lines of the שליח צבור of the Jewish synagogue. He is aware of the fact that to episcopalians the angel is the bishop and to presbyterians he is 'the symbol of the eldership or ministerial body'; but for Wesleyans he can only be the Circuit Superintendent. In any case, Barrett accepts the Angel passage as confirming the Wesleyan circuit system. He sees affirmed in scripture, 'the principle of a ministerial fellowship or union, held together by a nexus of a President or chief, who, as far as we can see here, is a permanent one'.[27]

There were aspects of the Superintendent's authority which chafed—three, at least, could be mentioned. First of all, there was the rule that he alone must preside at a

[25] Ibid., p. 253.
[26] Gregory, B., *Sidelights*, p. 191. See also M.C.A., letter from William Constable to Jabez Bunting, 30th December, 1828. It will be remembered that the Free Methodists had 'Plan Committees' where ministers and laymen made the plan together—quite a different conception of the operation from that held by Bunting.
[27] *Ministry and Polity*, pp. 245–55.

THE RESULTANT POLITY

Quarterly Meeting and if he left the chair, the meeting was thereby dissolved; in other words, he was essential to its constitution. At the same time, it ought to be remembered that this was not a rule which had been introduced under stress of agitation. It had been in the Minutes since 1806.[28] Secondly, arbitrary action of autocratic Superintendents in and after 1849 in withholding Class Tickets from members, Class Books from Leaders and Plans from Preachers, for the only offence of sympathizing with reform or contributing to 'aid for the expelled ministers'. Thirdly, under the rule that no subject could be introduced into a Quarterly Meeting for discussion but such as the Superintendent approved, he alone was judge of what was proper. These things irritated the Reformers and, of course, were made the most of by them.

(d) The Society

Methodist organization at local level was very simple. Individual members were grouped into classes under the direction of Class Leaders.[29] In a large Society, there would be many Classes—sometimes men only, women only, single women only and so on—and at regular intervals (weekly, monthly or quarterly) the Leaders would meet to pay their Class money to the Society Steward and to review the spiritual condition of the Society. Admission to a Society was on a simple confession of a 'desire to be saved from sin' followed by nomination by someone who was already a member. It will be noted that these terms of membership had no ecclesiastical reference and this raised the perennial question (it is still with us today) of the relationship of Society membership by ticket and membership in the Church of Christ by Baptism and Confirmation. To this question, perhaps of more importance to Methodists than to other Free Churches, we must now turn.

[28] *Minutes*, ii. (1806), p. 347.
[29] For Class Leaders and Class Meetings, see Peter D. MacKenzie, 'The Methodist Class Meeting' (thesis for M.Th at St Andrew's University, 1969: copy in M.C.A.). Also article in *Proc. WHS* xxxiv. 12, by the Rev. Henry D. Rack, 'The decline of the Class Meeting and the Problem of Church Membership in Nineteenth-century Wesleyanism'.

Membership of a Society, religious or secular, depends upon the rules, which it is perfectly free to make, especially about the admission and expulsion of members. The problem with Methodism was that tickets could be withheld; Baptism cannot be annulled except by excommunication. As Methodism became increasingly church-conscious this problem became more acute. Traditionally the Wesleyans never regarded Society membership as the equivalent of Church membership, hence their practice of infant baptism. There was a time when their emphasis upon attendance at Class laid them open to the charge that they substituted this for Baptism and the Lord's Supper as the marks of membership in the Church of Christ, but this was emphatically denied in the *London Quarterly Review* for 1873:

> Those who have asserted that Methodism knows no other test or conditions of membership in the Christian Church, or even in the Methodist branch of it, than its Class Meeting, have recklessly asserted what is not true, what indeed has been disavowed again and again (p. 173).

Or, again, as Theophilus Woolmer wrote:

> Meeting in Class is the ground of admission into the Methodist Society, but not into the Christian Church. The admission into that must ever be as God has appointed it, viz: so far as we can understand scripture—externally, by the use of the two Sacraments, Baptism and the Lord's Supper; and spiritually, by faith in Christ. Neither the Conference, nor any other body of Christian men has a right to alter this; and, so far as the Conference is concerned, such an attempt has never been made.[30]

Accordingly, while admission and expulsion of Society members was in the hands of the Superintendent in consultation with the Leaders, according to rules, the selection of candidates for Baptism was the responsibility of the minister alone. Admission to the congregation of Christ's

---

[0] Woolmer, T., *An Answer to some Complaints of a Friend*, p. 19. On this subject, see also my Wesley Historical Society Lecture for 1961, *The Lord's Supper in Methodism 1791-1960*, p. 26ff.

flock does not necessarily imply enrolment in the Methodist Society.

Another aspect of the same problem was the care of people who had been baptized and wished to attend the Lord's Supper, but were not inclined to join a Class. The Wesleyans were constantly having to face up to this. The rule still stood, 'no person shall be suffered on any pretence to partake of the Lord's Supper among us unless he be a member of Society or receive a note of admission',[31] and Conference repeatedly exhorted ministers to enforce it,[32] but a writer in the *London Quarterly* stated what actually happened:

> Never has the position and standing of a baptized person been dishonoured by either the Methodist constitution or its administration. Never has the Sacrament of the Lord's Supper been denied to a single soul because the ticket of membership in the class was not produced.[33]

The same writer attempted to define more clearly 'what constitutes Society membership, in particular whether it should be restricted to those who met in class'. Obviously not, so it had to 'include all godly persons who place themselves under the supervision of the pastorate and are willing to undergo the ordeal and be subject to the discipline that those are under who meet weekly in Class'. They would be members of Society, their names enrolled in books kept by the minister who would be their Class Leader, and they would stand in the same relation to the Leaders Meeting and the Society as the other members. 'Thus, in fact, the Methodist Churches and the Methodist Societies would be virtually and really one.'

This ambiguity between Society and Church membership remains with Methodism to the present day, making nonsense of statistical returns even when such terms as 'adherents', 'members of the community roll' are used to cover the fringe population of our churches. To require no

[31] Simon, J. S., *Methodist Law and Discipline* (1923 ed.), p. 39.
[32] As, for example, in the Report of a Commission on Church Membership —see *Minutes*, 1889, p. 412.
[33] October, 1875, p. 181.

subscription to a creed or confession, but only to profess to pursue 'holiness in heart and life'[34] was, in spite of its vagueness, often cited as the glory of the Methodists. Certainly it made them a 'peculiar people', but as Church-consciousness increased, baptism came also to be required as a basis for membership. Attendance at Holy Communion had, of course, been obligatory upon members from Wesley's first *Rules for the United Societies* (Green 43).

(e) Ecclesiastical Terminology
Methodism developed into a Church without adopting traditional ecclesiastical terminology. It employed none of the recognized terms such as Presbyter, Elder or Deacon; Moderator or Bishop: Presbytery or Synod. This was because it began as a Society, where the terms Preacher, Steward and Leader were correct and adequate; that was how Wesley wanted it and he railed at Jonathan Crowther for introducing Elders and Session into the Methodist Society at Glasgow.[35] The whole body of Societies was a Connexion, not a Church, and it was well after our period that the title Wesleyan Methodist Church came into general currency, and not until 1893 that the word 'Church' superseded 'Society' on the Class Tickets. Naturally, Wesley was unwilling to adopt Church terms to distinguish his office-bearers while the Methodist Societies constituted a kind of religious order with some allegiance (however vague) to the Church of England.[36]

The critics said that, without such offices as Bishops, Priests, Deacons, Moderators or Presbyteries, Methodism could hardly claim to be a Church. The reply was, 'We have the offices without the terminology'. Alfred Barrett was the chief exponent of this position. In a previous chapter we have seen that the office of Bishop in Methodism is fulfilled most nearly in the Circuit Superintendent. Presbyter and Elder will be discussed in a later chapter. The office of Deacon presents a different problem. In his

---
[34] *The Character of a Methodist*—Wesley's *Works*, viii. 340ff.
[35] *Letters*, viii. 136 (May 10th 1789)—a stinging rebuke!
[36] See Barrett, A., *Ministry and Polity*, p. 208.

earlier work, *The Pastoral Office* (p. 128) Barrett ventures the opinion that the Deacon's office in Methodism was filled by the Leaders and the Local Preachers. He came to this conclusion on the ground that 'Deacons were wont to preach'. In his later book, *Ministry and Polity*, he revised this judgement, 'inasmuch as the *original* ordination of deacons was not to the care of souls, but to the serving of tables, and, in economical matters, the serving of the Church'. He further argued that any spiritual ministry pursued by deacons was temporary and incidental.

Again, the distinction between Pastors and Deacons is that the former are 'directly ministers of Christ and responsible to Him', but Deacons are 'directly ministers of the Church and responsible to it'—though ultimately responsible to Christ as every Christian is. The Methodist Church (says Barrett) has 'deacons of its own', i.e. Society Stewards, who receive the contributions of the people, Circuit Stewards, who receive contributions from the Society Stewards, and Poor Stewards, who receive and administer the alms taken at the Lord's Supper. 'These are essentially diaconal duties,' says Barrett, 'only the holder is not ordained for life, but is elected annually.' He regards this as an advantage rather than a defect, as 'it does not aid aristocratical but democratical tendencies in the ordering of Church affairs'. Thus, he concludes, 'the duties of the diaconate are discharged in Wesleyan Methodism upon a scale larger than is known in any communion in Christendom'. In Anglicanism the diaconate is but a *gradus* hastily passing over towards the Presbyterate; in Presbyterianism it is almost unknown, as the real function of Deacons is performed by ruling Elders. His opinion is that the Deacons of the Congregational Churches 'approach the primitive pattern nearer than any other'.[37]

Its Nature

(a) It was not Independency

Wesleyan Methodism was essentially Connexional and,

[37] See also the chapter on Methodism and the Diaconate by Gordon S. Wakefield in *Service in Christ*, pp. 182ff.

as such, was at the opposite pole to Congregational Independency as a system of Church government. Wesleyan apologists believed that Connexionalism in some form or other could be traced back to the early Church, and they quoted New Testament evidence in support. It was therefore no great effort for them to dilate on the advantages of Connexionalism and show that Methodism and Congregational Independency were fundamentally irreconcilable. Methodist comments on Independency reflect a defence (and, not infrequently, a eulogy) of their own system, and criticism was made as follows:

i. Independency is unscriptural. We need not dwell on this; for obviously, if one is satisfied that the New Testament Church was 'Connexional', Independency must be unscriptural.

ii. Independency lacked adequate oversight, and found it difficult, if not impossible, to enforce discipline. Methodists attributed this largely to lack of ministerial authority. Independent ministers are appointed by election of the church on whom they are dependent for what authority they may possess. As every decision of the church is that of a majority of its members, the minister is but the mouthpiece of the people. As J. H. Rigg says:

> He has burden but not power; office without prerogative and responsibility without authority. He is a ruler only in name; in reality he is the hired servant and organ of the people.[38]

iii. In Independency there is 'no healthy circulation flowing from church to church; no common permeating life; no widespread sympathies or far-reaching arms of common enterprise'.[39] Independent churches tend to become isolated and then to stagnate and ultimately decline into antinomianism or Arianism. This had happened to many of the old Independent congregations of the eighteenth and nineteenth centuries.

iv. Independency took power from the minister and gave it to wealthy or dominating laymen. 'The power of the

---

[38] Rigg, J. H., *Church Organisation*, p. 72.
[39] Ibid., p. 24.

THE RESULTANT POLITY

purse and the power of the keys ... coalesced' and the minister became subject to 'the tyranny of the majority'.[40]

v. Independency was ill-adapted to evangelistic or missionary enterprise. Each church, being independent of its fellows, is *ipso facto* unable to embark on new enterprises, for no minister has a right to exercise pastoral functions in any congregation except that which has chosen him to be their minister. We know that, as a matter of history, Congregationalism has sponsored Overseas Missions and has spread from Church to Church; but to do this, it has had to overstep the bounds of strict Independency. Missionary enterprise must therefore be an exception rather than the rule of Independency.

vi. As Independency operates on the principle of 'one congregation, one minister', there is no need for the services of lay preachers. There can be no 'nursery' where candidates for the ministry give evidence of fitness for the work. As each congregation has no organic relation to any other, it can have no compelling interest in any congregation but itself. There is thus little inducement to discover and care for prospective candidates for the ministry.

vii. An important difference between Methodism and Independency was that of Itinerancy *versus* fixed Pastorates. The Congregationalist held that a fixed pastor is better able to exercise personal pastoral oversight than an Itinerant Preacher, that he can get to know his people better. The Wesleyans maintained that this apparent disadvantage is more than compensated for by the frequent interchange of ministers, giving variety, and sparing the congregation from being at the mercy of one man's foibles and emphases.

viii. Methodists held that Independency misunderstood the meaning of the Priesthood of all Believers and obliterated the distinction between minister and layman; that the civil and political principle that 'authority derives from the people' was mistakenly applied to Church government.

ix. Independency had no common authority to which ministers and people can appeal, giving no adequate

[40] Ibid., p. 28.

means of redress to either party. Any aggrieved person or party must be at the mercy of local prejudices.

Before we leave this topic of Independency, two comments ought to be made. The first is that we are not unmindful of the fact that Congregationalism is now largely 'Connexional'. This is evidenced by the recent change from 'Congregational Union' to 'Congregational Church' and now to 'The United Reformed Church'. The need for 'Union' itself demonstrated the growing inadequacy of out-and-out independency. The second comment is that it will be apparent that most of the criticisms levelled against Independency were applicable to the Free Methodists, especially to the Protestant Methodists, the Wesleyan Association and the United Methodist Free Churches. The constitution of the latter was the least Connexional and most Congregational of all the Methodist bodies. William Vevers in his *Defence of the Discipline of Methodism* said that the Protestant Methodist Connexion of 1835 was 'as essentially independent in its character as could have been proposed by any member of an Independent Church' (p. 39).

(b) It was not Presbyterianism

The obvious similarity in organization and ordination which exists between Methodism and Presbyterianism encourages the belief that, apart from particular Methodist terminology such as 'Leader', 'Steward', etc., the two systems are, for all practical purposes identical, and that Methodism could be classed in the Presbyterian tradition. Pronouncements by early Methodist Leaders support this. Samuel Bradburn quoted John Wesley as predicting that Methodism would become a regular Presbyterian Church. His argument was that as Methodists were neither Independents nor Episcopalians, they must be Presbyterians.[41] Charles Wesley, on hearing that his brother had ordained Coke and Asbury for America, remarked, 'What are your poor Methodists now? Only a new sect of Presbyterians'.[42]

[41] Bradburn, S., *Are the Methodists Dissenters?* p. 19.
[42] Tyerman, L., *Life of John Wesley*, iii. 440.

THE RESULTANT POLITY

In a previous chapter we have set out the arguments which were used by those who believed that Wesley favoured a Presbyterian order for Methodism, and we discussed the reasons why his followers after his death built the Connexion on certain Presbyterian lines. In 1839 Alfred Barrett wrote:

> Our general form of ecclesiastical polity is Presbyterian, combined with Episcopacy, *jure humano*. The Established Church of Scotland is not very dissimilar.[43]

Again, a writer in the *London Quarterly Review* for October 1875 (p. 169) says that Methodism is 'of the essence of Presbyterianism':

> ... first, that the Church is governed by the Presbytery; and, secondly, that the government keeps ever in view a systematic representation of the ministerial and lay orders of Christian People; and, thirdly, that representation extends to the combination of Churches in a Connexional form.

It is thus not difficult to draw parallels between Methodism and Presbyterianism—between Leaders Meetings and Kirk Sessions; between the Conference and the General Assembly; between Quarterly Meetings and Presbyteries; between the forms of ordination in both Churches. Yet, in spite of this, to say simply that Methodism was a Presbyterian Church would be a very superficial judgement. There are fundamental differences. The crux of the matter lies in the Wesleyan conception of the Pastoral Office,[44] and this takes us back again to John Wesley.

John Wesley was a Presbyter in the Church of England and the only sense in which he recognized a Presbyter or Elder was as the middle grade in the threefold order of ministers (as seen from his ordinations); but this was not the sense in which it was held in Presbyterianism. Here we may

---

[43] *The Pastoral Office*, pp. 132–3.
[44] See Gregory, B., *Sidelights*, p. 334, spurned any suggestion that 'the Wesleyan Methodist idea of the Christian Pastorate is identical with that of historical Presbyterianism'. Thomas Jackson in *The Wesleyan Vindicator*, 1852, p. 73 said, in a speech to the 1852 Committee, 'We never professed to derive our discipline either from Presbyterianism or Independency'.

refer again to the only attempt made by a Preacher to graft the Presbyterian office of Elder on Methodism, and Wesley responded in no uncertain manner. In 1789, John Pawson, who had decided leanings towards Presbyterianism, ordained seven Elders to regulate the affairs of the Glasgow Society. They were to meet weekly to review the state of affairs, and Pawson compiled a set of rules to which they were to conform. Unfortunately, he gave them too much power. One regulation was that no person should be admitted into the Society or expelled from it except by a majority of the Elders. The Itinerant Preacher may preside at meetings, but he was not allowed to vote.[45] When Wesley heard of the innovation he was furious. To Jonathan Crowther he wrote:

> Sessons! Elders! We Methodists have no such customs... I require you... immediately to disband that session (so called) at Glasgow. Discharge them from meeting any more.... We acknowledge only Preachers, Stewards and Leaders among us, over whom the Assistant in each Circuit presides.[46]

Nothing more was heard of Elders and Sessions in Methodism on either side of the Border!

It is not surprising, therefore, that although Methodism developed her polity along Presbyterian lines, the Presbyterian concept of Elder was never included. 'Assistants' became Circuit Superintendents and Itinerant Preachers in Full Connexion were simply known as ministers. Apart from the fact that the Methodist economy had really no room for Ruling Elders, tradition was heavily against them. Fundamentally, the term and the office was alien to the Methodist concept of the ministry, and to this we must now turn.

In Methodism, the terms 'Elder', 'Presbyter' and 'Minister' denoted the same office. When the Itinerant Preachers came to assume the office of ministers, they

---

[45] Tyerman, L., *Life of John Wesley*, iii. 581. In my book, *The Sacrament of the Lord's Supper in Early Methodism* I have discussed Wesley's dislike of Presbyterian customs; though he had to give way for Scotland.
[46] *Letters*, viii. 136.

THE RESULTANT POLITY

regarded themselves as Presbyters in the New Testament sense of the word. 'Presbyter' and 'Elder' are synonymous, and Wesley ordained his men to that office. So did Dr Coke and his associates. They believed that they were Presbyters, ordained to the Pastoral Office chiefly because they were separated from secular occupations and devoted full-time to the ministry. As we shall see in a later chapter, the Wesleyans regarded separation as one of the essential marks of the ministry. Barrett could 'find in the New Testament no mention of Elders who followed a worldly calling'.[47] Nor did they find in the New Testament a distinction between one class of Elders and another—that is, between Elders who only rule (lay Elders) and Elders who both rule and teach. He argued that, while certain isolated texts may support the idea of Ruling Elders in the Presbyterian sense, the general teaching of the New Testament was against it. He dealt with three passages which were frequently used by Presbyterian apologists, Romans 12:6–8, 1 Corinthians 12:28 and 1 Timothy 5:17.

i. Romans 12:6–8

> Having, then, gifts differing according to the grace that is given to us, whether prophecy, let us prophesy according to the proportion of faith; or ministry, let us wait on our ministering; or he that teacheth on teaching or he that exhorteth, on exhortation; he that giveth, let him do it with simplicity; he that ruleth, with diligence; he that showeth mercy, with cheerfulness.

Presbyterians stress 'he that ruleth'; Barrett contends that St Paul mentions the primary officers of the Church—prophets, ministers and teachers—who have charge of the flock of Christ and after that (as in Ephesians 4:11) certain gifts which were not necessarily the possession of any one class of church officer. Hence, 'he that ruleth' in this context does not denote a separate officer such as a Ruling

---

[47] *Ministry and Polity*, p. 137—unless it could be said that St Paul followed a worldly calling, but Barrett does not appear to class him among the Elders.

Elder, but a certain function (namely, oversight) which belongs to several officers.

ii. *1 Timothy 5:17*

> Let the Elders that rule well be counted worthy of double honour, especially they who labour in the word and doctrine.

Presbyterians (says Barrett) here infer that, as there are among the 'Elders that rule well' some who 'labour in the Word and Doctrine' so there must be some Ruling Elders who do not 'labour in Word and Doctrine'—hence, non-preaching Ruling Elders of the Presbyterian type. Barrett thinks this is a false inference, and produces the following considerations:

(a) In all other passages where the qualifications or functions of Bishops or Elders are mentioned, they both rule and teach—one class exercising both functions. From these, St Paul singles out some who are worthy of double remuneration (τιμῆς). From supporting evidence in Romans 12:8, 1 Thessalonians 5:12 and 1 Timothy 3:4, 5, 12, he argues that the word προεστῶτες has a wider significance than simply 'ruling'. It denotes general oversight. He quotes Dr Smith of the Westminster Assembly and Clement of Alexandria in support of the version, 'Those that execute the duties of their twofold office well'. The point is that the office includes both ruling and teaching.

(b) The word rendered 'honour' (τιμῆς) means 'pecuniary acknowledgement' or 'remuneration', which supports the theory that the Elders here referred to were full-time preachers. The whole tenor of New Testament teaching in general, and of St Paul's reference to Deuteronomy 35:4 and 1 Corinthians 9:14 in particular, is that they who preach the Gospel are to live of the Gospel. In other words, the office of non-preaching Elders finds no support in this text.

(c) Therefore, the distinction, thought by some Presbyterians to be implied in this text, between Ruling and Preaching Elders, is a false inference. Here we have (says Barrett) 'not a distinction between different offices, but

THE RESULTANT POLITY

between officers of the same description', and the office of Elder includes both preaching and ruling. It could be noted that J. H. Bernard, commenting on 1 Timothy 5:17 in *The Cambridge Greek Testament* says, 'There is no distinction between two classes of Presbyters, some who rule and some who do not rule . . .'.

Barrett then examines the word 'especially' (μάλιστα). He says it 'could never be made to bear the sense which the theory of Ruling Elder requires'—in other words, it indicates not a distinct class, but 'a selected portion of the same class distinguished by a specified particularity'. He is referring to his contemporary authorities, Wardlaw and Davidson. He also deals with arguments for Ruling Elders advanced by Dr King of Glasgow and Dr M'Kerrow, but they need not detain us here. Barrett's main point is that προεστῶτες must be taken in the full sense of 'those exercising pastoral care', and this involves both government and instruction.

Barrett regards Calvin's appointment of 'seniors, grave and approved men, appointed for the correction of manners and administration of discipline' as a 'novelty and an invention'. That some Presbyters in the early Church possessed a gift for ruling rather than for teaching, and that Bishops and ordinary Presbyters would take counsel with civil rulers before they administered discipline in certain cases is not denied, but:

> that a distinct class of Elders was created solely to rule and administer discipline, and for that purpose set apart in common with Pastors properly so called, and with them likewise sustained by the Church—this we entirely deny, as being a scheme having no evidence in its favour either from scripture or antiquity.

In all this, of course, Barrett is building up a defence of the Methodist conception of the Pastoral Office. This meant Presbyter in the sense of full-time Preacher, Pastor and Ruler, and that he to whom is committed the oversight of men and Societies must also be given authority. Furthermore, this authority is not to be shared with non-pastors.

Barrett does not like the Presbyterian system, where Elders have joint rule with Pastors. It is true that Elders are ordained, but as they are not set apart to the full-time ministry, Barrett will not regard them as ministers; they are still laymen.[48]

True to the high Wesleyan doctrine of the Pastoral Office Barrett will not have non-pastors associate with pastors in disciplinary cases involving the ministry. To mingle pastors with 'non-preaching or non-clerical persons' is wrong, for the latter 'are set to administer pastoral acts without *the Pastoral heart*'. A Presbyterian, of course, would reply that Eldership in his church is a pastoral office, as it involves regular visitation of the people in their homes and also the exercise of discipline. Be that as it may, Barrett thinks that the blending of 'spiritual authority with powerful lay oligarchy' inevitably leads to secularization (as in Lutheranism) or persecution (as with prelacy or unopposed Presbyterianism—e.g. in the New World). Barrett concludes:

> Taking all considerations together, it has been proved that the ministers of the New Testament are of one class and order; that is, so far as to exclude a prelatical authority or transmitted apostleship on the one hand, and the intervention of non-teaching rulers on the other. . . .
>
> In harmony with this conclusion, the founder of Methodism ever acted in all his disciplinary arrangements; and the Conference, in like manner, since his day. It has never recognized two classes of Elders.

To Methodists, the 'Lay Elder' was a contradiction of terms. One writer described it as 'a dexterous method of compromise by which the Church commits all its ample prerogatives to its ministry and yet will have its own lay presence conjoined with them'.[49] The same writer continues confidently, 'but there is no sanction for this in the

---

[48] Barrett will not allow the analogy between the Jewish system of rule by 'Priests and elders of the people' and the Presbyterian system. He maintains that it is one of the distinctions between Judaism and Christianity and a practice 'which we are forbidden to adopt'.

[49] *London Quarterly Review*, October 1875, pp. 170–1.

THE RESULTANT POLITY

New Testament'. It could well be argued that if Bishop and Presbyter/Elder are one office (as is generally conceded from New Testament evidence) then with equal propriety one could style a Ruling Elder a 'Lay Bishop'. On the other hand, if one regards a Presbyterian minister as a Presbyter/Elder, one relegates the Ruling Elder to the status of Deacon. Given John Knox's Superintendents, this would be possible.[50]

There was a tendency with some writers to draw a parallel between Methodist Class Leaders and Presbyterian Elders, and in so far as both are responsible for the periodical distribution of tickets there is a certain similarity of function. Beyond that, however, the similarity ceases and there are essential differences. To begin with, there is a difference in the relationship in which they stand to the church. The Ruling Elder is ordained to an office which is related not merely to the local church of which he is a member. He is a Presbyter (Elder) of the whole church, ordained for life, a co-pastor with the minister. The Methodist Class Leader is a Society officer only, related only to his own Class. He does not hold office for life, nor is he ordained. He is a member of the Leaders Meeting and so is in a position to advise and, if need be, to restrain the minister, but he is not a co-pastor. In view of the spiritual oversight exercised by a Class Leader over the members of his Class, this may seem to be a strange statement to make; nevertheless, for Wesleyan Methodism it was true. Co-presbyters exist in Methodism only within the colleagueship of ministers in a circuit, and the distinction between ministers and Elders in a Presbyterian Church is different from that which exists between a Wesleyan Superintendent and his colleagues.

Again, between the Methodist Leaders Meeting and the Presbyterian Kirk Session there is only a superficial likeness; in fact, the differences we have just noticed between

---

[50] Many Presbyterians regard the minister as the 'episcopos', and the Ruling Elder as the 'presbyter'. The relationship of Methodism to Presbyterianism was discussed at the Conference of 1842—see Gregory, B., *Sidelights*, pp. 333–4.

Elders and Class Leaders is reflected in the real difference which exists between the courts of the two Churches. The Presbyterian Kirk Sessions, the Synods and General Assembly consist entirely of ordained office-bearers of the Church—the ministers and Elders, that is the 'teaching' and 'ruling' Presbyters. This means that lay representation, as such, is absent; i.e. in the sense of elected representatives of the rank and file of the members. Calvin believed that the power of the keys rested in the 'whole church'; therefore, in Presbyterianism the people are represented by the Elders; but the Wesleyans denied that Elders truly represented the people. In modern Methodism especially, the laity have definite rights and duties as representatives of the people and they themselves are of the people. On the other hand, Methodism assembles its pastors alone to deal with pastoral matters. Presbyterianism knows nothing similar to the 'corporate pastorate' of the Methodist Conference, expressed and nourished by what is perhaps the most distinctive feature of all, the Itinerancy. We shall consider Itinerancy, its merits and demerits in a later section, so it is sufficient to note here that Methodist Itinerancy, unlike the more lengthy Presbyterian charges, requires a particular form of 'stationing'. In our period, it was unthinkable that the stationing of ministers should be done by a mixed committee. Until Methodist Union (1932) the Stationing Committee in Wesleyan Methodism was an all-ministerial body. J. H. Rigg argued that any arrangement in which the stationing of ministers was shared by laymen who were responsible for their maintenance was wrong. He said it was an arrangement which 'could not but lower the character and status of the minister'; that it was a 'degrading arrangement, quite incompatible with pastoral independence, pastoral fidelity or efficiency'.[51]

Underlying this is a fundamental difference in origin, reflecting itself in organization and in the concept of church and conditions of membership. Basically, Presbyterianism had its origin in controversy, and the claims of ecclesiastic

---

[51] *Church Organisation*, p. 240. After Methodist Union, the Stationing Committee included a lay representative from each District.

and secular politics shaped its structure. Methodism, on the other hand, sprang up as a revival of personal religion. Furthermore, Presbyterianism has no meetings for fellowship *as part of its official structure*. We are not saying that it has no meetings for Christian fellowship, but only that such meetings are not an integral part of its economy. The Class Meeting, however, was the very *fons et origo* of Methodism. W. B. Pope, one of the few outstanding theologians of Methodism, expressed this in his book *The Peculiarities of Methodist Doctrine* (1873). He said that while meetings for mutual confession, edification and counsel are found in all Churches of Christendom, 'we are the only community that has incorporated them in the very fibre of our constitution' (p. 18). The Class Meeting was not an incidental activity, meeting on church premises, but the primary cell of the constitution. Allied to this is the fact that membership in Presbyterianism is associated with a confession of Faith linked with a reputable character. The kirk is a community of such people who choose their minister by a formal election.

In Presbyterianism, 'Connexionalism' is maintained by the contacts which one Presbytery has with another—especially in the supervision of ministerial appointments—and also in the General Assembly. In this respect there is a kinship with Methodism. Perhaps it could be said that Connexionalism was maintained in Presbyterianism with its fixed pastorates by statute law but in Methodism by voluntary arrangement. Rigg thought that the Free Church of Scotland was more thoroughly Connexional and even came near to adopting the Itinerant system—that was in 1851.[52] In any case, in Methodism and Presbyterianism alike, no Church is independent.

There is, however, a difference in the basis of membership. Membership in Methodism involves no confession of faith, but only (to use Wesley's phrase) 'a desire to be saved from your sins and to flee from the wrath to come'. A company of such people assembled in Bands, Classes and Societies; the Societies were grouped into Circuits, and

[52] *Op. cit.*, pp. 50–1.

over all was the Conference. Thus the Methodist Connexion was composed of those who (to use another of Wesley's phrases) 'watch over one another in love'.[53] We shall consider this more fully when we discuss the Methodist concept of the Church; we quote it here simply to emphasize the distinctive marks of Methodism as compared with Presbyterianism and, incidentally, to show that Wesley's prophecy, that after his death Methodism would become a regular Presbyterian Church, was not fulfilled.

Finally, there was a difference in emphasis, especially in the concept of a minister's calling and duties. The Presbyterians laid much greater stress on teaching and very little, if any, on calling people from sin to salvation; that is, conversion.[54] Both churches lay great stress on preaching and have equally produced great preachers; but, traditionally, the Methodist Preacher was expected to regard the end of his preaching as the conversion of sinners. However much he took upon himself the Pastoral Office, he was still fundamentally an evangelist. The Methodists of our period (1791–1850) would read the liturgy in the morning, but the Sunday evening service seldom ended without an 'appeal for decisions'. Perhaps it could be summed up (allowing for the inadequacies of all summaries) by saying that Presbyterians emphasized the intellectual aspects of the Faith, Methodists the experiential.

(c) Wesleyan Connexionalism

'The word "Connexion"', says Charles Welch in his book on Wesleyan Polity, 'very aptly and felicitously designates the essential and intrinsic character of the Wesleyan body' (p. 59). Yet 'Connexion' is a term unknown to, and not easy to describe to a non-Methodist. Presbyterians and Anglicans have this 'Connexionalism' but not the word. In origin, it goes back to the Religious Societies which came within the law if they met 'in connexion with' a

[53] *Advice to the People Called Methodists—Works*, viii. 353.
[54] Calvin was very reticent about his own conversion, and in his letter to Sadoleto he said that people should be concerned about God's glory and not about whether they are personally saved—see *The Scottish Journal of Theology*, 1963, p. 381—an article by G. S. M. Walker.

clergyman of the Church of England. So, the early Methodists met 'in connexion with the Rev. Mr John Wesley'.[55] While he lived, the Methodists were still officially 'in connexion' with him, and after his death the word persisted and Methodism continued to be referred to as a 'Connexion'. When the Kilhamites broke away from the parent body, they styled themselves 'The Methodist New Connexion'. A working definition of the word is, 'A number of Societies who have agreed to unite themselves in a common bond of doctrine and discipline, under a common code of regulations and usages and under a common government'.[56]

Methodist Societies were never isolated, never independent of each other. Even where there was an 'enlightened' incumbent at the Parish Church,[57] Wesley would not detach the Methodist Society from the Connexion, for he knew that, independent of its fellows, it had no assured future, especially if the next incumbent was unsympathetic. Wesley's general supervision, together with the Annual Conference, gave a unity to the movement from the start. One often discusses the question of the separation of Methodism from the Church of England, but apart from the fact that it was never really within the Establishment, it was this conscious unity, the fact of acting in concert with each other,[58] the common organization, discipline and doctrine that not only made it a distinct and homogeneous body from the start, but more than any other single factor, gave it an independence from the Anglican Church.

Methodist Connexionalism was, therefore, a real unity. It was not mere federation, but co-ordinated effort and concerted action;[59] but what commended it most to

[55] Reginald Kissack, in his book *Church or no Church?* is wrong when he says that Methodism was originally called Connexional because each Society had some connexion with all others. This was, of course, true, but it is not the correct derivation of the word.
[56] *The Methodist Magazine*, 1835, p. 533.
[57] See Wesley's letter to the Rev. Mr Walker of Truro, 24th September, 1755. *Letters*, iii. 144.
[58] *Minutes*, i. 87 (1769).
[59] As, for example, in the opposition to Lord Sidmouth's Bill on the one hand, and in grand-scale missionary activity on the other.

Wesleyans was that, as they saw it, it was scriptural. Dr George Smith, for example,[60] shows that in Acts 15 the Apostle Paul acts in conjunction with James and John, and their decisions are binding on the whole church. Therefore, concludes Smith, 'the Christianity of the Apostolic Age, like Wesleyan Methodism, was a great Connexion'. He further believed that in New Testament days evangelists like Timothy and Titus were commissioned by and for the whole church, not for individual Societies. Financial arrangements, too, so far as the New Testament sheds light on these matters, were Connexional.

Alfred Barrett devotes the whole of Chapter VIII of *The Ministry and Polity of the Christian Church* to 'The Connexional Principle'. He includes the Old Testament in his discussion, for he believes that, from the Hebrew tribes to the Jewish Synagogue, there was a national unity. Independent local shrines were unknown. The early Christian communities could not have existed as isolated units. Discipline was uniform throughout. Barrett will not go so far as to say that the primitive churches 'so early as the Apostles' day actually existed in established connexions', but that 'under the sanction of the Apostles... the initial principle of church connexion involving central administration was affirmed'. He even thinks that there was something akin to the circuit system in the organization of the early church; beginning with the mother church at Jerusalem, many a city church consisted of a 'plurality of societies, yet merging itself into one assembly on occasion of great and common interest'.

Generally, these points are made in reply to the claims of Independency; as, for example, when J. H. Rigg wrote his book, *Congregational Independency and Wesleyan Connexionalism*, in which he develops the thesis that 'Connexionalism, not Independency, was the condition of the Apostolic churches'. So the Wesleyans found great satisfaction in drawing parallels between the ecclesiastical polity of the early church and their own.

Wesleyan Connexionalism was built upon three

[60] *The Polity of Wesleyan Methodism*, pp. 60-4.

THE RESULTANT POLITY

principles—episcopé, itinerancy and mutual help. Episcopé, in the sense of Watchfulness or oversight, was built into Methodism from the earliest days. Members were responsible to Class Leaders, Class Leaders to Ministers, and Ministers to the Conference. John Lawson, in the *History of the Methodist Church in Great Britain* (volume 1, page 206) has said that early Methodist Connexionalism 'was an admirable expression of the traditional Catholic quality of episcopé. . . .'

The second principle of Wesleyan Connexionalism was Itinerancy. The frequent movement of ministers in Methodism goes back to Wesley, the greatest itinerant of them all. He once said, 'were I to preach one whole year in one place, I should preach both myself and most of my congregation asleep'.[61] In his day, his preachers stayed no longer than a year in one place, but after his death a three-year limit was fixed, and that remained the custom in Wesleyan Methodism until 1932. While the Itinerant system welded the Connexion into a unity it had its disadvantages. On the credit side, it could be said that 'every Society is provided with a ministry of various gifts and talents, and its members are prevented from saying, at least for long together, "I am of Paul, and I of Apollos and I of Cephas . . .".'[62] So long as the primary mission of the church, and the basic function of a minister, was thought of in terms of evangelism pure and simple, Itinerancy presented no problems; but when there came a need for the shepherding and teaching of the souls thus won, the minister had to be pastor and teacher as well as evangelist; the original system of Itinerancy called for modification, for the Itinerant struck no roots in the community in which he lived. He was a bird of passage. Yet this was how it was meant to be. James Dixon believed that Wesley never intended his preachers to 'have the temptation of settling down in a limited sphere . . . gain for themselves mere local influence and respect or surround their ministry by attached admirers'. They were to exercise their

---

[61] Letter dated 3rd September, 1756 to Samuel Walker of Truro, *Letters*, iii. 195.
[62] Barrett, A., *The Pastoral Office*, p. 122.

ministry 'without the adventitious aids of residence, personal influence....'[63] Yet Barrett had to admit that the Itinerant system involved considerable hardship to ministers and their families, only piously hoping that 'those trials (would) be means of bringing them all nearer to God'! Through time, however, the limitations of the system became increasingly obvious and (less obvious) painful and frustrating. By the end of the nineteenth century, the Forward Movement, with its Central Halls, created the need for long-term ministries. Today the average stay of a Methodist minister is five to seven years.

Officially, the Wesleyans defended the Itinerant system on the grounds that ministers were 'the guardians of Connexional interests and rights and expounders and administrators of Connexional law', therefore, 'to secure their vigilance and impartiality ... (they must) be kept loose from all local interests and attachments'.[64] This might be a good thing, but it meant that the minister was almost powerless to exert effective local leadership—in contrast with the parish priest on the one hand and his Class Leaders and Trustees on the other. One of the factors which facilitated the spread of disaffection (as in the Leeds Organ Case) was the lack of ministerial oversight; but, what is more significant is that the ministers, almost to a man, were Connexional rather than local in their sympathies. William Longbottom, a prominent minister in the Methodist New Connexion, writing in the *Methodist Quarterly* for December 1871, remarked that while the relation of a minister to a circuit is temporary, his relation to the Conference is to last for a lifetime, 'let the conflict between Conference and people come, there can be little doubt on which side his influence will be ranged'.[65] There was much truth in this. In all the upheavals in Wesleyan Methodism, very few ministers seceded.

The Wesleyans also ruled that the Leaders and Stewards

---

[63] Dixon, J., *Methodism, Its Origin*, etc., p. 162. See, also, Henry Moore's *Life of John Wesley*, ii. 60.
[64] Rigg, J. H., *op. cit.*, p. 50.
[65] p. 13.

be changed every year, or every other year; thus (it was hoped) to prevent the build-up of power in individuals or groups. But it did not work out quite that way. What was designed to operate in theory was not achieved in practice. Trustees did not change or resign, and it was with them that local power often lay. So the Itinerant system may have brought variety to the pulpit and cement to the connexional structure, but not without disadvantages.

The third factor in Wesleyan Connexionalism was mutual help. From the beginning, Methodism pooled its resources, the strong helping the weak through Connexional Funds. The Yearly Collection, begun in 1749, was taken privately in the Classes and used to liquidate chapel debts. The July Collection, begun in 1815, was taken publicly in chapels and used for Home Missionary work. Together, these two formed a Contingent Fund. The Yearly Collection was later supplemented by the Chapel Fund (1818) and to all these we must add the School Fund for Kingswood and the Auxiliary Fund (1797) for the relief of aged Preachers and their widows.

It is impossible to exaggerate the effect of Connexional finances in binding the Methodist body together, especially when affluent laymen, most of whom were trustees of valuable property, took these finances in hand. The buildings themselves were Connexional property, so the trustees were really Connexional officers, the guardians of Connexional rights in a way which did not apply to Leaders and Stewards who were local officers.[66] Societies had very little local finance apart from what was needed to maintain their chapels and pay the stewards for ministerial allowances.

Three other factors ought to be mentioned about Connexionalism. It was able to enforce discipline, to maintain sound doctrine and to facilitate expansion—and herein lay its strength. It was able to enforce discipline. At times it did so with an iron gauntlet when a kid glove might have

---

[66] This was probably another reason why the trustees were on the Connexional side of the fence and the leaders with the Dissentients in the Leeds Organ Case.

achieved happier results; but at least it did endeavour to ensure that discipline was exercised evenly and impartially in every Society, to ministers and laymen alike, free from local prejudices. At the time of the Leeds Organ crisis, Richard Watson remarked that to hand over the administration of discipline to local courts would be to 'reject... the advantages of belonging to a Connexion'.[67] William Vevers said it would be the same as if one wished 'to abolish the right of appeal to the Court of the King's bench and confine the right of appeal exclusively to the Quarter Sessions'.[68]

Connexionalism also helped to maintain unity of doctrine. Wesleyan ministers were one as preachers of a common doctrine. Year by year the question was put to every minister in Full Connexion, 'Does he preach our doctrines and observe our discipline?'. The chapel deeds make it binding on every minister appointed by Conference to the circuit to preach the doctrines of evangelical Arminianism, 'a system of scriptural interpretation which acknowledges all our salvation to be of God's grace, and yet preserves the moral agency of man'[69] as expounded in the *Sermons* and *Notes on the New Testament* of John Wesley. Should a minister violate these doctrines, he was liable to suspension or expulsion. 'Wesleyan Methodism', says Alfred Barrett, 'appeals to one standard, and thus secures to its largely-extended societies of people the same lessons of Christian truth.'[70]

Finally, Connexionalism facilitated expansion at home and overseas. It moved as a single body, with all the resources of that body behind it. Independent ministers, tied to single congregations with access to no resources other than local ones, could not break new ground, either at home or abroad, as a nation-wide and worldwide Connexion like Methodism could and did.

This 'Connexionalism' was, and still is, the strength and

[67] Watson, R., *An Affectionate Address*, p. 20.
[68] Vevers, W., *A Defence of the Discipline of Methodism*, p. 40.
[69] Barrett, A., *The Pastoral Office*, p. 124.
[70] Barrett, A., *Ministry and Polity*, p. 125.

THE RESULTANT POLITY

one of the great characteristics of Methodism as a church; in fact Dr Frank Baker claims that it is 'one of the greatest contributions made by Wesley to ecclesiastical polity'[71] high praise indeed, and from one who is qualified to speak.

---

[71] *History of the Methodist Church in Great Britain*, p. 230.

CHAPTER TWO

THE PASTORAL OFFICE

'THE Pastoral Office', says Professor W. R. Ward, 'is an interesting problem in the transmission of ideas; more particularly in the respective roles of ideas and events in shaping institutions'.[1] So now we pass from the institution to the idea which shaped it; from Wesleyan polity to the Wesleyan doctrine of the Pastoral Office, without reference to which the history of nineteenth-century Methodism cannot be written. It was the immediate, though not the root cause of the Leeds Organ Case in 1828; Dr Warren's clash with the authority of the Pastorate in 1834 led to the disputes which centred round his name; the expulsions of 1849–52 were the last displays of power based on the same foundation, the Pastoral Office.

We are dealing with something which, in a sense, was uniquely Wesleyan, for it was neither Anglican nor Dissenting. Yet its antecedents lay in the Anglicanism to which Wesleyanism was the heir. The Anglican conception of the powers and duties of a parish priest flowed into Methodism via the Wesley brothers, so we must begin with John Wesley's conception of the ministry.[2]

Wesley's Conception of the Ministry

'What is the office of a minister?' This question was asked at the first Methodist Conference (1744) and the answer given was, 'To watch over the souls whom God commits to his charge, as he that must give account'. This is worth double under-lining as it is basic to any study of the ministry

---

[1] Chapter xvii entitled, 'The Legacy of John Wesley: The Pastoral Office in Britain and America'; in *Statesmen, Scholars and Merchants*, Lucy Sutherland's Festschrift, O.U.P., 1973.

[2] On Wesley's view of the ministry, see: Lawson, A., *John Wesley and the Christian Ministry* (1963), Kissack, R., *Church or no Church?* (1964), Kent, J., *The Age of Disunity* (1966), and Rack H., *The Future of John Wesley's Methodism* (1966).

in Methodism. It underlies the discipline which Wesley imposed upon his Assistants. It is the basis of that 'watchfulness' or episcopé which can be traced at every level of organization, from the custody of local finance to the general oversight of the Conference. It is the foundation of the doctrine of the Pastoral Office.

By 'minister', of course, Wesley was referring to a clergyman of the Church of England, for only ordained clergymen were originally present at this Conference.[3] Wesley's Assistants and Helpers (not synonymous terms) were as yet few, but their duties were defined as 'in the absence of the minister, to feed and guide, to teach and govern the flock'.[4] So, at the very outset of our study, we meet the terms which are destined to play such a large part in it, namely, 'feed', 'guide', 'teach' and 'govern'.

Wesley himself believed that, as a minister in the church of Christ, God had committed certain souls to his charge, and that for them he was accountable. This imposed a responsibility and bestowed an authority. In Wesley's case, however, there was a dual origin of both responsibility and power. First of all, he held them as an Anglican priest, and this fact underlies all his thought. He never outlived his Anglican heritage. A son of Samuel Wesley of Epworth could have no illusions about the seriousness of the ministerial calling. The old rector may have been a third-rate poet in everyone's estimation but his own, and as a farmer he was a pitiful failure, but no one can gainsay that he was a diligent pastor, dedicated to the 'cure of souls' and quite fearless in the administration of discipline.[5] John was a true son of his father when he repelled his sweetheart from Holy Communion at Savannah, regardless of the fact that she was the Governor's niece. It ended his mission to Georgia and he fled with a price on his head; but it was all part and parcel of his duties as he conceived them within the context of the Anglican conception of the Pastoral Office. Wesley

[3] *Minutes*, i. 1. The laymen, Thomas Richards, Thomas Maxfield, John Bennet and John Downes were later brought in—*Minutes*, i. 22.

[4] *Minutes*, i. 23.

[5] See his *Advice to a Young Clergyman*, reprinted in Jackson's *Life of Charles Wesley*, ii. 500ff.

displayed it in its most rigorous aspects, and much of it was assimilated by the Methodist Preachers.

Wesley had, however, another claim to power. He was the head of the 'people called Methodists', the leader of thousands who had *voluntarily* placed themselves under his care. This relationship was more precise and intimate than that which existed between the curé and his flock. With the curé, the parishioners were, willy-nilly, his flock; but Wesley's people were his of their own free will. Submission to his direction was undisputed,[6] but it is not surprising that, as the movement grew and Wesley aged, it was less and less taken for granted, and the way in which Wesley replied to his critics gives an indication of how he regarded his power.

> It is a power of admitting into and excluding from the Societies under my care; of choosing and removing Stewards; of receiving or not receiving Helpers; of appointing them when, where, and how to help me; and of desiring any of them to meet me when I see good.[7]

Here are all the seeds from which the Wesleyan doctrine of the Pastoral Office was to grow. Other points which Wesley made were that his power was given by God, unsought and unsharable, and that submission to it was entirely voluntary.

Further light on Wesley's views can be gleaned from his sermon 'On Obedience to Pastors'.[8] He begins by admitting that this is a subject with which but few Christians are familiar. Generally, the Christian Church has leant too much to the right or to the left. On the right are the Romanists (and, says Wesley, several eminent Anglicans) who demand implicit obedience. On the other hand, 'the generality of Protestants are apt to run to the other extreme, allowing their Pastors no authority at all, making them both the creatures and the servants of their congregations'. He believed that there were some in the Church of England

---

[6] See his words to his Assistants, 'sons in the Gospel'—*Minutes*, i. 24–25. Note also the way in which he drastically pruned the Newcastle upon Tyne Society in March, 1743, *Journal*, iii. 70.
[7] *Minutes*, i. 61–62 (1766).
[8] *Works*, vii. 108ff.

who supposed that Pastors are wholly dependent upon the people and that, therefore, the people 'have a right to direct, as well as to choose their minister'. Wesley, however, will follow neither the Romanists nor the extreme Protestants. He endeavours to find a middle way. 'Them that rule over you', he interprets as 'those who guide you . . . if not by your choice, at least by your consent'. His position is that, once a person has found a pastor who will feed him, he should submit to him in all things, save those which offend conscience or are contrary to what is prescribed in scripture.

Wesley exercised his unique authority until his death. Even when Conference had been given a legal constitution (1784) Wesley lost none of his authority; he was still the *episcopos*, the supreme *pastor pastorum*. It was after his death, when his powers had to be transferred to his Preachers, that tensions, hitherto repressed rather than absent, revealed themselves. Wesley's Itinerants were essentially Preachers, yet from the beginning they were more than Preachers; they were Pastors with all that the Pastoral Office meant. Under Wesley's general supervision, the admission and expulsion of members was in their hands. They were not elected by or subservient to local laymen. They were accountable to Wesley while he lived and to Conference after he died.

Wesley never intended his Itinerants to replace the regular clergy (how could they?). They were to be 'extraordinary messengers designed to provoke the regular ministers to jealousy and to supply their lack of service towards those who are perishing for want of knowledge'.[9] It is a matter of history that the regular clergy were not thus provoked, though they were provoked in other ways, and to those 'extra-ordinary messengers' there fell the pastoral work of visiting members and supervising Classes as they 'went their rounds'.

---

[9] Wesley would never allow his Preachers to be classed as ministers—see *Minutes*, i. 602. Yet he guessed that many would have ambitions in that direction. 'Who does not wish to be a little higher? Suppose to be ordained?'—*Minutes*, i. 493. (1789).

In this way, a conception of the Pastoral Office was taking shape in their minds; they came to know something of its responsibilities and powers. We have seen something of the turmoil through which Wesleyan Methodism passed as the Preachers sought more and more to be regarded as ministers, fulfilling the ministerial office of administering the sacraments. But the extent to which they were already Pastors, and had been since the early days of the movement is not always realized. What took place after 1791 was not so much the assumption of a new role as the development of what they had been doing from the beginning. The process in the nineteenth century was an exposition of the principles on which that function rested. The extra-ordinary messenger became, within his own denomination as much a regular minister as the clergyman of the Parish Church or the Pastor of a Dissenting congregation.

After Wesley

The development of the Wesleyan doctrine of the Pastoral Office after the death of John Wesley was essentially a growing awareness of status. Eventually this was defined in response to the challenge of those who held other views, chiefly the Free Methodists. In some respects, the process was yet another example of Methodist pragmatism. A doctrine which was implicit in Wesley's system was formulated as circumstances demanded. This is not to say that there was anything artificial about the doctrine, or that it was devised to defend an otherwise intolerable situation. Had it not been challenged, it would have continued as an accepted but more or less undefined tradition;[10] but, being challenged, some sort of formulation became necessary. Professor W. R. Ward in *Religion and Society in England 1790–1850*, p. 104, suggests the contrary. His view is that 'what took place was not so much the definition of a deposit

[10] Jonathan Crowther, for example, writing in 1796 says, 'The minister that does not assert and maintain the authority with which he is officially invested by God Himself is unfaithful to Him who put him in authority'— *Christian Order or Liberty without Anarchy*, p. 3.

from John Wesley as of the new pastoral functions which the Preachers were performing as they moved from the old-style itinerancy. . . .' On the other hand, the Rev. J. Munsey Turner, reviewing Dr Ward's recent books in *The Proceedings of the Wesley Historical Society* xxxix. 51, says, 'a case can be made out for a pre-dating of the high Wesleyan view of the ministry'—i.e. earlier than Dr Ward would allow. So we adhere to our position that, in spite of the lack of literary references from 1791–1820, the Pastoral Office had its roots in what Wesley thought a minister ought to be and in the responsibilities and powers he gave to his assistants. It was not without discernment that Dr John Kent has called Jabez Bunting 'The Last Wesleyan'—the title of his Wesley Historical Society's Lecture for 1955. On the other hand, Dr Robert Currie, who is no admirer of Bunting, admits that 'Buntingism was little more than a development of Wesley's own autocracy, an autocracy essential to his system' (*Methodism Divided*, p. 76, see also pp. 31–43).

After the death of Wesley, the claims of the Itinerant Preachers to exercise the office of a Christian minister was challenged from two entirely opposite positions. In the first place, the 'Old Planners' who wished Methodism to remain a federation of Societies within the Church of England, opposed the ministerial idea altogether. Preachers were to remain Preachers only, with pastoral duties amounting to little more than general oversight of the Societies. This was an intolerable position, acceptable to neither Preachers nor people. On the other hand, the Kilhamites would have made Methodism quite independent of the Church of England. The Preachers would have been pastors but with only such authority as could be shared with the laity. The Plan of Pacification (1795) was a compromise with the trustees and as such did not altogether satisfy the Kilhamites, who left the old body in 1797 to form the Methodist New Connexion. When the next disturbance rippled the surface, a new star was rising in the Wesleyan firmament. This was Jabez Bunting, whose thinking was clearly behind the *Statement of Facts* (1806)—the clearest exposition to date of the Pastoral Office—and the 'Liverpool Minutes' of 1820. It was not until the Leeds Organ affair of 1828 that it became necessary to state the case more openly and in Richard Watson there was a first-rate theologian to do it. His *Affectionate Address* contained thoughts which were later expounded more authoritatively in his *Theological Institutes*.

Throughout the period 1791–1828, there is little in the way of the formulation of a doctrine of the ministry. Methodism was in search of a doctrine. There were no clear precedents which exactly fitted their situation, and what they were aiming at (at least for some years after Wesley's death) was very indeterminate. The Preachers could not adopt the Anglican form *simpliciter*, for not only did they lack episcopal ordination, but they had thrown overboard Wesley's system of superintendent/presbyter/deacon without giving it a trial. They greatly hesitated on whether to wear gown and bands and in the end decided against it.[11] On the other hand, the Dissenters' conception of the ministry was alien to all they had learned from Wesley, as well as ill-fitted to the Connexional system. Dissenting ministers were too much at the mercy of their congregations. Therefore, with neither Anglican nor Dissenting forms to guide them, it is not surprising that it took nearly forty years for them to hammer out a doctrine of the ministry; but what did emerge, namely, 'The Pastoral Office' was the offspring of both heredity and circumstances.

In the meantime, a variety of ideas floated in the air, but apart from the Manchester *Statement* of 1806, conspicuous by its absence is the authoritarian conception which began to be officially formulated around 1828 and was so confidently proclaimed thereafter. One would have expected to find, in the period between, say, 1791 and 1820 in some form or other the ideas which Watson, Beecham and Bunting developed in and after 1828. We know that, in

[11] Bradburn and Roberts wore gowns and bands for the opening of Portland Chapel, Bristol in 1792 but objections were raised and in 1793 all clerical attire was banned by the Conference—see, Blanchard, T. W., *The Life of Samuel Bradburn*, pp. 146f; also the Embury Edwards correspondence; and *Minutes*, i. 290 (1793).

THE PASTORAL OFFICE

practice, the essentials of the Pastoral Office were there—and had been since Wesley's time. For one thing the distinction between pastor and non-pastor had been maintained but not expounded fiercely or authoritatively. Again, the *Form of Discipline* preserved the authority which Wesley gave to his Assistants in admitting and expelling members. But it would appear to us that the working of the system was much more liberal than the later apologists were prepared to admit. In the literature of this period there is no belittling of the ministerial office, but a much more tender note is struck than we get in the later writers. Perhaps this is because the latter were defending positions which were at the time under severe attack. Be that as it may, let us look at one or two of the commentaries of the pre-Beecham/Watson/Barrett period and note how they treat texts bearing on the nature of the ministry.

Matthew 20:25, 26 is used by Adam Clarke to enforce discipline in the Christian ministry. Acts 15, as interpreted by Benson, almost lends support to the 'whole church' idea so beloved of the Free Methodists. Dr Coke has much to say about the office of Presbyter but nothing of its power. Respect is due to Christian ministers[12] whose duty is to feed the flock.[13] The strongest reference to the authority of Pastors is that in Coke's note on Hebrews 13:17,

> Where Pastors, in all respects, behave themselves as Christians; where they are qualified with sufficient gifts, and faithfully perform all the duties of their pastoral office; where they do not lord it over God's heritage, but are examples of all holiness and virtue to the flock, and heartily labour to promote the salvation of their people ... the people are bound to obey them, i.e. to hearken to their good advice, to submit to their just reproofs, as to men who, like parents, have a right to exhort and reprove them.

Adam Clarke writes in a similar tone:

> ... submit to their authority in all matters of doctrine and discipline, on the ground that they watched for their souls

[12] See Clarke on 1 Cor. 4:21, Coke and Clarke on 1 Thess. 5:12.
[13] See Clarke on 1 Peter 5:1–4.

and should have to give an account of their conduct to God.

Joseph Cownley and Joseph Benson believed that the call to preach implied authority to administer the sacraments.[14] Daniel Isaac virtually argued for the abolition of an ordained ministry altogether.[15] Perhaps the nearest we get to the authoritative conception of the Pastoral Office[16] is Joseph Benson's sermon to the Conference of 1796, entitled 'The Character and Office of Ministers':

> Ministers are not servants of the people. He has entrusted the ship of His church, properly speaking, not to the people who are but, as it were, passengers in it, but to the ministers of the Gospel, to be conducted over the tempestuous ocean of the world to the port of eternal bliss; and they are not at liberty to give up the steering or government of it into other and less skilful hands....

We give these quotations as evidence of the fluidity of ideas which circulated after Wesley's death. When we come to Bunting of the period 1806–20 we do get the germ of the authoritative doctrine of the Pastoral Office. We have already noticed the Manchester Preachers' *Statement of Facts* (1806) which is unmistakably by Bunting, but the ideas emerge again in the Liverpool Minutes of 1820 which we know to be the work of Bunting:

> We are under solemn obligation to conduct ourselves... not as mere chairmen of public meetings, but as Pastors of Christian Societies, put in trust by the ordinances of God and by their own voluntary association with us... with the scriptural superintendence of their spiritual affairs.[17]

W. B. Carter maintained that the germs of all future claims

---

[14] Wesley, of course, would not have agreed. His invariable maxim was 'no administration without ordination'. See *Letters between Joseph Cownley and Robert Grey*, p. 6, and Benson, J., *A Farther Defence of the Methodists* (1793), p. 62.
[15] See Isaac, D., *Ecclesiastical Claims* (1816).
[16] Apart from the writings which we can ascribe to Jabez Bunting and which will be dealt with below.
[17] *Minutes*, v. 151. Bunting's biographer, in his *Life of Jabez Bunting*, i. 275, ii. 177 admits Bunting's mind behind these two documents. See also M.C.A. letter from Bunting to Humphrey Sandwith, 10th February, 1825.

for the Pastoral Office lurked in this paragraph.[18] At the same time, it is easy to over-estimate Bunting. He was not alone in his sentiments. He epitomized what others felt. His conceptions were congenial to Wesleyans on the whole, and it only required a Beecham or a Barrett to expound them. Just how this was done, we must now enquire.

The Office of a Pastor

(a) A Separated Order

The opening sentence in Alfred Barrett's essay *The Pastoral Office* reads, 'from the very beginning there has been an order of men consecrated to the service of religion' and Edmund Grindrod in his book *The Duties of Class Leaders* says, 'God has ordained that there should be an order of men in His Church separated from all secular callings, devoted wholly to the study of His Word and to the discharge of various pastoral functions' (p. 11). This appeal to history and scripture was fundamental to the Wesleyan apologists. The supreme examples of this separated order are the Jewish priests in the Old Testament and the twelve Apostles in the New Testament. 2 Timothy 2:4 is quoted to support a twofold argument, (a) that the duties of a Pastor are so numerous that he must devote his whole time to them, and (b) that separation from worldly activities is necessary so that Pastors may be preserved from the 'deadening influence' of secular employments.

The Wesleyan writers would have nothing to do with a priestly caste, nor did they regard men who are engaged in secular work as precluded from occasional preaching; but separation from secular employment was regarded as 'the normal condition of the ruling and teaching office'.[19] Alfred Barrett finds New Testament support for this separated order in Mark 1:18 and Luke 5:11 (the disciples forsaking their nets) and also in Romans 1:1 (St Paul's separation for the work). He quotes 1 Corinthians 9: 12–25

---

[18] *Methodism, Past and Present*, p. 41.
[19] Barrett, A., *The Ministry and Polity of the Christian Church* hereafter referred to as 'M & P', p. 133.

as evidence of St Paul's freedom from the care of procuring the means of temporal support, yet not ashamed to work with his own hands. St Paul's charge to Timothy was to give himself wholly to the work of the ministry. Barrett examines a series of texts, Mark 3:13-14, Romans 1:1, 2 Timothy 2:4, Hebrews 5:4 and Acts 13:2 from which he draws the conclusion that, 'calling and separation are concomitant'. Furthermore, only Apostles, Prophets, Evangelists, Pastors and Teachers[20] are thus separated; separation does not apply to other church officers, not even to Deacons. Barrett interprets the term κλητος as 'the occupation of the whole man'.[21]

Given this separated order of men, it was further maintained that, 'It is God's ordination that ministers should be supported by those to whose service their lives and labours are devoted'.[22] In support of this, 1 Corinthians 9:7ff is quoted. Barrett used this text to defend the Wesleyan position against those who deny a separated ministry altogether (e.g. the Quakers) and those who assert that ministerial power can be exercised by anyone (e.g. the Free Methodists).[23]

Furthermore, within this separated order, there have always been two types of ministry—an ordinary and an extra-ordinary. In Jewish times, there were priests who officiated in the Temple, but from time to time God raised up extra-ordinary messengers, the Prophets. These men were generally quite unconnected with the priesthood, but it was not unknown in earlier time for an extra-ordinary messenger to perform the divine ordinances—Elijah, for example. In origin, Christianity represented the rise of a company of extra-ordinary messengers, for such were the early apostles and evangelists. Later, the Christian Church developed its own ordinary and extra-ordinary messengers; evangelists and prophets being the extra-ordinary; bishops, elders, pastors and teachers, being the ordinary. Wesley

---

[20] Barrett regards 'Pastor and Teacher' as one office.
[21] M. & P., pp. 116-38.
[22] Grindrod, *op. cit.*, p. 13.
[23] P.O., pp. 14-16.

had said that his Preachers were of the former class, and Barrett saw them as successors of the Prophets and Apostles, possessing an irregular but divine commission.[24] But here he got confused, for the whole conflict in Barrett's time was due to the passing of the Itinerant from the extra-ordinary messenger of Wesley's time to the ministerial or Pastoral character for which Barrett was arguing—he did not quite face up to this.

That the Christian pastor should devote the whole of his time to the work was never questioned in Methodism. At the Conference of 1768, the question was asked, 'Should Itinerant Preachers follow trades?'.[25] There was apparently a long discussion, but it was concluded that trading as such was not an evil, but with 1 Timothy 4:15 and the ordinal of the Church of England in mind, it was judged improper for a Methodist Preacher to engage in any occupation other than preaching the Gospel and supervising the Societies. So Methodist Preachers fulfilled the first requirement of a Christian Pastor—separation from secular employment. This made the transition from Preacher to Pastor so much the more natural and easy.

(b) The Divine Call

'To be called of God for the work' was regarded as an indispensible necessity for the Christian minister, for 'the whole Pastoral system is based on this; it is a condition *sine qua non*'.[26] It is well known that the Anglican clergy charged Methodist ministers of being 'self-appointed'; part of the reply to this charge was the fact that all candidates for the Methodist ministry must initially have felt and responded to the call of God to the work, for it is this call alone that can give meaning or efficacy to any outward act of commissioning.[27] At the same time, this call must be attested by men who themselves have already responded to it. Wesley had had his fill of enthusiastic young men who professed to

[24] *Methodist Magazine*, p. 198—article by Alfred Barrett.
[25] *Minutes*, i. 78. (1768).
[26] M. & P., p. 140.
[27] See also, Vevers, W., *The National Importance of Methodism*, p. 49.

be called of God to preach; it would have been unkind to them and disastrous to the Societies to have accepted them for the ministry. So when the third Conference came round (1746) regulations were laid down for the testing of 'those who think they are called of God to preach'.

George Smith argued that the Christian Church had its very origin in a divine call and not in a popular election. It began, not with a group of people choosing their minister, but by a divinely-called preacher proclaiming the Good News. The New Testament Church, he said, 'is not begun by a people who elect a teaching class, but by a divine appointment of a minister to announce the mercy of God to fallen sinners'.[28]

Social factors, too, were not irrelevant. The first half of the nineteenth century saw the rise of the affluent Wesleyan layman who belonged to the second and third generation of Methodists and worshipped in his mahogany 'Brunswick'[29] where only ministers were appointed to preach. This gave more than a little relevancy to such invectives as the Wesleyan Association production *A Catechism for Wesleyan Methodists*. *The Illuminator* was not above sneering at the managers of its contemporary *The Watchman's Lantern* because they were men of 'lowly social origin, of vulgar occupations' who 'dared to defy the collective wisdom of the ministerial Conference'.[30] The Wesleyans believed in a divine social order of sorts—that the minister's place was 'to feed and rule', and that of the lower orders to submit and be fed. This was a real, but unexpressed assumption of the doctrine of the Pastoral Office.

(c) Invested with Authority

In the Wesleyan economy, the Conference had supreme power in the stationing and disciplining of ministers. This was because it held that ministerial authority came from

[28] Smith, G., *The Polity of Wesleyan Methodism*, p. 50.
[29] The name indicates a loyalty to the house of Hanover, allegiance to the establishment against 'radicalism' and reform.
[30] *Proceedings of the Wesley Historical Society*, xxxv. 142—an article by Ian Sellers, 'The Wesleyan Methodist Association in Liverpool 1834–35'.

above and not from below.[31] The Conference of 1835, after warning the Methodist people against slanders 'which had been thrown against the Pastoral Office', told them that they should regard the Pastoral Office as 'an ordinance of God for the perpetuation of religion and the salvation of the world'. While it was possible (continued the Conference Pastoral Letter) to justify this on the grounds of its fruits, 'it is not on the mere grounds of its good effects that we claim for the office the respect of our people, but on the fact of its divine appointment...'. To acknowledge this divine appointment was, furthermore, 'essential to your comfort and edification in receiving their message'.[32] The people had a right and an opportunity to object, but this was not democracy; in fact, it is 'as far from democratical authority as the pastoral is from absolutism'.[33] Jabez Bunting's 'Angel of the Church', as expounded by Alfred Barrett, was not a representative or a delegate of popular opinion, but 'the messenger or angel of Christ to the Church'.[34] In fact, the laity had their own share in the government of the church.

There can be no doubt that, in Wesleyanism, the minister's authority was supreme. In fact, it was argued by some that the ministry could not exist without this absolute authority unshared with laymen. Joseph Entwisle remarked after the Leeds organ affair, 'I am sure that our Connexion could not exist if lay delegates were admitted in our Conferences; and that the power exercised by the Conference is absolutely necessary to the perpetuation of the Itinerancy'.[35]

This pastoral authority expressed itself in many ways:

i. It was to feed and rule. Having been called of God, and approved by those in the ministry before him, a minister must feed and rule the church. It was on the nature and

[31] Barrett said 'it came not from the feet upwards but from the head downwards'—M. & P., p. 309.
[32] These quotations are from the Pastoral Letter of the 1835 Conference. *Minutes*, vii. 596.
[33] M. & P., p. 310.
[34] M. & P., pp. 248–49.
[35] *Memoirs*, p. 355.

extent of this power that the Wesleyan doctrine of the Pastoral Office foundered. The Wesleyan apologists built their arguments on the New Testament evidence; though it must be remembered that living before the days of the modern critical approach to scripture, they handled their evidence differently, and drew conclusions more confidently than scholars do today. However, it is our business to demonstrate how they reasoned, not to say how we think they should have acted, or even what we would have done.

In the Old Testament, the Hebrew word for pastor, רעה is often translated by ποιμήν and used of kings as well as of shepherds. The New Testament word for pastor was also ποιμήν and the corresponding verb ποιμαίνειν meant, 'to do the work of a pastor', or 'to be a shepherd'. In Matthew 2:6, this verb is translated 'to be a shepherd', but in some translations it is rendered, 'to rule', a meaning which it bears in Revelation 2:27. Thus in both Hebrew and Greek, the concepts of feeding and governing are inherent in the word for pastor.[36] Matthew 28:19, 20 commissions Christian ministers to exercise discipline in the church. John 20:21-23 undoubtedly commissions them to admit and exclude members. Wesley's comment on this passage in his *Notes on the New Testament* agrees:

> a power of declaring with authority the terms of pardon etc; a power of inflicting and remitting ecclesiastical censures, that is, of excluding from and re-admitting into a Christian congregation.

Beecham observes that 1 Peter 5:2 directs Christian ministers, πρεσβύτεροι, to feed and govern the flock, ποιμάνατε το ποίμνιον, but care must be taken that it is done with the right motives. Here also we get the word ἐπισκοπεω, the root from which we get the word for 'Bishop' or 'Superintendent'. Beecham continues:

> To regulate the Church by wholesome discipline is thus as much the work of a Christian Bishop or overseer as to instruct and nourish it by the Word and Sacraments.[37]

[36] E.C.W.M., p. 83.
[37] *Op. cit.*, p. 85.

THE PASTORAL OFFICE

Thus, St Paul, while forbidding lordly rule, does not forbid pastoral authority. From Hebrews 13:7, 17 it is understood that this authority must be accepted and acknowledged by the people, 'those who rule the Church are the same who nurture it with the Word of life'.[38] Finally, an appeal was made by Alfred Barrett to Richard Baxter's *Christian Ecclesiastics* in a passage which we wish to quote in full:

> The right of the Christian Pastor, not only to perform the baptismal act, but also to determine who are fit subjects for the sacred ordinance, is forcibly stated by Richard Baxter in his *Christian Ecclesiastics*. 'It is the Pastor's office', he observed, 'to bear and exercise the keys of Christ's church; therefore, by office, he is to receive those that come in; and, consequently, to be the trier and judge of their fitness. 2. It belongeth to the same office which is to baptise, to judge who is to be baptised; otherwise, ministers would not be judges of their own actions, but the executioners of other men's judgement. It is more the judging who is to be baptised, that the minister's office consisteth in, than in the bare doing of the outward act of baptising. 3. He that must be the ordinary judge in church admissions is supposed to have both ability and leisure to make him fit; and authority and obligation to do the work. 4. The ordinary body of the laity have none of all these four qualifications, much less all. (1) They are not ordinarily able so to examine a man's faith and resolution with judgement and skill, as may not tend to the wrong of himself nor of the church; for it is great skill that is required thereunto. (2) they have not ordinarily leisure from their proper callings and labours to wait on such a work as it must be waited on; especially in populous places. (3) They are not therefore, obliged to do that which they cannot be supposed to have ability or leisure for. (4) And where they have not the other three, they can have no authority to do it. (5) It is therefore as great a crime for the laity to usurp the Pastor's office in this matter, as in preaching, baptising or other parts of it.'[39]

ii. It carries an authority to administer the Sacraments. A logical deduction from the foregoing arguments is that

[38] *Op. cit.*, p. 90.
[39] *Methodist Magazine*, 1835, p. 751.

the pastor, and only the pastor, has the right to administer the sacraments to the flock; that is, to judge who should be baptized and who is to be admitted or excluded from the Holy Communion. This, of course, had always been the practice of the Wesleyans; the Free Methodists, on the other hand, allowed Local Preachers to administer. The Wesleyan position was expounded by Barrett in *The Methodist Magazine* for 1835:

> As the sacrament of baptism is the door of admission into the general church, the Lord's Supper is the pledge of continued membership. And it being the business of the Pastor to admit persons to membership, and remove them from it, it must necessarily remain for him to give the pledge of membership to the approved members of the church, as well as refuse it to those whom he deems unworthy. Were others than the Pastor allowed to perform this act, it might sometimes happen that the pledge of membership would be given to such as he had excluded and denied to others whom he might judge worthy of communion with the church.[40]

The same writer, in his *Wesleyan Tracts for the Times* No. 9 used this point in replying to the Tractarians:

> He on whom the responsibility devolves of providing for the stated preaching of the Word, and of preparing, through the other ministrations of the Gospel, penitent and believing individuals for the obsignation of the Christian Covenant must himself most appropriately confer the sign.
>
> If the ministers of Christ are called to feed the flock of God over which the Holy Ghost hath made them overseers or Pastors, well may it be reckoned a pastoral act to administer unto the members of that flock the sacramental emblems of His body and blood.[41]

In his larger work, *The Ministry and Polity of the Christian Church*, Barrett develops this theme.[42] He begins with a forthright rejection of the notion of priesthood in the Christian ministry, and of any *ex opere operato* or *ex opere operantis* in the sacraments. He concedes, however, quoting Tertullian, that any baptized Christian can himself

[40] *Op. cit.*, p. 752.
[41] *Wesleyan Tracts*, No. 9, p. 4.
[42] See also Barrett's *Catholic and Evangelical Principles*, pp. 51ff.

THE PASTORAL OFFICE

baptize others, although normally this is the duty of the Pastor. Barrett makes four points:

The first point is that the administration of the sacraments is a pastoral act. The pastor, as guide, teacher and mentor, is the only proper person to administer what is 'the seal of affirmation upon the profession of faith'. The sacraments concern 'the recognition of membership in the Body' and 'that recognition is one which no company of Christians apart from the Pastor and without his distinct affirmation can give'.

Barrett's second point was that to administer the sacraments to a company of people 'apart from the sanction of their own proper pastor or contrary to it' is to set up 'a different altar' and is plainly schismatic.

Thirdly, no objection could be raised to 'any holy man of God' administering the sacraments 'if there were no ordained or responsible pastor near'.

His fourth point was that whereas the Free Methodists have reduced the Lord's Supper to 'nothing more than a Feast' which any two or three of their own will might institute, from the beginning the Wesleyans have allowed none but their pastors to administer.

iii. It was an authority to admit and expel members. We need not dwell upon this, as it has already been discussed in connection with the Leeds Organ Case and the Warrenite secession. In spite of the attacks which came from both these quarters, the Wesleyans adhered to the principle which they claimed went back to Wesley and the authority which he gave to his Assistants.[43] The principle was that he who admits to the Church in Baptism and administers the Lord's Supper is the proper person, the only person, to admit into and expel from the Society.[44]

As the Liverpool Minutes of 1820 expressed it, Wesleyan

[43] See *Large Minutes*, 1753 in *Minutes*, i. 596.
[44] Watson, R., *Institutes*, p. 197; *The Wesleyan Vindicator*, 1852, p. 61. The Free Methodists, rejecting this doctrine of the Pastoral Office, denied that ministers had the exclusive right to administer the sacraments. It was said that the Wesleyans were alone in giving such power to the Pastorate but Barrett replied that Calvin 'asserted our principle, though he created a new class of Presbyters in order . . . to carry it out' (M. & P., p. 406).

ministers were to regard themselves as being more than chairmen, they must rule. In a discipline case, for example, though the verdict of guilty or not guilty lay with the Leaders Meeting, to the pastor was given the authority of determining the sentence. John Scott, when giving evidence before the 1852 Committee, regarded this as 'the last and highest exercise of the supreme authority in the Church, for the proper performance of which the Pastor is responsible to the Chief Shepherd'.[45]

Once the exclusive right of the Pastor (or a collective Pastorate like the Methodist Conference) to rule the church is conceded, it follows that this function cannot be transferred to, or shared with the laity.[46] The Free Methodists appealed to Acts 15:6 in support of the 'whole church' view, but Smith answers for the Wesleyans by an appeal to Adam Clarke's comment on that same verse, 'This was the first council ever held in the Christian Church and we find that it was composed of Apostles and Elders simply'.[47] It is not denied that the people have rights; the point is that the Pastor 'is not at liberty to divest himself or allow others to divest him of his legitimate scriptural rights to govern the church'. Laymen may assist Pastors by preaching under their direction, but this does not confer the Pastoral Office and its legitimate authority. 'The persons to whom Jesus Christ has given the keys are the regular and stated ministers of the Gospel who are fully set apart to the sacred office.'

iv. It was an authority to teach and interpret sound doctrine—and always had been so in the Christian Church. Barrett observed that doctrine and discipline go together.[48] He points out that in the New Testament all the warnings against a corrupt ministry have to do with doctrine, and the faithful are constantly warned against false prophets and teachers.[49]

[45] *The Wesleyan Vindicator*, 1852, p. 61.
[46] See, Watson, R., *Institutes*, p. 196.
[47] See M.C.A., Bunting's reply to a letter from William Beal, 3rd May, 1821. Barrett again appeals to Baxter—see his article in *The Methodist Magazine*, 1835, pp. 756–57.
[48] Watson, op. cit., p. 200; M. & P., 31.
[49] M. & P. p. 34.

The preservation of 'our doctrines', as contained in Wesley's *Forty-four Sermons* and his *Notes on the New Testament* played a large part in shaping the character and preserving the ethos of Methodism. A pledge to maintain an evangelical Arminianism against the claims of the Latitudinarians on the one hand and the Calvinists on the other, gave the Methodist Preachers a sense of both unity and mission. A sense of belonging to a disciplined order was an important factor in establishing Methodism as an independent body, separate from both the Church of England and Nonconformity. Responsibility for preserving sound doctrine lay, in the first place, with the ministers; but a second line of defence was to be found in the trustees, who were pledged to see that only 'our doctrines' were preached in the buildings of which they had charge. Yet the trustees only preserved doctrine; it was for the ministers to regulate, teach and interpret it. As the *Methodist Magazine* for 1835 put it, 'the right of Christian ministers to be the judges of the doctrines which they are called to preach is perfectly compatible with the right of the people to judge of what they hear' (pp. 749–50).

(d) Safeguards to Purity and Power

The responsibility and authority which were given to the Methodist Preachers were constantly in need of oversight and safeguards. We deal first with safeguards to purity, by which we mean purity in doctrine and morals. While Wesley lived, his Itinerants exercised their authority under his personal supervision, and after his death under that of the Conference. A candidate for the ministry was carefully examined, and then the outward seal was set upon the inward call; henceforth, he was under the constant vigilance, or episcopé, of the collective pastorate in District Meeting or Conference. 'Wesleyan Methodism', said George Turner, 'guards the morality of its ministers with a strictness bordering upon severity.'[50]

There had also to be safeguards to power, and the

[50] Turner, G., *Wesleyan Economy*, p. 7; see also *Methodist Magazine*, 1835 p. 618.

Methodist constitution provided checks to any minister who might be tempted to exercise his authority with undue severity. Barrett sees that ministerial despotism might arise from such factors as youthful indiscretion, love of power, prejudice or even decline in piety; but checks come from four directions—from the Leaders Meeting, from the fact that the minister is dependent upon the voluntary support of his people, from the oversight of District Meeting and Conference, and from the fact that he is liable to be called to account on the accusation of an aggrieved party.[51] In addition to this, the Quarterly Meeting has a veto on candidates and the trustees have power to check false doctrine. Therefore, while pastoral power is never surrendered, it is always surrounded by effective safeguards against abuse.

(e) Summary

In general, the Wesleyan concept of pastoral authority endeavoured to avoid two extremes—despotic power on the one hand and 'power delegated to the people' on the other. It may be instructive to end this section with Barrett's summary of the duties of a pastor:

i. To receive candidates into church fellowship, having first judged of their fitness;
ii. To remove from the body the disobedient and incorrigible;
iii. To inflict censures in cases of flagrant transgression, and
iv. To appoint church officers.[52]

Beecham's summary ran:

i. Pastoral fitness for the work, personal religion and competence (natural and acquired);
ii. A divine call;
iii. Recognition of that call and formal committal to him of the sacred trust by those authorised to make it—i.e. ordination;
iv. Separation from all secular business.[53]

[51] P.O., p. 218 and E.C.W.M., p. 126 (second edition).
[52] P.O., p. 190.
[53] E.C.W.M., pp. 105ff.

Pastoral and Civil Rule

The Free Methodists maintained that in an age when Parliamentary government was becoming more democratic, church polity ought to keep in step.[54] From the days of Alexander Kilham they held that the right to a representative ruling body should exist in religious as well as in civil affairs. The Wesleyans adopted lay participation at committee level, but they stood firm by the principle that only an all-ministerial conference, the collective pastorate, ought to rule. That it was a position which proved increasingly difficult to defend does not exonerate us from examining the arguments on which it rested.

The Wesleyans argued that the relationship between a minister and his people is essentially different from that which exists between civil governments and the people. George Turner's reply took the line that while civil laws are binding on every member of the State, the laws of a religious community are binding only on those who voluntarily assent to them. This was Wesley's position when he defended the right of a Christian to choose his own pastor.[55]

Turner's second point was that members of the State are bound to support its various institutions, but Christian ministers are dependent upon the voluntary support of their people'[56] Barrett takes up the same theme with the premise that while God is the source of all government, sin has made necessary a coercive government on earth. This leads to some strange assertions on his part. He maintains that Romans 13:1 and 1 Chronicles 29:11, 12 do not give 'sovereign power to the whole community' except so far as the community contains those who are destined by God to be judges and rulers. This is surely a doctrine of 'the divine right of class distinctions'! He asserts, rather optimistically, that church government is of a spiritual character for regenerate men, standing close to the Kingdom of Heaven. Furthermore, civil rulers are raised up by 'ordinary methods

---

[54] See, Allin, T., *Exposition of Church Government*, p. 6.
[55] *Minutes*, i. 27 (1745).
[56] *The Wesleyan Economy*, p. 5.

of divine providence' but spiritual overseers are called direct by the Holy Spirit. This is a strange argument, but it leads him to make an interesting comment on ordination. The Wesleyan view, he says, is that ordination is neither 'a sacrament conveying grace' (as with Rome and Pusey), nor is it merely a 'solemnising of popular election' (as with the Free Methodists and the Dissenters); rather, it is setting a seal on the divine call and the bestowal of authority to rule the church.

The aim of civil law is to guard society against evil and to promote the 'social elevation of society'; church government is designed to 'training the baptised, edification of believers, censure of unfaithful'. The civil law can punish, church law can only censure and exclude. All this is said in support of the role of pastors as rulers of the church. Barrett firmly believed that the Bible was opposed to democracy so far as church government was concerned, and that an 'eternal law of arrangement and subordination' prevails throughout the universe. He said that 'a man who has the Lord for his shepherd has a right to demand that no under-shepherd but one of the Lord's appointing shall be placed over him'.[57] George Smith said, 'The church is not a democracy but the Kingdom of God'.[58] Welch believed that 'in civil society the rulers derive their existence from the people, but in religious society the people owe their existence to their teacher' and carried his conviction to the logical conclusion that 'the subordinate officers of a church, generated by a Christian ministry, can exist no longer than the ministerial functions continue to be exercised'.[59] Has any devotee of Rome ever said anything stronger than this? It is tantamount to saying that if a church were suddenly deprived of its ministry, it would cease to exist. The hypothetical 'desert island' situation has always to be allowed for—as the venerable Hooker realized.

---

[57] M. & P. p. 17.
[58] *The Polity of Wesleyan Methodism*, p. 55.
[59] *Wesleyan Polity*, pp. 43 and 50.

The Place of the Laity

Their high view of the Pastoral Office enabled the Wesleyans to define the place of the laity in the church. At every outbreak of dissension, the Conference party was charged with denying the laity its rightful share in church government. In reply it was stated that the laity had considerable responsibility, though it stopped short of pastoral power.[60] While Conference never shed its ultimate responsibility, it had, from time to time, given the laity an increasing share in the government of the church. For example, the Leaders had a right to declare any candidate for membership unfit. Laymen entirely disbursed the funds of the Connexion and sat with ministers on all committees. They could invite ministers and memorialize Conference without being members of that court. 'Where', asks Barrett, 'is there a communion... whose laity has so wide, intelligent and influential a sphere?'[61]

The duties of Local Preachers and Class Leaders were such that some democrats urged that they should be given a status equivalent to that of the pastor: conversely, they regarded the pastor as merely a Preacher-cum-Class Leader in full-time service. The Wesleyans resisted this tendency; the difference between a minister and layman was not simply one of degree, but of kind.

The Free Methodists believed that government was invested in the 'whole church' and that Local Preachers and Class Leaders were co-pastors with the minister; that all officers, including the pastor, operated on a common level. The Wesleyans, on the other hand, held that the Pastoral Office implied a divine call to which the Local Preacher had not responded.[62] The New Testament also convinced the Wesleyans that occasional preaching does not authorize a person to administer the sacraments and that deacons who sometimes preached were not pastors.

[60] See Barrett, A., P.O. p. 131.
[61] M. & P., p. 353.
[62] According to Beecham, E.C.W.M., p. 112, Local Preachers 'are not, in the proper sense of the expression, Pastors of the flock'. He also quoted Baxter's *Christian Ecclesiastics* on the point.

Nor can Class Leaders, even though they be guides to the flock, be regarded as co-pastors with the minister. Beecham felt that to make Local Preachers and Class Leaders co-rulers with the minister, would be to reduce him to the status of a chairman. It would leave the Pastor, 'stripped of his rightful authority, without help and without redress'.[63]

This distinction between ministry and laity had no sacerdotal significance whatever; it was purely a separation to the office of teaching and ruling; not of priestly mediation, but of feeding and guiding. Hence, the pastoral duty of administering discipline, at times involving the unpleasant duty of expelling a member, could never be given to laymen. In such cases one must seek the collective opinion and concurrence of the church in its collective pastorate; and this cannot be shared with non-pastors. Says Theophilus Woolmer:

> Christ has made His ministers accountable for the purity and good discipline of the church, and unless it can be shown from scripture that He has made others equally accountable with His ministers, the latter cannot share their responsibility with others.[64]

For the same reason, only the ministry can try the ministry. This was well illustrated in a discussion which took place in the 1852 committee. Thomas Jackson suspected that there was a move on the part of some laymen to provide a mixed court to which a superintendent could appeal when faced with what he may regard as a factious Leaders Meeting. The very idea, however, of a minister appealing to a court composed partly of laymen brought Jackson to his feet for a weighty speech in which he said:

> I consider this proposal as neither more nor less than a project for putting a Superintendent upon his trial before laymen whenever he may perform an act of discipline upon an offending member of the church. You may call this arrangement an appeal or what else you please, but to this course of humiliation we would be liable whenever a case of offence

[63] E.C.W.M., p. 117.
[64] M. & P., 214 and 294; also Woolmer, *Wesleyan Pastors*, p. 18.

THE PASTORAL OFFICE

should occur. . . . A complaint against him is heard by a body of men who are themselves under his pastoral charge. . . . They perhaps censure him. . . . From that day this Superintendent is an humble, degraded man. . . .[65]

Jabez Bunting would not allow his name to be called at the Circuit Local Preachers Meeting. 'When I am tried', he declared, 'I will be tried by my peers.'[66]

The Free Methodist View

Having studied in detail the Wesleyan concept of the Pastoral Office, we can now review ideas on the ministry as held by the various non-Wesleyan bodies, many of whom have been noted in previous chapters, but whose ideas on this subject are much in accord, partly because they were all protests, in one way or another, against the Pastoral Office of the Wesleyans.

To begin with, the Free Methodists denied the sole right of the minister to rule; 'power-sharing' was their maxim. They rejected such terms as 'overseer' and explained away such texts as 'submit to them that rule over you'. They denied that ποιμαίνω included 'rule' in the sense the Wesleyans gave to it.

The Free Methodists were also at variance with the Wesleyans on the appeal to the methods of civil government, for in a sense they were all experiments in ecclesiastical democracy. An ardent Methodist New Connexion expositor based his apology upon the argument that the people ought to have as direct an interest in Church government 'as they possess in civil society'.[67] To the Wesleyans this was entirely false; 'no man of God', said Alfred Barrett, 'would consent to adopt his view of pastoral authority from secular politics'.[68]

All the Free Methodists stood by representative govern-

---

[65] *The Wesleyan Vindicator* (1852), p. 71.
[66] *L.Q.R.*, January, 1888, p. 220; This was the answer which Wesley gave to the Dewsbury Trustees in 1788—*Letters*, viii. 77.
[67] Allin, T., *Principles of Church Government*, p. 5.
[68] P.O., p. 189.

ment. They refused to believe that perfect wisdom resided in any single class of people, ministerial or lay; therefore, representation at every level of administration was a necessity. They were quite sure that 'this association of churches with the ministry is distinctly recognised in the New Testament'.[69] So they removed the government of the church from the pastor and made him 'one among many'. This was 'the whole church' doctrine which was advocated by all Free Methodist writers of this period.[70]

On the other hand, the Wesleyans would not divide the spiritual authority of the pastor with anyone who did not share his responsibility. They felt that to do so would mean that the pastor would be, 'depressed far below his just level ... considered merely in the light of a speaking brother ... no official distinction or authority'.[71]

After the disruption of 1849, the Reformers carried the argument even further by asserting that the Itinerants, by the very fact that their stay in any one circuit was necessarily brief, could not possibly be pastors; that the real pastoral work was done by the Class Leaders. 'They do not, neither can they, know the flock. Their public ministrations do not reach the sick, the infirm and those who for other reasons absent themselves.'[72] There was some point in this, though they were on less secure ground when they tried to claim that Local Preachers were co-ordinate with pastors and therefore ought to administer the sacraments. The Reformers said that the quarterly visitation of the society by the ministers for the distribution of tickets 'comes nearer the pastoral work than anything yet noticed', but they also pointed out that this was but a monetary and superficial contact with the people. The real pastors, they claimed, were the Class Leaders whose weekly contact with each member provided a degree of 'watchfulness' or episcopé which the Itinerant could never give. There was, of course,

[69] Allin, *op. cit.*, p. 6.
[70] See, e.g., Leach, J., *Remarks on Richard Watson's Views*, p. 16. E.C.W.M. devotes eleven pages to a criticism of the 'whole church' idea.
[71] See, Turner, G., *The Wesleyan Economy* (a reply to Allin), p. 26; Welch, C., *The Wesleyan Crisis*, p. 18.
[72] *The Wesleyan Reformer*, 1851, p. 89.

THE PASTORAL OFFICE

some force in that argument. It even found support in the Liverpool Minutes of 1820 and in the Conference Pastoral Letter of 1822, 'We hope that our Class Leaders will endeavour to watch over the souls committed to their charge, as those who are to give an account to the Great Shepherd'.

This is an interesting comment on the ambiguity of the role of the Methodist minister. He was still, officially, a Preacher assigned to a circuit rather than a pastor in charge of a particular congregation. By the very nature of his itinerancy, he has not fitted comfortably into the accepted role of a pastor, yet upon him tradition has thrust, and he has accepted, pastoral authority as well as a preaching mission. The Reformers saw the weakness of this dual role and the incongruity of what they called 'the shepherd with the keys'.[73] The Wesleyans, nothing daunted, maintained the duality of Pastor (Ruler) and Preacher. The Free Methodists resolved the tension by retaining the 'Preacher' part of the ministerial office and rejecting the 'ruling' element; thus, for them, the difference between a minister and a Local Preacher was simply that 'the former is supported by the people, the latter supports himself'.[74]

It is regrettable that the Free Methodists fed the flames of dissension by setting minister and Local Preacher against each other as unequal rivals, always to allege that the Local Preacher was the underprivileged.[75] They saw a sinister design behind the Theological Institution. It was designed, they alleged, 'to assist in the overthrow' of Local Preachers as a body.[76] They read equally sinister motives into the adoption of laying-on of hands in ordination. They alleged that it was intended to serve as 'a demarcation

[73] *The Wesleyan Reformer*, 1851, p. 91.
[74] *A Catechism for Wesleyan Methodists*, p. 6.
[75] It happened in the Leeds Organ controversy when Local Preachers and ministers were on opposite sides. Ministers discouraged Local Preachers Mutual Help clubs on the grounds that the Local Preachers would unite against the ministers—see Ward, W. R., *The Early Correspondence of Jabez Bunting* and Mrs Margaret Batty's Leeds M.A. thesis on Local Preachers in Wesleyan Methodism.
[76] *A Catechism for Wesleyan Methodists*, p. 8.

between ministers and Local Preachers'.⁷⁷ When the London Circuit Plan began to print the ministers' names in capitals to distinguish them from the Local Preachers, the Reformers denounced the move as the work of 'the man of sin in the Wesleyan Connexion'.⁷⁸ We mention these unsavoury incidents as some of the more regrettable reactions to the doctrine of the Pastoral Office.

Conclusion

Much of the present-day thought about the Christian ministry is polarized on two conceptions. By some, the ministry is thought of as an authoritative priestly caste; the minister as a man apart vested with mysterious power and surrounded by the mystic aura of the cultus. On the other hand, there are those who regard the minister as little more than the representative of the church, the 'speaking brother', a full-time servant *vis-à-vis* the Local Preacher who serves part-time. This view of the ministry is bolstered by an emphasis on the Priesthood of all Believers which really is meant to imply the non-priesthood of the ministry. This latter view is reflected in the Deed of Union of the Methodist Church (1932):

> Christ's ministers... hold no priesthood differing in kind from that which is common to the Lord's People, and they have no exclusive title to the preaching of the Gospel or the care of souls....

The Free Methodists would have said Amen to this, but the Wesleyans of our period would have wondered what had happened to the Pastoral Office and what had become of the significance of ordination. But is there no middle way between these two views?⁷⁹ We believe there is, and that it is to be found in the Wesleyan doctrine of the Pastoral Office.

---

⁷⁷ *The Wesleyan Reformer*, 1851, p. 104. They regarded the imposition of hands as 'a very close approximation to Romish transubstantiation'.
⁷⁸ *Op. cit.*, p. 188.
⁷⁹ We are reminded of Wesley's views on the middle way between Rome Geneva—see above, pp. 200–1.

THE PASTORAL OFFICE

The Wesleyans would have been among the first to acknowledge that Methodist ministers were not priests, because they held that the function of mediator between God and man was the work of Christ.[80] As they read their New Testament, they found that ἱερεύς is never used of Christian ministers, and the Minutes of Conference had said:

> Denying the sacerdotal character of the Christian ministry, we claim no priesthood because we know, and the New Testament knows, no priest but the One in heaven: we claim not to offer sacrifice at the altar, for we know of no altar but the Cross and of no atoning or propitiatory sacrifice but the Saviour's blood.[81]

However, from this denial of a sacrificing priesthood, the Wesleyans did not adopt the concept of The Priesthood of all Believers. They did not empty the Pastoral Office of all meaning, or obliterate the distinction between Pastor and non-pastor.[82] Between the two extreme positions we have mentioned, the Wesleyans found a middle way which was scriptural, which respected the conscience of the individual and retained for the minister a considerable degree of authority. This the Priesthood of all Believers did not do. Barrett saw that it was one thing to say that in Christianity 'a priestly caste in the ministry ceased',[83] but quite another thing, and quite unjustified, to discredit the idea of a class of men separated to teach and guide the flock of Christ. He maintained 'the universal priesthood of God's people' but not without a clear distinction between minister and people which is warranted by scripture. We repeat that this is not a sacerdotal distinction, but one which is based on 'the separation to the work of teaching and ruling'. Hence a Local Preacher, 'not separated to the work is not a pastor endued with the authority of the Pastoral Office'. He may

---

[80] M. & P., p. 213. See next chapter for the argument that Christ transmitted his work of Pastor, but not his Priesthood to his Apostles.
[81] *Minutes*, ix. 404 (1842).
[82] See Rigg, J. H., *Congregational Independency*..., p. 60.
[83] The ministry was, in a sense, a 'caste' all the same; by the principle that 'the ministry appoint the ministry'.

have 'grace in abundance . . . but not THE grace which is needful to sustain the anxieties, joys and sorrows of the pastoral care'.[84] Similarly with Class Leaders, whom the Wesleyans would never concede to be co-pastors with the minister. John Scott said, 'the minister is as much the pastor of the Leaders as of the members; his, therefore, is not a co-ordinate position and authority'.[85]

To sum up—the Wesleyans were steering a middle course, between High Anglicanism and Dissent (or Free Methodism, whose views of the ministry were much akin to those of the Dissenters). Shorn of some of its over-emphases, the Wesleyan Doctrine of the Pastoral Office could give us a conception of the ministry which we could profitably recover today—a ministry with authority and a mission. The minister would be regarded not as a religious psychologist or a quasi-social worker, but one recognizably 'sent from God' with a self-authenticating authority bestowed by God through the Church.

---

[84] M. & P., pp. 215, 125 and 225.
[85] *The Wesleyan Vindicator*, 1852, p. 61.

CHAPTER THREE

THE IMPACT OF THE OXFORD MOVEMENT

IT is as remarkable as it is regrettable that the effect of the Oxford Movement on Methodism has been so scantily treated by historians.[1] A sentence is sometimes sufficient, 'The Oxford Movement drove the Wesleyans into the arms of the Nonconformists' and Thomas Jackson's reply to Pusey seems to be the only literature on the subject of which they are aware.[2] Yet in the Methodist Archives there are over fifty publications which were the direct outcome of the Oxford Movement. They are practically all written from the Wesleyan point of view, or by Anglican writers addressing themselves to the Methodist People.[3] The neglect of this rich storehouse means that the deeper effects of the Movement have gone largely unnoticed. These 'deeper effects' touched Methodism in many ways—culturally, socially, theologically, ecclesiastically—but what we are concerned with is that it drove the Wesleyan theologians to re-examine their doctrines of the Church and ministry. In a sense, they had been doing this since the early 1820s—the internal disruptions had forced them into it, but this had been on the level of domestic, practical politics. The Oxford Movement presented a theological challenge. The disruptions drove the Wesleyans to look at

[1] Smith's three-volume *History of Wesleyan Methodism* devotes two pages to the subject, largely quoting from Jackson's reply to Pusey. Townsend's *New History of Methodism* in two volumes, devotes only one page, cursory references and bare mention of Jackson's pamphlet. Gregory, J. R., *A Student's History of Methodism* in two volumes contains only two passing references. Rupert Davies's recent book, *Methodism*, can spare only a passing reference.
[2] Smith devotes one paragraph (iii. 424) to *Wesleyan Tracts for the Times*, concluding, 'Some of these tracts were written with great ability, and, although as a whole they do not exhibit the most successful literary defence of the Connexion, they rendered important service at the time of publication'.
[3] To these add the vast collection of pamphlets and tracts, including the Jackson library, many from Anglican sources, which have now come into the Archives from Richmond College.

the nature of their office *within* their own body; the Oxford Movement drove them to look at its validity in the wider sphere of the Church Universal. To the Free Methodists the Wesleyans had to reply in terms of the power of superintendents, the authority of the District Meeting, the supremacy of the Conference and the nature of the Pastoral Office. To the Tractarians, their apology was framed in terms of, *inter alia*, the authority of the scriptures, the validity of the sacraments, together with such topics as apostolic succession, episcopal ordination and the nature of schism. They also had to answer the charge of being untrue to the intentions of John Wesley. So they had to take stock of themselves. They were driven to justify their claim to be a church and to examine the bases on which their own doctrine of the ministry was founded—and do it on a much higher intellectual level than ever they had been called upon to do it before. But before we deal with the various points in the controversy, we must look at the relationship between the Methodists and the Tractarians in general.

Methodists[4] *and Tractarians*

Strange as it may seem, and however unrecognized by the protagonists themselves, there was a certain amount of common ground between them. Both Methodists and Tractarians regarded themselves as a bulwark against the rising tide of liberalism, reform and infidelity (with socialism sometimes included in this unholy alliance) as expressed in the Reform Bill on the one hand and the suppression of the Irish Bishoprics on the other. As Gordon Rupp once remarked, 'In protesting against the swelling Liberalism, Bunting anticipated the Oxford Movement and the Papal Syllabus of 1864'.[5] Again, they both protested against what R. W. Church calls, the 'blot' on the nineteenth-century Anglican Church, 'quiet worldliness'. Both Tractarians and Methodists sounded a call to holiness.[6]

[4] Throughout this chapter the term 'Methodist' refers to the 'Wesleyans'.
[5] *Ideas and Beliefs of the Victorians*, p. 110.
[6] See my book *The Sacrament of the Lord's Supper in Early Methodism* for the kinship between Wesley and Newman and the percipient remark of

The former, however, interpreted holiness rather starkly and forbiddingly in terms of sacraments and Church ordinances. They were anxious, of course, to recall the church to her mission as the Body of Christ and her ministers to the correct pedigree of apostolic succession. The Methodists, on the other hand, interpreted holiness in terms of godly living for the individual, and pure doctrine, pastoral oversight and scriptural organization for the church—not forgetting all the warmth and enthusiasm of that new life in Christ which they called 'conversion'.

Methodist and Tractarian, in fact, each supplied what was lacking in the other. In the search for salvation, for example, while the Methodists regarded the sacraments as subordinate to the personal acceptance by faith of Christ as Saviour, the Tractarians regarded them as 'efficacious vehicles of grace and . . . through these material channels the righteousness of Christ is not merely imputed but imparted to us'.[7] It is a tragedy that neither should see the merits or the sincerity of the other, for they were at one in their contest with 'the world, the flesh and the devil'.

Part of the trouble was that the Wesleyan idea of the Church[8] was so different from that of the Tractarians; in fact, as Dr Outler has pointed out, the early Methodists had no distinctive doctrine of the Church, for the very simple reason that they did not need one. 'They were not a

---

Brilioth, 'It was in some measure his (Wesley's) spirit which was so to fertilize the organism of old High Churchmanship that it once again could bear offspring'. See also Webb, C. C. J., *Religious Thought in the Oxford Movement*, 'Not only was Wesley's teaching, like that of the Tractarians, inspired by this passionate desire for holiness, but it also like theirs, emphasised the acceptance of moral obedience, even when not accompanied by mature Christian faith'. Also, Dearing, T., *Wesleyan and Tractarian Worship* and my review in *Proc. W.H.S.*, xxxv. 159f.

[7] Webb, C. C. J., *The Religious Thought of the Oxford Movement*, p. 73. The Tractarians dismissed the Methodist attitude as mere 'feelings'—an accusation which was not new, as seen from correspondence between Walker of Truro and Charles Wesley in 1756, see Sidney, E., *Life of Walker*, p. 214.

[8] For Wesley's theology of the church, see Williams, C., *John Wesley's Theology for Today*. For definitions of the Church by Wesleyan theologians —Watson, Barrett, Treffry, Dixon and Rule—see my Leeds Ph.D. thesis where the Wesleyan doctrine of the church is discussed more fully.

church and they had no intention of becoming one.'[9] But, as we have seen, events after the death of Wesley compelled Wesley's successors to make up their minds on the nature of the church and whether they themselves were part of it or not. As early as 1792, Kilham was for declaring Methodism a church there and then, 'If a number of serious persons meet in a Methodist chapel where the pure word of God is preached and the sacraments duly administered, they are the true church'. Wesley's version of Article XIX of the *Book of Common Prayer* was printed in Wesleyan service books of the nineteenth century:

> The visible Church of Christ is a congregation of faithful men in which the pure Word of God is preached and the sacraments duly administered according to Christ's ordinance, in all those things that of necessity are requisite to the same.

Wesley once defined the Catholic Church as, '... the whole body of men endued with faith working by love, dispersed over the whole earth—and the church is "ever one". In all ages and nations it is the one body of Christ. It is "ever holy".'[10]

In practice, the Wesleyan conception of the church was strangely eclectic; it was at one with the Presbyterians in its insistence upon the preaching of the Word and the need for pure doctrine; it was also at one with the 'gathered church' school of thought, for the Methodists were, in a broad sense 'gathered' from the world and in a narrower sense they were 'gathered' from the Church of England. But in the last analysis the Methodist definition of the Church emphasized *function* rather than *nature*. To them, the Church *is* what it *does*. The Wesleyans did not quarrel with the Established Church about the nature of the church, they protested against its failure to *be* the church in any real sense of the word. Alfred Barrett once said that the Methodists would have remained in the church (a) if none were admitted to Holy Communion but converted men and women, (b) if delinquent ministers were promptly

---
[9] Kirkpatrick, D. (Ed.), *The Doctrine of the Church*, p. 12.
[10] Letter to the editor of *The London Chronicle—Letters*, iv. 137.

removed, (c) if erroneous doctrine had been suppressed, (d) if ordination vows had been fulfilled, and (e) if pastoral care had been exercised over the weak and unconverted. These were tall demands, but Barrett claimed that Methodism *did* these things; and in doing them it was 'a humble revivisence of the spirit of the Church of England, viewing that church as a spiritual community'.[11]

The Tractarian Movement is generally thought to have begun with Keble's Assize Sermon at Oxford in 1833 and the first Tract appeared on 9th September in the same year; but the Methodists were slow to waken to its significance. In fact, a contributor to the *Methodist Magazine* for 1840, writing on the dangers of Popery, thought that he had been regarded as a scaremonger five years previously. He admitted that the new movement had 'come upon us in great measure by surprise'.[12]

According to the index to the *Methodist Magazine*, 'Popery' had been consistently discussed since 1820, but not until 1837 does the entry 'Oxford Tracts' first appear. By 1841, however, the Magazine is in full cry. A review of 'Pamphlets on Puseyism' begins by saying that the effects of the Methodist Revival on the Church of England had been, (a) to create a care for a pious ministry, (b) to devote attention to the condition of the heathen, and (c) to encourage a willingness to co-operate with other bodies. Now, however, Puseyism has emerged with the avowed object of destroying the Evangelical Party and substituting the ritualism of Laud, the theology of Jeremy Taylor and the politics of Sacheverell for the Articles and Homilies of the Church.[13] It was acknowledged that some of the Tractarians were godly men and benefited their church by their personal character, in their meekness under reproach and in their theological protest against liberalism; but in the subordination of scripture to tradition, belief in the Real Presence, practice of prayers for the dead, confession and penance, in their ascribing magical powers to the

[11] *Methodist Magazine*, 1841, p. 202.
[12] Ibid., 1840, p. 138.
[13] Ibid., 1841, p. 39.

clergy and the assurance of salvation through the church, they were on the verge of Roman superstition. Above all, when it was said that 'the sacraments and not preaching are looked on as the sources of divine grace'[14] the Methodists began to take notice. By 1842, there were many in the Connexion who were wondering how far they could maintain what associations and affections they still had for the Church which cradled the Wesleys:

> We have been accustomed, hitherto, to look with veneration and love upon the English Establishment, and to regard her as being ... 'the great breakwater against the swelling tide of Popery'; but now that she fails to afford us protection, now that her best sons are filled with alarm as to the issue of passing events, what can we say? If the breakwater gives way, what is to become of the harbour?[15]

Or, as Jabez Bunting expressed it: 'Unless the Church of England will protest against Puseyism in some intelligent form, it will be the duty of the Methodists to protest against the Church of England.'[16]

In the meantime, the Tractarians were creating other barriers between themselves and the Methodists. To dismiss Methodism as a schism, its ministers as 'self-appointed' and its sacraments as invalid were allowable deductions from Tractarian theology; but when incumbents, infected with Puseyism, actively persecuted Methodists in their parishes, the effects of the Movement extended beyond the ecclesiastical to the social sphere. An alienation, hitherto unknown, between Methodists and Anglicans, was created, from the effects of which we are only just recovering today. One writer said that the Oxford Movement had so 'warped the minds of a considerable number who formerly frequented Church in the morning and chapel in the evening, that now they never enter a Methodist chapel'.[17] In 1844, a Methodist, Stephen Kay, wrote a pamphlet entitled *Puseyism in Power* and followed it by *The Self-*

[14] *Tracts*, vol. i., preface, p. iv.
[15] *Methodist Magazine*, 1842, p. 683.
[16] Gregory, B., *Sidelights*, p. 317.
[17] *Papers on Wesleyan Matters*, i. 7, 13.

convicted Curate in which he gives instances of Methodists, especially in rural parishes, being severely ostracized by Puseyite incumbents. Tradesmen and farmers were starved out of employment, villagers were refused, or excluded from charitable grants to the poor. Local Preachers were particularly vulnerable to this form of victimization. Another writer tells how two Methodist theological tutors, one at Richmond and the other at Didsbury had each a son at Oxford where they were told to regard their fathers as unauthorized teachers.[18] It is therefore not surprising that in 1843, the Conference itself should take note of what was happening.[19] Even *The Times* which was once in the habit of publishing 'fulminating articles' against the Tractarians had now been silenced;[20] Puseyism had become 'accepted'!

It was in this atmosphere that *Wesleyan Tracts for the Times* appeared in 1842,[21] as the official reply of the Wesleyans to the Puseyite 'Tracts'. In the controversy there were four main points at issue, (a) the scriptures, (b) episcopacy, including ordination and Apostolic Succession, (c) the sacraments and (d) whether Methodism was a schism and true to the intentions of its founder. We shall now consider these.

Attack and Defence
(a) The Scriptures

For the Methodists, the scriptures were the supreme rule

[18] *Methodism as It Is*, p. 24.
[19] See the Conference Address to the Societies for 1843—*Minutes*, ix. 557.
[20] Fish, Henry, *Jesuitism in the Oxford Tractarians*, p. 19.
[21] These Wesleyan Tracts were published anonymously, but from the Minutes of the Book Committee in the Methodist Archives we have been able to establish authorship. The full list of titles and authors is as follows:
  1. *Why Don't you come to Church?* by George Osborn.
  2. *Wesleyan Methodism not a Schism* by Dr Hannah.
  3. *Apostolical Succession* by W. L. Thornton.
  4. *Wesleyan Ministers true Ministers of Christ* by George Turner.
  5. *Modern Methodism, Wesleyan Methodism* by George Osborn.
  6. *Justification by Faith an Essential Doctrine of Christianity* by George Cubitt.
  7. *Lyra Apostolica, an Impious Misnomer* by Dr Humphrey Sandwith.
  8. *Baptism not Regeneration* by Francis A. West.
  9. *Wesleyans have the true Christian Sacraments* by Alfred Barrett.
  10. *A Letter to 'A Country Curate'* by John McOwan.

of faith and conduct. This was good, traditional Anglican teaching on which Wesley himself had been nourished. The Methodists knew their Prayer Book which was largely scriptural; they were also familiar with the Thirty-nine Articles of which Article VI was retained in Wesley's *Sunday Service of the Methodists* as Article V:

> Holy Scripture containeth all things necessary to salvation: so that whatsoever is not read therein, or may be proved thereby, is not to be required of any man, that it should be believed as an article of faith, or be thought requisite or necessary to salvation.

Although he read widely, Wesley always regarded himself, fundamentally, as *homo unius libri*, and after his death his followers sought to fashion their emerging church on scriptural principles. At times, the teaching of scripture is not clear, and its ambiguities led some of the Dissenters from Kilham onwards to come to conclusions which did not concur with those of the Wesleyans, but they all (in spite of their differences) appealed to scripture in support of their contentions. The Wesleyans argued that their church principles—polity and doctrine alike—were modelled on scriptural lines. They knew, as Wesley did, the Homily of 1726 which said, 'In Holy Scripture is fully contained what we ought to do, and what to eschew, what to believe, what to love and what to look for at God's hand at length'.

So one can imagine the reaction of the Methodists when they read in Newman's Tract XC, 'In the sense in which it is commonly understood at this day, scripture is not, on Anglican principles, the rule of faith'; or this from Tract LXXVIII, 'Scripture and tradition, together, are the joint rule of faith'; or when a young Puseyite remonstrated with his fellow-clergymen because they supported the Bible Society—he called it, 'a league of all sects and shapes of mischief'.[22] In the face of such statements, the Wesleyans had no alternative but to emphasize their belief in the scriptural nature of their church, as one writer in the

[22] *Methodist Magazine*, 1841, p. 1008.

Methodist Magazine for 1835 said, 'No form of Church government... has been framed with stricter regard to those great New Testament principles which are essential to the constitution of a Christian Church'. (p. 748.)[23]

Of course, there were over-emphases and over-simplifications on both sides. The Methodists failed to appreciate the excellence of some of the elements which the Tractarians were recovering from the past; the Tractarians, on the other hand, 'bent the bow too far' (as Wesley said of himself in his Oxford days); but we shall now see how the Wesleyans applied their appeal to scripture in other spheres.

(b) Episcopacy

Within a period of about fifty years, the Methodist ministry had emerged from the status of 'Preachers', 'Mr Wesley's Assistants and Helpers' into that of ministers of the church, endowed with the authority and privileges of the Pastoral Office. It came as a profound shock to them to be told by the Tractarians that, without episcopal ordination, they were self-appointed and that the sacraments administered by them were invalid. When such claims as these were made by Rome, they were understood, but detested; but for them to be advanced seriously by scholars of the Church of England must have been to the Methodists, as well as to many within the Anglican Church itself, an innovation the impact of which we can hardly estimate.

The Tractarian claims on episcopacy were, in brief:

i. That there are, by unalterable divine appointment, three distinct orders of ministers in the Church of Christ—bishops, priests and deacons.

ii. That only bishops have authority to ordain.

iii. That where there is no bishop, there can be no valid ordination, no true ministry, church or sacraments.

iv. That there has been a regular and unbroken series of valid episcopal ordinations, commencing with the Apostles and extending to the present time.

[23] See also Shrewsbury, W. J., *An Essay on the Scriptural Character of the Wesleyan Methodist Economy* (1839).

v. That all those, and none but those, who have been ordained by a bishop in this succession, are true ministers of Christ.

The Tractarians accused the Wesleyans of being even further removed from a valid ministry in that they lacked true Presbyterian succession. The reference was, of course, to the fact that the Methodists had suspended laying-on of hands in 1792, and when they resumed it in 1836 they did not invite Henry Moore, who had been ordained by Wesley, to take part in the ceremony and so establish a tactual succession.[24] Not that there was much point in this argument for, in any case, in the eyes of the Tractarians all non-episcopally ordained ministers had, 'assumed a power which was never entrusted to them: and have presumed to exercise the power of ordination and to perpetuate a succession of ministers without having received a commission to do so'.[25]

The Wesleyans brought a considerable amount of scholarship to bear upon these claims, quoting freely from the scriptures and the early Christian Fathers. They demonstrated that an unbroken succession cannot be proved from either, and that episcopacy was never intended to be the only form of church government. What weighed with the Methodists more was that to sustain an unbroken succession, men of questionable faith and morals had to be included in the list. They also knew that during the Elizabethan period, the ordinations of Scottish Presbyterian and other Reformed Churches were accepted by the Church of England.[26]

Nor were the Wesleyans without their own criteria of ministerial validity. In the first place, they did not object to episcopacy as a form of church government;[27] what they contested was the theory that, 'the right of the Christian

---

[80] On the question of Henry Moore and the succession, see my article entitled 'Ordination in Wesleyan Methodism 1791–1850' in *The Proceedings of the Wesley Historical Society*, xxxix. 121. Moore's letter to the Conference is printed in *The Life of Henry Moore*, p. 326.

[81] *Tracts*, VII, p. 2; quoted by *Wesleyan Tracts for the Times*, No. 4, p. 9.

[82] *W.T.T.*, No. 3, p. 12, quoting Statute XIII, Eliz., chap. xii.

[83] For the American Methodists had organized themselves accordingly.

ministry belongs exclusively to the episcopal clergy, because they have descended in unbroken succession from the Apostles ...'.[28] Secondly, they did not deny the value of ministerial succession, but not by 'arbitrary contact or imposition of hands'.[29] A lengthy passage from the pen of Thomas Jackson is worth quoting:

> There is ... an Apostolic Succession ... in which every minister should be careful to stand, or he will be found an intruder into the sacred office ... The true Apostolical Succession is a succession to a ministry which is characterised by Apostolical truth, by Apostolical zeal and faithfulness, by Apostolical efficiency and power, by Apostolical labour and self-denial, and by Apostolical success. In this succession we believe that our fathers stood and we ourselves are in it as far as we are actuated by the same spirit, and tread in their steps....[30]

In other words, the Wesleyans held that 'the ministry appoints the ministry' and therein lies a valid succession, and in so far as they stood in a succession of godly men who were appointed by Wesley, they were not, as the Tractarians alleged, 'self-appointed' men.

When the Wesleyans asked the further question, 'What sort of ministry appoints the ministry?', they fell back upon their system of discipline, and insisted that the marks of a true minister were, as they had been since Wesley's time, 'gifts, grace and fruit'. As the writer of the Wesleyan Tract No. 2 wrote (p. 11):

> A ministry, though it may in some things seem irregular, is proved to be valid where these ('Gifts, grace and fruit')

[28] *W.T.T.*, No. 3, p. 4.
[29] Barrett, A., *Wesleyan Church Principles*—an article in the *Methodist Magazine*, 1841, p. 197. We recall Wesley's belief in Apostolic Succession, but the theory of an 'unbroken succession' he 'knew to be a fable which no man ever did or can prove'—*Letters*, iv. 139.
[30] Jackson, T., *Wesleyan Methodism a Revival of Apostolic Christianity*, p. 35; the whole passage, of which this is an extract is worth reading. The Wesleyans were with Luther and Calvin here in the belief that succession was one of doctrine, not of office. Luther said that what makes a man a bishop is not that he succeeds to a certain office vacated by a previous bishop, but that he teaches the Gospel rightly—Weimar edition of Luther, vol. 39, II. 177; Calvin *Institutes*, IV. 2, 6.

unquestionably exist and abound; but, without these, even the ministry which is deemed most regular in its official transmission, can scarcely be otherwise than defective and inefficient. We value order and regularity; but we must prefer ministerial grace and fruit.

Ministerial validity must therefore evidence itself in ministerial 'fruit'; just as St Paul told his Corinthian readers that they were his 'seal of Apostleship in the Lord' (1 Cor. 9:1, 2), so the Wesleyans pointed to the people who had been won for Christ at home and abroad through their ministry. Christ's dictum, 'by their fruits shall ye know them' (Matt. 7:16–20) 'is a rule that is equally applicable to the man and his ministry'.[31] As to tactual succession, Barrett said convincingly that it is 'not necessary that the servants of Christ should touch each other, or be locked into each other as links. Enough that the individual has the vocation of the body.'[32]

Another serious criticism which the Wesleyans laid against the Tractarians was that their conception of episcopacy and Apostolic Succession 'unchristianized' others. Methodism had little to learn about the nature of true catholicity; Wesley's sermon on The Catholic Spirit had not been lost upon them. While they freely criticized both Anglicanism and Dissent and belonged to neither, they never for a moment doubted that these two great bodies of Christians were within the one holy catholic church. To the Tractarians, however, this meant that the Methodists were neither one thing nor the other. As Conference remarked in 1840, 'By many, our Catholicity has been reckoned our infirmity, if not our sin; and hence the censures which have been heaped upon us because of our independent position with respect to the Established Church on the one hand and to the different classes of Dissenters on the other'.[33] This was painful; but Methodism could not recognize any true catholicism in a system which

[31] *W.T.T.*, No. 4, p. 3.
[32] Barrett, A., *Catholic and Evangelical Principles*, p. 25. See *W.T.T.*, No. 4, pp. 4–7 for a useful summary of the Wesleyan definition of a valid ministry.
[33] *Minutes*, ix (1840), p. 111.

unchurched millions of fellow-christians in all parts of the world:

> To unchristianise more than one half of all the Protestant Churches in the world; to include thousands of pious, learned and devoted ministers of Christ in the sin and condemnation of Korah, Dathan and Abiram; to harass the souls of the simple, on subjects of eternal moment, with doubts which never can be resolved; and to induce an universal scepticism with regard to Christian ordinances, are, with these men, matters of no practical moment.[34]

A people who had learned to sing: 'Names and sects and parties fall' had not so learned Christ.

(c) The Sacraments

For the Tractarians, the validity of the sacraments was bound up with Episcopacy and Apostolic Succession. From the belief that the only valid ministry was that bestowed by episcopal ordination, it followed that only sacraments administered by such ministers were valid. Furthermore, as only episcopally ordained ministers could constitute the true church, salvation could not be found outside their ministrations. One could quote extensively from the Oxford Tracts, but the following are sufficient for our purpose.

> It is only this (apostolic commission) that can give any security that the ministration of the word and sacraments shall be effectual to the saving of souls. The Dissenting teachers have it not.[35]
>
> The Eucharist, administered without apostolical commission, may to pious minds be a very edifying ceremony, but it is not that blessed thing our Saviour graciously meant it to be.[36]

In reply, the Methodists argued that if Methodism was a Church and its Itinerants were ministers, to administer the sacrament is a necessary pastoral function. 'If we have a right to the ministry', said James Dixon, 'we have a right to

[34] *W.T.T.*, No. 4, p. 13.
[35] *Tracts*, vol. i., No. 35, p. 4.
[36] Ibid., No. 4, p. 5.

this particular function.'[37] In other words, the administration of the sacraments was the prerogative of the Pastoral Office; to the Pastoral Office even more than to the Priestly Office. The Wesleyans made much of this—and it was a telling argument. To the Tractarians, the Lord's Supper was a priestly act exercised under the High Priesthood of Christ. The Wesleyans denied this on the grounds that 'Christ never transmitted his priesthood'. To administer the sacraments was to them, 'a pastoral act, performed by authority delegated from Christ as Chief Shepherd, for his pastorate he *has* transmitted and put into commission'.[38] As Barrett said, '... the Christian ministerial commission is a commission held under Christ in His office of prophet and chief Pastor or Bishop of souls.... In the New Testament, the transmission of ministerial authority is never spoken of as the conveyance of a mere office and dignity, irrespective of the character of those who fill it but rather as the transmission of the truth through the medium of faithful men.'[39]

The next charge laid against the Methodists was that their sacraments were 'no sacraments' because they were administered by men not episcopally ordained and so outside the authentic apostolic succession. The reply was again a resort to the argument that they were not self-appointed men, but commissioned by those already in the ministry:

> The scripture knows of no consecration except the separation of the elements to their intended use by a Christian Pastor, and in the exercise of prayer, and the use of liturgical or other scriptural exhortation and declaration....
> ... although they are not episcopally ordained, yet they are not without ordination. The Methodist ministers are as much in the succession of God's true, apostolical, evangelising ministers as are the national clergy, and as much conformed to apostolical order, as it would be easy to show from the Acts of the Apostles. Nor did they put themselves into this position.

[37] Dixon, J., *Methodism, its origin*, etc., p. 94.
[38] *W.T.T.*, No. 9. pp. 4–5.
[39] Barrett, A., *Catholic and Evangelical Principles*, pp. 9–10.

Their right to administer the sacraments flows by apostolic sequence from their being placed in the Pastoral Office.

... every Methodist minister from the beginning has been put in his position by those who were in the ministry before him, and therefore in the succession before him.[40]

Finally, the charge that the Methodists were guilty of what the Tractarians called 'Justification by Feeling'. There was just enough truth in this jibe to make it bite, and one of the services which the Oxford Movement rendered to the church of its day was to administer a corrective to what has always been a weakness of the Evangelicals—an over-emphasis on the subjective elements in the Christian Faith.[41] They sought to restore the objective factors in the sacraments—both Baptism and the Eucharist. But the Tractarians overplayed their hand. It was not logical to argue that because the Methodists attached so much importance to feeling, 'the feelings of those who communicate are a proper test of validity'; less still is it right to allege that the Methodists believed that even the sacraments of Wesleyan Association Local Preachers were valid if they create the right feeling![42] For one thing, the Wesleyans did not allow Local Preachers to administer the sacraments; but even the Wesleyan Association, who did, would not have grounded the validity of their sacraments on the test of feelings alone. This Tractarian comment showed a sad ignorance or misunderstanding of the Wesleyan doctrine of the Pastoral Office.

The Methodist conception of a valid sacrament began with the scriptures. 'Not the hands which administer it, but its conformity to the original institution, to the ordination of Christ, and especially its containing and setting forth the very grace and blessing intended by our Lord.'[43] The only sacraments to be observed are 'those signs and seals of the evangelical covenant which are expressly recognised as such

---

[40] *W.T.T.*, No. 9, pp. 4–5.
[41] See Webb, C. C. J., *op. cit.*, pp. 116, 121.
[42] *Remarks upon a Wesleyan Tract*, No. 1, p. 18. The Methodists did, on occasion, emphasize feeling; see, e.g., Dixon, *op. cit.*, p. 51, 'We glory in the reproach that our people manifest feeling'.
[43] Dixon, J., *op. cit.*, p. 94.

in the sacred book'.⁴⁴ They are 'covenant transactions', 'illustrations by action and visible confirmations of a compact entered into by God with His redeemed creatures'.⁴⁵

> As far as a sacrament contains a *signum significans* (or signifying sign), it is emblematic... but as far as a sacrament contains a *signum confirmans* or confirming sign, it is a divine pledge or security that God will give unto the receiver all the grace of the covenant to which it refers... according to his obedience to its proposed terms; and thereby it may be, though always it is not, the channel through which it is conveyed, inasmuch as the traitor Judas partook of the Last Supper and Simon Magus, though baptized was 'in the gall of bitterness and bond of iniquity'.
>
> In one point of view they are tests of our Christian obedience; in another the instruments of Christian fellowship; in another, bonds of charity; in another, incentives to devotion; in another safeguards against sin; in another, memorials of Christ's purchased benefits; in another, aids to our feeble faith; in another, badges of discipleship. They are all these but chiefly they are appointed to be channels by which the Holy Ghost shall convey to every faithful receiver that measure of covenant grace which his circumstances at the time shall require, and accordingly, as he shall comply, in the exercise of penitence and faith, with the evangelical conditions of salvation.⁴⁶

This is a full and fair statement of the Wesleyan conception of the Sacrament of the Lord's Supper.

(d) *Was Methodism a Schism and untrue to Wesley?*

Time and time again, pamphlets appeared from rather naïve Puseyite incumbents, imploring the Wesleyans to 'return to the Church'. They argued that John Wesley was an episcopally ordained priest, that he never intended his people to form a separate sect and that in separation, the Wesleyan Connexion was not a church at all; it was, in fact, in schism. Coming from the Tractarians, this was not

⁴⁴ *W.T.T.*, No. 9, p. 1.
⁴⁵ Ibid.
⁴⁶ Ibid.

unexpected for to them all non-episcopal bodies were in schism from the one, true church. It was the Apostolic Succession alone which enabled 'the most simple-minded and unlearned person to discriminate between the true Church of Christ and the unauthorised sects which call themselves Christ's followers'.[47] A certain 'Epaphras' rather shallowly remarked that whereas the Church of England goes back to Apostolic times, Methodism was scarcely a century old and is 'plainly a schism *in* a Church and *from* a Church which is undeniably scriptural in its principles'.[48]

Thomas Jackson's reply was that Methodism, in principle, was as old as Christianity, 'for it is Christianity itself'.[49] As for Methodism being a schism, he made three points. His first point was that no one should use the word 'schism' of separation, for it is never thus used in the New Testament; secondly, he maintained that it is begging the question to say that 'to separate from a Church which is scriptural in principles is schism', for a church may be 'scriptural in its principles yet corrupt in administration'; his third point was that the majority of the Methodist people formerly attended no church at all. They were never in the church, 'and therefore have not separated from it'. Jackson concludes:

> Methodism . . . is not a schism *from* a Church. It appeared as a revival of apostolical Christianity . . . in the Established Church. The Church cast it forth . . . in consequence of which it was thrown upon its own resources, gradually assumed a distinct and definite form and grew up by the side of the Establishment as an independent body. Men may call it 'schism' and 'separation', but it stands before the world as a national blessing.[50]

Methodism had developed its own life apart from the Church of England and organized its own worship, but it

---
[47] *Tracts*, vol. i, No. 29, p. 10.
[48] Epaphras: *The Church of England compared with Wesleyan Methodism*, p. 2.
[49] Jackson, T., *The Wesleyans Vindicated*, pp. 7–11.
[50] Ibid., p. 12.

did not devise new doctrines.[51] 'When the Methodists separated,' wrote Barrett, 'it was because the doctrine of the Church was no longer preached, and its discipline was not exercised and when its ordinances (particularly the Sacrament of the Lord's Supper) to them (i.e. the Methodists) at least was not administered. There was no breach of love....'.[52]

It was when the Wesleyans took the battle into the Anglican camp that they became most telling. It was the Tractarians themselves, said *The Wesleyan Vindicator*, who were causing schism—and that within their own church. As Alfred Barrett wrote:

> We think the charge (of schism) may be preferred with fearful truth against the Church of England; not only because of her sacrifice of charity in her treatment of the early Methodists, but also on account of the painful dissentions *within* her pale at the present day.[53]

In contrast to the Church of England, Methodism was a unity; not only was it one with the Church of England in essential and traditional Anglican doctrine (and therefore not in schism), it was also a unity within itself. Doctrinal unity was a strong point with the Wesleyans, and had been since Wesley's day. It was laid down in the Deed of Declaration and in every Conference Model Deed, that the Preachers must be true to Wesley's *Forty-four Sermons*, and that nothing contrary to those sermons must be preached in Methodist chapels. At every District Meeting and at the Conference, Preachers were called to account for their loyalty to this basic system of doctrine.[54] There was no such unanimity in the Church of England; and even if there had been, there was no disciplinary means of ensuring it. The writer of Wesleyan Tract No. 1 could say of the Church of

---

[51] See *W.T.T.*, No. 5, p. 10.
[52] Barrett, A., *Catholic and Evangelical Principles*, pp. 38–9.
[53] Hall, S. R., *A Wesleyan Minister's Address to Methodists at Tunbridge Wells*, p. 11; see also, Layman: *Reasons why Wesleyan Methodists separated from the Church of England*.
[54] 'No deviation from (Methodist doctrines) has ever been tolerated in any of our ministers'—Grindrod, E., *Wesleyan Methodism in Retrospect*, p. 12.

England, '... when we go to church, unless we know beforehand who is the minister, we are never sure what doctrine we shall hear'.[55] On the other hand James Dixon claimed that Methodism's 'unity is more complete than that of any community of Christians',[56] and in spite of all the deep and painful divisions over church organization, this claim is true so far as doctrine is concerned.

So it was claimed that while Methodism may be separated from the Church of England, it is not a schism in either origin or nature. As defined in Article XIX, Methodism claimed its place in the Church of Christ.

Conclusion

More than a century has passed since the Oxford Movement burst upon the Church. We are therefore better able to judge both its achievements and its excesses. The good it did lives on, and the Church of England owes much to the saintliness and the energy of its leaders. They restored an objectivity to the sacraments, a dignity to its worship and a sense of corporateness to the Body of Christ. They did much to offset the narrowness of the Evangelicals and reminded the Church that the Incarnation, as well as the Atonement, was part of 'the whole Gospel'. They recovered the holiness of beauty, as well as the beauty of holiness, especially when holiness was not always beautiful.

It is, of course, too much to expect that the nineteenth-century Methodists should see this. What was true, as well as what was bizarre, in Tractarianism was as great a shock to them as Wesley's preaching was to eighteenth-century latitudinarians. What the Wesleyans rightly protested against in Tractarianism was the unscriptural elements in its doctrine, its intolerance towards non-episcopal denominations and its pro-Roman leanings; and —what is more important—they did more than merely protest. They answered with positive concepts of their own. They showed that Tractarian ideas of Church and ministry

[55] *W.T.T.*, No. 1, p. 22.
[56] Dixon, J., *Methodism, its origin*, etc., p. 86.

were not the only ones to be reckoned with; and a valid alternative was the one they themselves put forward—namely the Wesleyan Doctrine of the Pastoral Office.

As an expression of the mind of the Methodist leaders on the Oxford Movement in 1841, we end this section with the judgement of Alfred Barrett, who was not blind to the merits of those whose views he is denouncing:

> Are the Tractist Divines learned? I would respect their learning. Are they meek? In opposing them, I would imitate that meekness. Are they diligent pastors? May I have grace so far to be like them!
>
> But when, in order to make out the line of the ministers of the Lord Jesus Christ, they drag me through crowds of some of the worst men the world ever saw, and meekly denounce unnumbered holy men, with their evangelical fruits of holiness around them, as intruders into God's fold, and unchurch their communions; when, according to them, religious experience is fanaticism, and communion with God only certainly and safely maintained in outward 'ecclesiastical expression' [Newman's Sermons]; when preaching the Word is only tradition, only the conveyance of objective truth, and not a channel of living influence; and when there is no certain ground for attaining the divine favour in the case of sin after baptism—there are, in all these, consequences ... fearful and anti-scriptural....[57]

---

[57] *Methodist Magazine*, 1841, p. 204.

CHAPTER FOUR

CONCLUSIONS

IT will be noted that we have made a practice of discussing the significance of each period or topic as it has been dealt with in the relevant chapter, and this relieves us of the necessity of having to write a lengthy summary here. The period covered by this study saw the evolution of Wesleyan Methodism as a Church. The Societies which met 'in connexion with' John Wesley developed into what Dr J. S. Simon once described, rather eulogistically, as an 'immense organization which wields such a powerful religious influence throughout the world'.[1] It was this slow process from Society to Church (so slow that the word 'Society' has only recently disappeared from our official terminology),[2] which more than anything else delayed the formulation of a doctrine of church and ministry in Methodism. Until the theologians and administrators accepted the fact that Methodism was no longer a federation of Societies, but a Church, such doctrines could never take shape. So precept moulded practice; the theologians forced the hands of the administrators. It was not that a certain doctrine of the ministry emerged from a particular ecclesiastical polity; on the contrary, Wesleyan polity was fashioned to express a certain conception of the ministry. The turmoil over the expulsion of members, the supremacy of the Conference, the authority of the District Meeting, the office of Superintendent, is incomprehensible without an understanding of what the Wesleyans meant by the Pastoral Office. On the other hand, the doctrine of the Pastoral Office could never have taken any practical shape had it not been exercised through Wesleyan polity.

When one reflects upon Wesleyan Methodism of the first half of the nineteenth century, one is acutely aware of tensions; tensions within the Connexion itself and tensions

[1] *London Quarterly Review*, January 1884, p. 268.
[2] See the new C.P.D., 1974.

between the Connexion and its environment. The very nature of its polity created a tension between the rulers and the ruled. With its high court composed of senior ministers, it was a highly centralized government by clerics. Yet the governed were local laymen who held the purse-strings and who were often men of independent spirit. The clerics believed in strong central government, as Bunting once wrote to Joseph Entwisle, advocating a strong executive:

> I am against increasing the power and multiplying the administrative functions of Leaders Meetings. A government carried on by endless debates and majorities would ruin the real work of God among us. . . .[3]

Many a creak and groan in the elaborate machinery of government can be traced to tension between the powerful ministerial Conference and determined local Leaders and Trustees. Generally, the government held a high view of the Pastoral Office and the governed a much lower view. Robert Currie, in his book *Methodism Divided*, has diagnosed the tensions between 'Chapel' and 'Connexion' as due to many factors, some of which are social rather than religious. The local chapel was a rallying point for the people; they 'owned the chapel' and the minister was a 'bird of passage'. Currie is generally anti-Bunting and shows little understanding of the Pastoral Office; if he has read any pro-Bunting literature he gives little evidence of it as compared with the extensive use he makes of Free Methodist books and pamphlets. We feel that there was much more rank-and-file loyalty to the ministers than Dr Currie allows for; surely it is an exaggeration to say, 'The position of the minister in Methodism created copious grievances which . . . never failed to shock the officials'.[4]

The central figure in this internal tension was, of course, Jabez Bunting. The image of this undoubtedly able man, as depicted by his detractors (and there were many), is too often accepted as authentic in every respect. We decline to regard him as the tyrant and self-seeker portrayed in the

[3] M.C.A. letter from Bunting to Entwisle, 24th October, 1828.
[4] pp. 46, 47.

CONCLUSIONS

Fly-sheets and *Centenary Takings*. The fact that he could be mistaken for a Kilhamite suggests that there is another side to his character. The writer of Fly-sheet No. 3 believed that Bunting had fallen into Kilhamitism of an extreme and dangerous kind in that he was at the mercy of lay lords of his own creating. Yet Joseph Hargreaves asserted that Bunting had 'done more to connect laymen with the working of Methodism than any other man ever attempted';[5] he admitted, however, that he allowed the lay lords to influence him.

The truth probably lies somewhere between the two extremes. William Arthur, a reliable judge of Wesleyan affairs, reported Bunting as once saying to him:

> My policy has been misunderstood. My real policy has been to secure the just rights of the people or the proper representation of the people ... and many of the old Preachers thought I went too far.[6]

Bunting saw the 'just rights of the people' not as the Free Methodists did, that is in the rule of the people by the people, but in a paternal Conference of Pastors who possessed all the authority necessary to rule and watch over those committed to their charge.

Again, that is why Bunting sensed the danger of too readily transferring to the church modes of government which happen to be current in the world of politics. Democracy was a 'live' word of the social reformers of his day. It was also a catchword of the Methodist 'gallery', to play to which is a constant temptation to any preacher; but, as the social reformers and the Free Methodists understood the word, Bunting regarded it as incompatible with both the Pastoral Office and the Crown Rights of the Redeemer.[7] His championship of the former was mistaken for tyranny; what was forgotten was that he was as doughty a champion of the latter as any John Knox. To Bunting, the claims of the Chief Shepherd alone gave meaning and

[5] Hargreaves, J., *Misrepresentations and Falsehoods of the Fly-Sheets Exposed*, p. 45.
[6] *Report of the Proceedings of a Special Committee on Lay Representation* (1875).
[7] See Bunting's Manchester *Statement* of 1806, p. 22.

authority to the Pastoral Office. The weakness of his position was that at that particular time he was defending a system of government much more autocratic than that of the State and it was not difficult for his enemies to call him a tyrant.

Internal tensions, however, were much more destructive. It was the tension between the Conference and the people which, in its more demonstrative form, led to the Leeds Organ Case, the Warrenite secession and the Fly-sheet controversy; in its less demonstrative form it resulted in a loss of confidence between ministers and laity. A church in which the governors and the governed were at one would have been much better equipped to deal with dissent. In Wesleyanism, the Conference party were too rigid, over-protesting and 'touchy'. With each successive revolt there was a certain loss of nerve, until we get the remarkable reaction to the Fly-sheets. It was those deep tensions within the system that occasioned the rumblings of dissent and made the outburst inevitable.

This brings us back to that fundamental quality, that 'watchfulness' or episcopé which was said to be of the very essence of Methodism; that 'watchfulness' against the lack of which in eighteenth-century Anglicanism Methodism itself was a protest. The question we ask ourselves now is, 'Was this watchfulness as effective as it was claimed to be?'. On matters of spiritual oversight, it probably was effective, and it would be true to say that the Wesleyans did their best to fulfil their Founder's maxim of 'watching over one another in love'. Yet here was a system which not only bred much disaffection but left too much room for it to fester. Lack of ministerial oversight (episcopé!) was probably one cause. In Leeds, for example, at the time of the organ dispute there were only four ministers for over five thousand members. Discontent spread unchecked. Ministers had no means of gaining the ear of the people or of winning their confidence. Erroneous and slanderous gossip about the Preachers and the constitution went unanswered.[8]

The same was true in 1849, so that the Chairman of the

[8] See *Sound Thoughts for Sound People*, p. 5.

Leeds District (the Rev. John P. Hare) once said, 'If this agitation teaches us anything, it teaches us the very slight hold we have of our people; the leaders who live among the people seem to have the power'.[9] The Free Methodists had a point when they insisted that the Class Leaders were the real Pastors; the Wesleyans denied this but came perilously near to contradicting themselves in 1822 when in the Conference Pastoral Letter they said, 'We hope that our Class leaders will endeavour to watch over the souls committed to their care as those who are to give an account to the Great Shepherd'—language used almost exclusively of the Pastoral Office.

Peter Prescott, who reported that saying of the Leeds Chairman, was once stationed in Scotland and he remarked that Presbyterianism could never understand 'how large bodies of people could be brought to array themselves in hostility against their minister'. The strong ties between a minister and his people, together with the power and prestige of the minister himself, made disputes like those which tore Methodism, unknown in Presbyterianism. Methodism lacked those 'strong ties' and 'power and prestige' just referred to and preferred to cultivate detachment from local prejudices on the part of its ministers. That was cited as one of the advantages of the Itinerant system, but it was also an unrecognized limitation.

It is a matter of history that the Wesleyan doctrine of the Pastoral Office did not survive the nineteenth century and when Methodist Union came in 1932 some of the Standing Orders on the ministry might well have been written by Kilham—so much for the victory of Dissent! To trace this disintegration would take us beyond our period, but we can discern the seeds of it there.

For one thing, as Dr W. R. Ward points out in his *Religion and Society in England*, the doctrine of the Pastoral Office, as expounded by Barrett, and Beecham, failed to stand up to the social tensions of the age. It was partly a question of leadership as well as of episcopé. People who

[9] Quoted by Prescott, P., *Does Methodism need Lay Representation?* (1875) p. 10.

were slowly emerging from illiteracy and non-enfranchisement were not likely to sit complacently under an autocratic ministry drawn from their own social stratum. The Church of England had traditionally bred a race of leaders (the Wesleys among them!) who were able to assume authority much more easily than the newly-risen Wesleyan minister. Then there was the strange situation between the 'leader' and the 'led' which must have arisen in many a local class meeting. It was not unknown for the 'master' to sit at the feet of one of his 'men' when the latter was a godly man who had been appointed the Class Leader of the Society Class of which his 'master' was a member. This reversal of roles, in a day when class distinctions meant something, sometimes created tensions of which we have little or no conception today; indeed, here lay one of the factors which made for the decay of the Class Meeting in Methodism.

Apart from this, however, the Wesleyans were too complacent and too self-satisfied for the Pastoral Office to endure. *The Eclectic Review* was not greatly exaggerating when it said that the Wesleyan ministry 'too largely partakes of a feeling of unparalleled excellence'.[10] Individual ministers, it said, were 'far too exclusive in their views of Wesleyan excellence and of ministerial authority'. They were right, too, in regarding the Wesleyan ministry as 'too much cut off, by their Itinerant Plan, from the play of those sympathies, than which nothing is more essential to the success of ministerial labours'. The Wesleyans were sure that their Orders were the most scriptural in Christendom. They ignored the fact that their opponents could use the same scriptures and arrive at different conclusions. The Free Methodists, for instance, believed that the doctrine of the 'Whole Church' might as properly be drawn from the New Testament as the doctrine of the Pastoral Office.

Reference to the scriptures prompts us to overstep the bounds of our period and remark that this very use of scripture contained within itself the seeds of its own destruction. Any system built upon a belief that the New

[10] *Methodism as it is* (1847), p. 39.

CONCLUSIONS

Testament contains a clear picture of the early Church, at least clear enough for us to emulate it in detail, was bound to feel the full impact of the Higher Criticism. When John Scott said in Manchester in 1851, 'Our constitution is the Bible'[11] he did not realize the frailty of the foundation on which he built. The Tractarians, less given to bibliolatry, were better able to withstand the impact of historical criticism. To them it was a mere graze; to the Methodists, indeed to all Evangelicals, it was a head-on collision.

But to return to this question of Wesleyan complacency, a forgotten factor is that they had so little to fear from the splinter groups, whose growth was not at all spectacular. Dr Robert Currie has shown that the history of these dissenting movements was not at all discouraging to the Wesleyans. None of them drew off any great numbers from the parent body and, withal, they were sadly divided among themselves. In 1852 at least, the Wesleyans could ignore the agitators.[12]

In 1831, an ill-informed attack was published by the British and Foreign Unitarian Association, which likened the Wesleyan Conference to a priest-ridden order and Wesley to a Pope. There was nothing new in this, but amid the invective, some comments were shrewd enough to hit hard. As outsiders, they could see that the Wesleyans were blind to the fact that 'the spirit of the times is such as not long to endure despotism in the church any more than in the nation'.[13] Their call to the Methodist people to 'rise and shake off their chains' was typical of the times:

> The great error of your rulers is that they strive to perpetuate a government suited only for the commencement of the system.... The Methodist community would have been much larger had its government been more liberal.

Strangely enough, this is just what Alexander Kilham had said in 1797.[14] In spite of what we have said about Bunting's

[11] *The Wesleyan Reformer* (1852), p. 2.
[12] Currie, R., *Methodism Divided*, pp. 222-4.
[13] *The Rise, Progress and Present Influence of Wesleyan Methodism*, pp. 52ff.
[14] Kilham argued that a mature society needs more liberal government than

refusal to play to his own gallery, the Wesleyans undoubtedly mistook, ignored or underestimated the power of the current of reform. They could hardly turn a blind eye to its effect in the political world, but they miscalculated on its ability to infect the religious world. So they were lulled into a belief that their people were satisfied with the system as it was. Alfred Barrett could complacently assert, 'The ministers . . . presume that the Societies are satisfied with their long-tried system—a system in whose details they have acquiesced'.[15] In 1863, Thomas Jackson could still speak of the divine right of the Wesleyan Conference,[16] yet only fifteen years later laymen were admitted, and that was virtually the end of 'Classical Wesleyanism'.

Furthermore, as we have said, Bunting might labour the point that ecclesiastical polity and secular government do not proceed *pari passu*, but in actual fact ecclesiastical politics and politicians are influenced by contemporary social patterns. Authoritarian systems like the Roman Catholic Church may be able to survive independently of changing social forms, but for comparatively young and voluntary systems like Methodism, this was virtually impossible. The Methodists had behind them less than half a century in which to work out a viable relationship between pastor and people, between the rulers and the ruled—and the time was too short, internal and external pressures too great. More than once they stressed the family spirit of the Connexion and the paternal relationship of the Conference to the Societies; but they did not see that this very situation required a high degree of rapport between pastors and people. To fall back upon the divine right of the Pastoral Office was not enough. The Free Methodists at times slandered the Wesleyan hierarchy in terms which were, to say the least, unworthy of the faith they professed, but the Wesleyans, on the other hand, were much too high-

---

an infant society does. The Wesleyans contended that a mature society needed pastors as much as preachers, and pastors meant rulers to them—see Kilham's *Paul and Silas*, p. 16.

[15] *The Pastoral Office*, p. 224.
[16] *Recollections*, p. 511.

handed. Bunting's 'like us or leave us' attitude comes out in his correspondence as early as 1803[17] but his famous phrase, as reported in Gregory's *Sidelights*, p. 193, was 'It is no sin for a man to think our discipline wrong, provided that he quits us'.[18]

The Wesleyans saw things too much as either black or white, with their opponents as irredeemably black! Said the *Methodist Magazine* for 1851:

> The men who have thus troubled once peaceful societies and who have spread sedition through some of our ranks, are, on every New Testament principle with which we are acquainted guilty before God (p. 644).

This displayed a regrettable underestimation of the merits and of the power of the democratic cause. It is perhaps too facile for us to say that a compromise should have been worked out; even easier for us to suggest what that compromise should have been. Yet, if the democratic workings of the Free Methodists could have been reconciled with the finer ideals of the Wesleyan doctrine of the Pastoral Office, the story of religion in England during the second half of the nineteenth century would have been very different.

At the same time, the Wesleyan conception of church and ministry is worthy of consideration, especially in these days of great fluidity of thought on such matters. In 1944, Canon Leonard Hodgson said that the outstanding feature of theological development since the First World War was the conception of the Church as 'a society called into being by God', 'to be the instrument of His work on earth'.[19]

[17] M.C.A. letter to George Marsden, 13th December 1803 in which Bunting regretted that Bramwell had not been expelled as one 'enthusiastically or schismatically disposed'; also letter to Richard Reece, 15th July, 1803 in which Bunting says 'the temporary loss of members would probably be more than recompensed by the increase of real scriptural piety, the restoration of good order and the establishment of brotherly love'.

[18] This, of course, is merely echoing Wesley when he wrote in the Minutes of 1766, 'Every Preacher and every member may leave me when he pleases; but while he chooses to stay, it is on the same terms that he joined me at first'.

[19] The *Guardian*, 18th August, 1944, quoted by Roger Lloyd in *The Church of England 1900–1965*, p. 271.

Allowing for the fact that the Wesleyans of our period were pre-Tractarians, this well expresses their view of the Church as expounded by Watson and Barrett. Canon Hodgson's church has given expression to that phrase in terms of the Eucharist; the Wesleyans saw it in terms of Christian experience and witness. They had no doubts about the church as a whole, and their own church in particular, being 'called into being by God to be the instrument of His work on earth', and the seriousness with which they endeavoured to fulfil their calling indicates the sincerity of their convictions. It is a timely reminder to us that the Church is more than a get-together of fellow 'do-gooders'; nor is it a civic convenience or a state ornament. Its ministers are more than would-be psychiatrists or religious welfare workers. The basic tenet of the Pastoral Office, as the Wesleyans conceived it, was that ministers must be called of God, 'to serve the present age' in the saving of souls and their nurture in the fellowship and discipline of the Society. Or, to return to the words of that first Methodist Conference, he is a man sent from God, 'to watch over the souls whom God commits to his charge as he that must give account' and one with a commission 'to feed and guide, to teach and govern the flock'.

A final word must now be said about the Wesleyan conception of the Church. As with most denominations of that pre-Tractarian period the Wesleyans lacked a vision of the church as the Body of Christ. We cannot, of course, blame them for that, as it was typical of the age in which they lived, but their intensely pragmatic nature, together with their tragic neglect of Wesley's spiritual legacy, aggravated this deficiency and it was left to the Tractarians to recapture it. Wesley's greatness lay in his synthesis of the priestly and the prophetic in the ministry, of the liturgical and the free in worship and of the Catholic and the Evangelical in churchmanship.[20] In later Methodism this balance was lost, and failure to see the Church as the Body of Christ was one of the causes of the terrible fissiparousness of nineteenth-century Methodism. Its emphasis on indi-

[20] See my book *The Sacrament of the Lord's Supper in Early Methodism*.

vidual conversion and personal holiness (rather narrowly conceived) its rigid demarcation of the sacred from the secular, its stern Sabbatarianism, its withdrawal from the world, a slipping of its moorings with such Catholicism as the Church of England was able to provide (and did provide for the Wesleys)—all made for the same effect; though they were redeemed by a quasi-allegiance to the Church through the use of its liturgy and the hymns of Charles Wesley. The Wesleyan hymn book in use until 1876 was 87 per cent Charles Wesley, though it had no separate section on the Church. The hymn, 'Christ from whom all blessings flow' was in the section headed, 'For Believers Praying'!

The lack of the vision of the Body of Christ was certainly a defect, yet the deficiency was not total. Methodism, as a whole, made only a limited use of music, liturgy and art; yet it never assumed the severity of Calvinism. Calvinistic austerity had a theological basis; Methodist austerity was largely a matter of economic necessity. Rural chapels were plain, indeed, but there was nothing in the theology or ethos of Methodism to prevent the affluent town members from erecting their neo-gothic churches and saying the liturgy on Sunday mornings, complete with the Anglican chants. Any consideration of the plainness of Methodist buildings must take into account the social and economic conditions of those who made up the bulk of the congregations.

We have had several opportunities to comment on the unique contribution of Wesleyan Methodism to our conception of church and ministry. This uniqueness lay in the policy of her statesmen to steer a middle course between Anglicanism and Dissent. The Wesleyans held to a conception of the ministry, for example, which lay mid-way between the priestly and the prophetic, between the autocracy of the priest and the 'hired servant' of the Dissenters; between the sacerdotalism of the extreme Catholic and the 'priesthood of all believers' of some modern Methodists.

As far as ecclesiastical polity is concerned, just as Wesley's organization was a synthesis of many different elements, so the Connexion that succeeded him was a strange amalgam. Alfred Barrett said that Wesleyan Methodism was episcopal in the oversight it gave to the ministry, Presbyterian in the parity it gave to its ministerial orders, and Independent in the recognition of the call of ministers and the voluntary contributions of the people towards their support.[21]

That is why the Methodist concept of the Church cannot readily be accommodated in any of the categories which were current at the time. It owed much to many traditions, yet it belonged to none in particular. Dr Outler has said that Methodism is 'a church after the order of Melchisedek', meaning that it became estranged from its Anglican heritage without possessing any 'blood ties with any other mode of Christianity'. It was too 'worldly' to make common cause with the radical Protestants and the Pentecostalists, so 'we are churchmen whose institutional forms are uniquely our own, but whose theological apparatus has been assembled from many quarters'.[22]

Wesleyanism, then, was neither Anglican nor Dissenting, yet it combined elements from both—a voluntary principle with an authoritative government, a Presbyterian polity with an Arminian theology, a gathered congregation without formal separation from the Established Church. As Dr Hannah told the Tractarians:

> The Wesleyan Methodists are not Dissenters, *in the ordinary sense and application of that term*; for they do not dissent from the principle of a national ecclesiastical establishment . . . nor do they dissent from the doctrine or general formularies of the Church of England; and they are not schismatics *in the* Church, for this plain reason, that, to a considerable extent and degree they are separated from the Church. They would not affect names which mark parties and distinctions, but they cannot entirely avoid using them; and they are satisfied with the one that has descended to them, including the hope, at the same time, of that better day when every sectarian distinction shall cease, and all Christ's disciples shall be one

[21] *Ministry and Polity*, p. 283.
[22] *The Doctrine of the Church*, p. 24.

CONCLUSIONS

in mind, in heart, and in name. *They are not, then dissenters from the Church of England in the customary use of that expression;* and they are not *SCHISMATICS in the Church of England*: but they *are*

WESLEYAN METHODISTS.[23]

---

[23] *Wesleyan Tracts for the Times*, No. 2 p. 10.

BIBLIOGRAPHY

Only a very selective bibliography is possible. In the Methodist Archives alone there are well over 1,200 books, pamphlets, magazines and newspaper articles which deal with the subject under discussion in this book.

I. Collections in the Methodist Church Archives

On the Sacraments and Kilham Controversies—140 items
On the Tent Methodists—7 items
On the Band Room Methodists—2 items
On the Church Methodists—11 items
On the Leeds Organ Case—50 items
On the Warrenite Secession—180 items
On the Fly Sheet and Reform—over 600 items

II. Contemporary Items (1791–1858)

Rules and Regulations of all the denominations discussed—various editions and dates
Biographies of Joseph Benson, Samuel Bradburn, Jabez Bunting, Adam Clarke, Thomas Coke, Joseph Entwisle (Sen), James Everett, Thomas Jackson, Alexander Kilham, Henry Moore, Richard Watson and others
The Magazines and Quarterlies of the various Methodist bodies
The Proceedings of the Wesley Historical Society (1898 to date)
The Watchman (1835–84)
The Wesleyan Times (1849–52)
Barrett, A., *An Essay on the Pastoral Office* (1839)
  Catholic and Evangelical Principles (1843)
  The Ministry and Polity of the Christian Church (1854)
Beecham, J, *An Essay on the Constitution of Wesleyan Methodism* (1st edition 1829: 2nd, 1850; 3rd, 1851)
Benson, J., *A Defence of the Methodists in five letters to Dr Tatham* (1793)
  A Farther Defence of the Methodists (1793)
  The Discipline of the Methodists Defended (1796)
  An Apology for the Methodists (1801)

BIBLIOGRAPHY

Carter, W. B., *Methodism Past and Present* (1852)
Crowther, J., *The Methodist Manual* (Halifax, 1810) later issued as *A Portraiture of Methodism* (1811, 1815)
Crowther, J. (Jun.), *A Defence of the Wesleyan Theological Institution* (1834)
Dixon, J., *Methodism, Its Origin, Economy and Present Position* (1843)
Eckett, R., *An Exposition of the Laws of Conference Methodism* (1846)
Everett, J., *Methodism as it is* (2 vols, 1863, 1865)
Jackson, T., *The Centenary of Wesleyan Methodism* (1839)
Wesleyan Methodism, a Revival of Apostolic Christianity (1839)
A Letter to the Rev. Edward B. Pusey, D.D. (1842)
The Wesleyan Conference, its Duties and Responsibilities (1849)
Christian Presbyters, their Offices, Duties and Rewards (1850)
Kilham, A., (Martin Luther) *To the Methodist Preachers Everywhere* (1795)
The Progress of Liberty and Outlines of a Constitution (Alnwick, 1795)
Manchester Preachers, *A Statement of Facts* (1806)
Myles, W., *A Chronological History of the People Called Methodists* (1st edition 1798 followed by later revised editions)
Nightingale, J., *A Portraiture of Methodism* (1807)
Peirce, W., *The Ecclesiastical Principles and Polity of the Wesleyan Methodists* (1854 and subsequent editions)
Rigg, J. H., *The Principles of Wesleyan Methodism* (1850)
Congregational Independency and Wesleyan Connexionalism Contrasted (1851)
Robinson, M., *Observations on the System of Wesleyan Methodism* (1824)
Sandwith, H., *An Apology for the System of Wesleyan Methodism* (1825)
Smith, G., *Wesleyan Ministers and their Slanderers* (1849)
The Doctrine of the Pastorate (1851)
The Polity of Wesleyan Methodism (1851)
A History of Wesleyan Methodism—3 volumes (1864)

BIBLIOGRAPHY

Taylor, T., *A Defence of the Methodists who do not attend the National Church* (Liverpool, 1792)
Turner, G., *The Constitution and Discipline of Wesleyan Methodism* (1851)
The Wesleyan Economy (1835)
Vevers, W., *Observations on the Power possessed and exercised by the Wesleyan Methodist Ministers* (1828)
An Essay on the National Importance of Methodism (1831)
A Defence of the Discipline of the Methodists (1835)
Vipond, W., *The Doctrine, Discipline and Mode of Worship of the Methodists seriously considered* (1807)
Warren, S., *Remarks on the Wesleyan Theological Institution* (1834)
Watson, R., *Institutes* (1828)
An Affectionate Address to the Trustees of the London South Circuit (1829)
Welch, C., *Wesleyan Polity*
Anon., The Fly Sheets (1844, 1846, 1847, 1848, 1849)
Proposals for the Formation of a Theological Institution (1834)
The Vice-Chancellor's Decision on the Warren Case (n.d.)
Wesleyan Tracts for the Times (10 papers, various authors, 1842)

III. Later Works

Baker, F., *John Wesley and the Church of England* (1970)
Bowmer, J. C., *The Lord's Supper in Methodism 1791–1960* (1961)
Currie, R., *Methodism Divided* (1968)
Davies and Rupp (Ed.), *A History of the Methodist Church in Great Britain* (1965)
Gregory, B., *Sidelights on the Conflicts of Methodism* (1898)
Kent, J., *The Age of Disunity* (1966)
Jabez Bunting, The Last Wesleyan (1955)
Kissack, R., *Church or No Church?* (1964)
Semmel, B., (Editor and Translator) Halevy, E., *The Birth of Methodism in England* (University of Chicago Press, 1971)
The Methodist Revolution (1974)

BIBLIOGRAPHY

Semmens, B. L., *The Conferences after Wesley* (Melbourne 1971)
Taylor, E. R., *Methodism and Politics 1791–1851* (Cambridge 1935)
Ward, W. R., *Religion and Society in England 1790–1850* (1972)
   The Early Correspondence of Jabez Bunting 1820–29 (1972)
   The Religion of the People and the Problem of Control 1790–1830, from 'Studies in Church History', volume 8 (Cambridge 1971)
   The Legacy of John Wesley: The Pastoral Office in Britain and America, from Lucy Sutherland's Festschrift, *Statesmen, Scholars and Merchants* (Oxford 1973)
   The French Revolution and the English Churches, from Miscellanea Historiae Ecclesiasticae IV (Louvain 1972)
Williams, C. W., *John Wesley's Theology Today* (1960)

INDEX

References to information in the footnotes are indicated by the addition of 'n' to the page numbers.

adherents, 72, 73–4, 95–6, 106
allowances, ministerial, 169
American Methodism, 55, 63, 238n
'Angel of the Church': *see* Circuit Superintendent
Apostolic Succession, 239, 245
Arthur, William, 158n, 251
Assistants: *see* Circuit Superintendent
Atlay, John, 23
Atmore, Charles, 26n
Auxiliary Fund, 195

Baker, Dr Frank, 197
Band-room Methodists, 71–4
baptism, 96n; as condition of membership, 173–4, 214
Barr, John, 108
Barratt, T.H., 36
Barrett, Alfred: on apostolic succession, 240, 242, 248; on Church of England, 232–3, 246; on lay participation, 221, 223; on Methodist polity, 181, 192, 194, 196, 256, 260; on the Pastoral Office, 149, 176–7, 183–6, 207–9, 213, 218, 219–20, 227, 253, 258; on Superintendent as 'Angel of the Church', 172, 211
Baxter, Richard, 213, 216n
Beaumont, Dr Joseph, 144n
Beecham, John, 118, 130, 149, 204, 207, 212, 218, 221n, 222, 253
Bennet, John, 23
Benson, Joseph, 24n, 28, 29, 32n, 33–4, 35, 50, 65, 66, 205, 206
Bernard, J.H., 185
Beverley, Church Methodists of, 75–80
Bible Christians, 84, 84–5
Birmingham: Circular (1791), 21n; secession at, 34n
Bogie, James, 66n
Book List for preachers on trial, 90–91, 122
Bourne, Hugh, expulsion of, 82–4
Bradburn, Samuel, 21n, 22n, 26, 28–9, 30–1, 42n, 45n, 92, 180, 204n
Bramwell, William, 81
Brettell, Jeremiah, 122n
Brilioth, Y., 231n
Bristol, 34, 39, 204n; circular (1791), 21n; Trustees, 22n, 52, 60
British and Foreign Unitarian Association, 255
Broadhurst, John, of Manchester, 71–2
Bromley, James, 109n
Bunting, Dr Jabez, 65–6, 71n, 86, 97, 203, 204, 223, 230;
 and Fly-sheet controversy, 147, 149, 150, 154n, 155, 250–1;
 and Leeds Organ Case, 110, 118, 171; and 'Liverpool Minutes', 94; and Theological Institution, 119, 122, 124;
 on Conference, 52, 77, 165; on lay participation, 98, 159n, 169, 251; on Methodist discipline, 81, 256–7; on the Pastoral Office, 72–3, 83, 149, 170–2, 206–7, 211, 251–2, 255–7; on Puseyism, 234
'secret Kilhamite', 47n, 137n, 251
Burslem, 82
Byker, Newcastle Circuit, 26n

Calvin, John, 185, 190n, 215n, 239n
Calvinism, 259
Canons, Anglican, 30, 32n
Carmarthen, 39
Carter, W.B., of Birmingham, 141–2, 146, 149–50, 206–7
catholicism, nature of, 240–1
Chapel Fund, 195
Cherry Burton, Yorks, 75
Christian Advocate, 121n
Church, R.W., 230
Church, doctrine of, 231–3, 236–7, 246, 249, 258–61 (*see also* whole church)
Church, use of term, 176

INDEX

Church Methodists of Beverley, 75–80
Church of England: discipline in, 27; relationship of Wesleyanism to, 78–80, 244–7 (*see also* 'Old Plan'; Oxford Movement)
Circuit plan, 171–2; 'Plan Comtee', 172n
Circuit Stewards, 98, 169
Circuit Superintendent ('Assistant'), 40–1, 44; 'Angel of the Church', 171–2, 211; powers of, 46, 55–7, 63–4, 138, 140n, 159, 170–3
civil authority, analogy with, 219–220, 223, 251–2, 256
Clarke, Dr Adam, 25n, 42n, 65, 78–9, 122, 205–6, 216
class leaders, 46, 99n, 173, 187, 194–5, 221–2, 224–5, 228, 253, 254 (*see also* Leaders Meeting)
class meeting, 86, 173, 189, 254
Coke, Dr Thomas, 35, 42n, 45n, 55n, 63, 64–5, 66, 205; and Church of England, 33, 34; ordinations by, 44, 183
Committees of Management, 98
Conference, Wesleyan, 19, 35, 47, 49, 51–2, 58, 108–9, 136, 152–5, 156–8, 159–60, 251, 252, 255; of 1744, 58–9, 122, 152–3, 198–9, 258; of 1745, 122; of 1746, 210; of 1768, 209; of 1790, 24n; of 1791, 40–1; of 1792, 41; of 1793, 28, 57, 59–60; of 1795, 35; of 1796, 206; of 1797, 45n, 51, 114–15, 126–31; of 1810, 98; of 1820, 93–5, 204, 206; of 1822, 225, 253; of 1827, 91; of 1829, 115; of 1833, 119, 122–3; of 1835, 129, 137–43, 211; of 1839, 144n; of 1840, 240; of 1842, 187n; of 1843, 235; of 1849, 146, 154; of 1851, 151, 157, 158; of 1852, 158–60; of 1853, 160; of 1955, 45; authority of, 111–12, 133, 135, 163–7, 210–11, 218; lay representation in, 136, 150, 160, 211; 'Legal Hundred', 39, 45, 52n, 63, 93, 144n, 165–6n (*see also* Deed of Declaration; Flysheet controversy; *Minutes*; Pastoral Address; Warrenite Secession)
Conference Model Deed, 97, 246
'Connexion', origin of term, 191n
connexional funds, 47, 97, 195, 221
connexionalism, 190–7; compared with Independency, 177–80; compared with Presbyterianism, 180–90
Contingent Fund, 195
Cooke, Joseph, 92
Cownley, Joseph, 26n, 206
Crowther, Jonathan (sen.), 32, 45, 57, 59n, 124, 137n, 176, 202n
Currie, Dr Robert, 203, 250, 255
Cusworth, Joseph, 144n

deacon, office of, 176–7
Deed of Declaration, 19, 39, 40, 42, 64, 67, 201, 246,
Deed of Union (1932), 226
democracy, 220, 251 (*see also* representative government)
Departmental Committee of Review, 169
Dewsbury trustees, 223n
discipline, 195–6; ministerial, 91–3
Dissent, Methodism and, 29–34, 204, 228, 253, 259–60
District Chairman, 39–45, 46–7, 52–5, 56, 64, 91, 122, 159, 168; called 'President', 39
District Meeting (Committee), 47, 53–5, 90, 91–2, 98, 122, 138, 151, 166n, 168–9, 218; function and powers of, 108–11, 132–4 (*see also* Leeds Organ Case; Minor District Meeting; Special District Meeting; Warrenite secession)
Districts, Methodist, 39, 169–70
Dixon, James, 63, 193, 241–2, 247
doctrine: safeguarding of, 216–17, 218; unity of, 196, 246–7

Eckett, Robert, 128, 150, 156
Eclectic Review, 254
Edmondson, Jonathan, 35
Elder, office of: *see* Presbyterianism
Emmett, Robert, 136
Entwisle, Joseph, 34n, 106, 129, 211

INDEX

episcopacy, 43, 62–3, 237–41
episcopé, 19, 37–50, 55, 85, 152, 167n, 170, 193, 199, 217, 224, 252
Everett, James, 78, 86, 92n, 96n, 120–1, 146, 152, 154, 156

Financial District Committee, 168
Fly-sheet controversy, 143–4, 145–160, 252
Form of Discipline, 48, 51–61, 67, 76, 88, 104, 109–10, 112–15, 121, 125–34, 136, 205
Forward Movement, 194
Free Church of Scotland, 148n

Gaulter, John, 122
Glasgow, 176, 182
Grand Central Association, 120, 137
Gregory, Dr Benjamin, 118n, 144, 156, 157, 170–1, 181n, 257
Grey, Robert, of Newcastle upon Tyne, 21n
Grindrod, Edmund, 109, 207

Haigh, Charles, of Bradford (Wilts), 159n
'Halifax Scheme', 37–41, 45n
Hannah, Dr John, 260–1
Hare, John P., 253
Hargreaves, Joseph, 157, 251
Hodgson, Leonard, 257
holiness, Tractarian and Methodist, 230–1
Home Mission Committee, 170
Huddersfield, 50n
Hughes, John, 122n
Hull, 75; circular (1791), 20–1, 26

Independency, 177–80
Ingham, Benjamin, 23; societies, 105n
Inglis, Andrew, 34n
Ireland: *see* Primitive Wesleyan Methodists
Isaac, Daniel, 92–3, 206
itinerancy, 188, 193

Jackson, Samuel, 158n
Jackson, Thomas, 90n, 93, 122, 153, 158n, 181n, 222–3, 239, 245, 256

Jenkins, William, 71
Johnson, Matthew, of Leeds, 103–4, 109, 111n
July Collection, 195
'Justification by Feeling', 231n, 243

Kay, Stephen, 234–5
Kent, Dr John, 57n, 146, 203
Kilham, Alexander, 24n, 25n, 26, 28, 30, 55–6, 58, 60n, 61, 65, 66, 75, 78, 88, 89–90, 97, 154n, 170, 232, 253, 255; expulsion of, 34, 46–50
Kilhamites, 52, 55, 59, 86, 129, 132, 134–5, 137n, 191, 203 (*see also* Methodist New Connexion)
Kingswood School Fund, 195
Kissack, Reginald, 191n
Knox, Alexander, 22, 23

Lamb, Mr, of Ireland, 136
Large Minutes, 22, 90, 126, 134
Lay Elders, 186–7
laymen: representation in Conference, 75–6, 77–8, 135, 136, 150, 160, 188, 211, 219; role of, 59–61, 98–9, 168–70, 210, 221–3
Leaders Meeting, 56, 73, 187–8, 218, 222, 250; and Kirk Session, 187–8; powers of, 60, 117, 126–31, 138, 216, 221, 250 (*see also* class leaders; Leeds Organ Case; Warrenite Secession)
Leeds, 39, 45n, 97n, 252–3; Organ Case, 24, 88, 96, 103–18, 128, 132, 135, 164, 171, 195n, 196, 198, 204, 225n, 252
Leeds Regulations, 126n, 131–2 (*see also* Form of Discipline)
Legal Hundred: *see* Conference
Lichfield Plan, 24, 42–5, 54n, 62, 64, 65
Liverpool Circular (1792), 29
'Liverpool Minutes', 93–5, 171n, 204, 206, 215–16, 225
Local preachers, 225n; administration of sacraments, 243; duties of, 221–2; pastoral responsibility, 224–5, 227–8; persecution of, 235; trial of, 109
Local Preachers Meeting, 223

269

INDEX

Local Preachers Mutual Aid Association, 158n
London: Circular (1791), 37; City Road Chapel, 25; Great Queen Street Chapel, 25; trustees, 22–23, 25
London Circuit, 226
London District, 148
Longbottom, William, 194
Lord's Supper, 27, 35–6, 175–6, 214–15, 244 (*see also* Sacraments)
Lumb, Matthew, 66n
Luther, Martin, 239n
Lyndhurst judgement, 131, 133, 134, 136, 164

Manchester, 31, 39; preachers' *Statement of Fact*, 204, 206; trustees, 23, 132 (*see also* Bandroom Methodists)
Mansfield, Lord, 22
Martindale, Miles, 79n
Mather, Alexander, 24, 25n, 35, 42n, 63, 64, 65, 66,
members, admission and expulsion of, 46, 88–9, 117, 125–31, 138–140, 156, 173–5, 182, 200, 201, 215–16
Methodist New Connexion, 49n, 77–8, 87, 123n, 191, 203, 223; Conference, 52n, 135, 136; membership figures, 88; 'Tom Paine Methodists', 50n (*see also* Kilhamites)
ministry, Methodist: authority of, 210–17; call to, 209–10; candidates for, 89–91, 132n, 218; criticism of, 147–50; discipline, 91–3; duties of, 94–5, 114, 116–117, 121–2, 125, 182–90, 190, 218; reception into Full Connexion, 91; secular employment, 183, 207–9; stationing, 188; training, 122–5; validity of, 239–40 (*see also* allowances; Conference; itinerancy; ordination; Pastoral Office; preachers)
Minor District Meeting, 139, 168
Minutes of Conference, 166–7; obituaries in, 58n

Moore, Henry, 28, 32n, 35, 42n, 63, 66
Murlin, John, 28
Myles, William, 53

Nature, Design and General Rules of the Methodist Societies (1798), 127
Newcastle upon Tyne, 200n; circular (1791), 26, 30; Orphan House, 25, 26n
Newman, J.H., 230n
Nightingale, Joseph, 95
Norwich, 28

O'Bryan, William, expulsion of, 84–5
'Old Plan', the, 20–6, 34n, 63, 75, 203
ordination, 48, 57, 80, 90, 117, 220, 225–6, 226, 242–3
ordinations: unauthorized, 21, 41n; by Wesley, 19, 22, 28, 180, 183 (*see also under* ministry)
organs, installation of, 96, 105–6; Organ Rule (1820), 107 (*see also* Leeds Organ Case)
Original Methodists, 84n
Outler, Dr Albert, 231, 260
Oxford Movement, 214, 229–48 (*see also* Tractarians)

Paine, Thomas, 50
'partial separation' from the Church, 27
Pastoral Letters, 166–7, 211n, 225, 253
Pastoral Office, 29, 57–9, 71, 73, 77, 80, 84, 86, 87, 93, 99, 114, 115–117, 126, 135, 137, 138–43, 144, 146, 149–50, 151, 157, 181, 185–6, 198–228, 242, 248, 249, 253, 256–7, 258
Pawson, John, 24, 25n, 28, 32, 34n, 35, 41n, 42n, 43, 44, 55n, 63, 64, 65, 66, 97n, 183
persecution by Puseyites, 235
Plan of Pacification, 35–6, 48, 65, 76, 95, 96, 112, 132–3, 203
Pocock, George, of Bristol, 80–1
Pope, W.B., 189
Prayer Book, 31

INDEX

preachers, itinerant: character of, 64–7; stationing of, 47; status of, 79–80, 201; trial of, 46, 223; wives of, 89n, 169 (*see also* Circuit Superintendent; ministry)
preaching licenses, Wesleyan attitude to, 82–3
Presbyterianism, 31, 63–4, 65, 67, 180–90, 253
Prescott, Peter, 253
President of the Conference, 46, 54, 167
priesthood: in the Church, 214, 227; in New Testament, 29, 207–8, 227; in Old Testament, 207, 208; of all believers, 179, 226, 227, 259; of Christ, 242
Primitive Methodists, 82–4
Primitive Wesleyan Methodists, 75
prophets, 208
Protestant Methodists, 52, 72n, 104, 115, 117, 135–6, 180
'Providential Way', the, 20, 26–9
purity, concept of, 74

Quarterly Meeting, 46, 47, 56, 61, 90, 218; constitution of, 142, 159, 173

Redruth circular (1791), 46
Reece, Richard, 129
representative government, 223–4 (*see also* democracy)
revivalism, 74, 83–4
Rigg, J.H., 178, 188, 189, 192
Roberts, Thomas, 204n
Robinson, Mark, of Hull, 75–7, 79–80
Rogers, James, 42n
Rule, W.H., 166, 170
Ruling Elder, 183–7
Rupp, Professor Gordon, 155–6, 230

sacraments, administration of, 19, 48; validity of, 241–4 (*see also* baptism; Lord's Supper)
Sandwith, Dr Humphrey, 77, 79
schism 244–7 (*see also* Church of England)
School Fund, 195
Scott, John, 216, 228, 255

Scripture, appeal to, 178, 235–7, 254–5
Shaw, John, 20n
Sheffield, 165; circular (1791), 21n
Sidmouth Bill, 83, 191n
Simon, Dr J.S., 21n, 93, 96, 128–9, 133, 134, 249
Smith, Dr George, 94, 143, 192, 210, 216, 220
society, 191–2; membership of, 173–6 (*see also* members)
society meetings, admission to, 73–4
Society Stewards, 46, 194–5
Southern, George, 151
Southwark, 109, 111
Special Circuit Meeting, 159
Special District Meeting, 104, 109–11, 119, 132, 139
special meetings, 103, 140–3
Sunday Schools, in Leeds, 104–5
Sunday Service of the Methodists, 63
'Superintendent', use of the term, 55n (*see also* Circuit Superintendent)
Sutcliffe, Joseph, 24n, 25n, 85

Tatham, Edward, 34n
Taylor, Thomas, 20n, 30, 32n, 42n, 66
Tent Methodists, 80–1
Theological Institution, 119, 124–5, 225
Thom, William, 65
Thompson, William, 24, 41n, 43–4; and the Plan of Pacification, 35, 65
Times, The, 93, 146, 155, 235
Tractarians, 214, 255, 258 (*see also* Oxford Movement)
Trowbridge, 28
Trustees, 24, 35, 98, 129, 159, 195; duties of, 97, 217, 218 (*see also* Leeds Organ Case)
Trustees Meeting, 56
Turner, George, 217, 219
Turner, J. Munsey, 203

Unitarians, 255
United Methodist Free Churches, 143, 145, 156, 180

Vevers, William, 118, 180, 196

271

INDEX

Walton, Daniel, 146
Ward, Professor W.R., 33, 34, 59n, 84, 149, 198, 202-3, 253
Warren, Dr Samuel, 119-21, 123, 124, 127, 131, 136; suspension of, 132-3
Warrenite secession, 114, 119-44, 148, 198, 252
Watson, Richard, 79-80, 86, 110, 111, 114, 115, 116-17, 118, 122, 149, 167, 196, 204, 258
Welch, Charles, 77, 79, 164, 190, 220
Wesley, Charles, 180, 259
Wesley, John, 30, 49, 78, 124, 176, 181-2, 191, 232, 236; and his assistants, 58, 121, 122, 193, 209-10, 215, 217, 257n; autocracy of, 51; concept of the ministry, 198-202, 203, 206n, 212, 239n, 258; and Dissent, 30; intentions for the Methodist connexion, 22, 27, 28-9, 41, 43, 62-4, 123, 133, 151, 180; ordinations, 19, 22, 28, 180, 183; pastoral oversight, 53, 200, 252; sermon 'On Obedience to Pastors', 200-201
Wesleyan Centenary Takings, 86
Wesleyan Methodist Association, 120, 136, 145, 150, 151, 180, 210, 243
Wesleyan Reformers: *see* Fly-sheet controversy
Wesleyan Tracts for the Times, 214, 229n, 235, 246-7; authorship of, 235n
'whole church', doctrine of, 224, 254
Wood, James, 129, 130
Woolmer, Theophilus, 174, 222
worship, 35-6, 95-7

Yearly Collection, 195